Red Lights and Green Lizards

RED LIGHTS
and
GREEN LIZARDS

A Cambodian Adventure

Liz Anderson

GREEN PRINT

© Liz Anderson, 2009

First published in1998 by Wayfarer Publishing
Second revised edition 1999
Third edition with epilogue
published by Green Print in 2009
an imprint of
The Merlin Press
6 Crane Street Chambers
Crane Street
Pontypool
NP4 6ND
Wales

www.merlinpress.co.uk

ISBN. 978-1-85425-096-4

The author has asserted her right under the
Copyright, Designs and Patents Act 1988
to be identified as the author of this work.

British Library Cataloguing in Publication data
is available from the British Library.

Printed in the UK by Imprint Digital, Exeter

For Tim

Illustrations

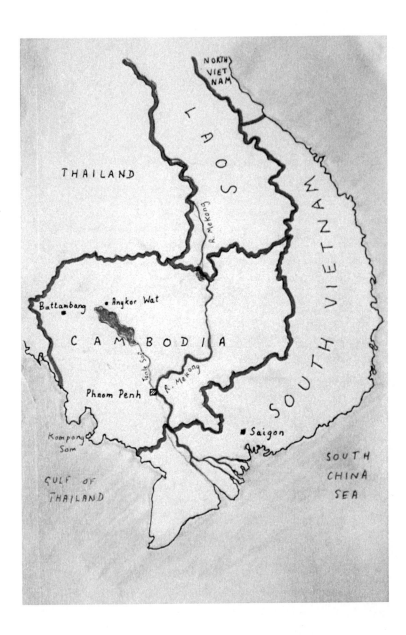

Prologue

How It Came About

The old man smiled as he looked up at me. His tall frame was spreadeagled behind the door, the shiny pink amputation stump jutting out at an odd angle below his pyjama jacket. It had jammed itself against the doorpost when he fell and as I knelt and held it gently between my hands I could feel the newly-broken ends of bone grating like a handful of gravel. There was no change in his expression, though the whisky that had unsteadied him had been his only pain-killer. The anaesthetic effect seemed absolute, and I marvelled at his composure.

While we waited for the ambulance, his wife, her tongue loosed by the emotion of the moment for as a rule they were a silent self-effacing couple, told me a little of his story. A landmine had been at the root of it; little did I know then just how familiar I was to become with the effects of these dreadful weapons. As a young man he had fought in the Second World War against the Japanese in South East Asia. On a jungle patrol he had led his men out of an ambush before himself treading on a mine, thereby winning an award for bravery in the face of severe hardship. No wonder he smiled now for how infinitely worse that must have been.

The ambulance took a long time in coming and dawn was breaking when I finally left the suburban semi where the consultation had taken place, sandwiched in the dimly-lit bathroom between door and lavatory pan. That night, everything had seemed more than usually unpleasant. The telephone bell had screeched more harshly as it dragged me from fathomless depths of slumber, the rain was wetter, the darkness darker, and the torch at its most feeble as its wan little beam searched along rows of identical front doors, their jumbled numbering in perfect keeping with my feelings. But duty at last was done, and as I drove home through the glistening streets, deserted but for the milkman and one solitary police car, I asked myself for the hundredth time why I was doing this. Sleep would not come easily in the few hours that remained before morning surgery at the start of another busy day. I was past retirement age; what was it that made me go on?

The answer I gave myself was always the same. The privileges of general practice were, I believed, almost unique. The constant revelations of the extraordinary hidden beneath the ordinary never failed to humble and amaze; tonight's episode had been just one more example. In short the work was satisfying and rewarding and I was enjoying it. Unless something equally absorbing beckoned the decision to make the break would be very difficult. But I was lucky. My gynaecologist husband Tim and I had always hoped to round off our working lives by spending some time in a third world country, and retirement from the national health service would allow us to set about our enquiries. Our search finally led us into circumstances so fascinating that it seemed a pity to keep them to ourselves, and it is the purpose of these pages to take you, the reader, with us on our adventures.

To find the right job, or indeed any job at all, was easier said than done. We had a dual problem. To use his experience to the full, it was important for Tim to be employed as a specialist, and such posts for Western doctors overseas are few and far between. Also the two of us were not exactly in our first youth, our combined ages totalling one hundred and twenty six years, and sixty apiece seems to be the cut-off point for many aid agencies and governments. We had nearly given up the search when we read an advertisement placed by Voluntary Service Overseas for a mature obstetrician in Phnom Penh, the capital of Cambodia. The job entailed working for two years alongside local doctors in the Women's Hospital, helping to bring their professional knowledge and practices up-to-date. It seemed to be exactly what Tim was looking for. Surely his maturity was a perfect match for their necessity, and the post would be his for the asking.

Determined this time to succeed for it seemed that it was now or never, my husband combed his hair over the bald patch and presented himself at the agency's big red-brick offices, prepared to put his foot in the door until he received an audience. But there was no need. Age at last was no problem. VSO was certainly interested but this posting was urgent and he must move fast. What about work for his GP wife? That would present no difficulty provided we both satisfied the selectors. But please hurry. We duly filled in application forms, bullied referees to perjure themselves quickly on our behalf, and waited...... and waited. We might well still be lurking in the dusty depths of some forgotten file had we not eventually become impatient and reached for the telephone. And then there was no holding them. In the twinkling of an eye we were pulled out, dusted down, and invited for interview. We passed. Then there were just two months in which to get ready, to leave jobs, to clear a generation's clutter from our house in preparation for its new tenants, and to prepare ourselves for the fray to which we were rashly committed. By the end of that time it felt as if our combined ages had risen dangerously near to the two hundred mark.

This particular agency is careful to give its volunteers as much preparation for individual postings as time and circumstances will allow. Tim and I went on several short courses which were instructive and enjoyable. Not only were our minds and skills nourished, but our stomachs as well. At Bristol University, for instance, where teaching sessions were held at that time, the food was so good that I suspect they were fattening us up against the rigours ahead. We began to meet others who would be coming with us, total strangers at that time but whose lives were soon to become inextricably entangled with our own.

Then I went off alone to the Liverpool School of Tropical Medicine for a five-day pathology course. A stranger to Liverpool and not yet restricted by the constraints of a volunteer's grant, I took a taxi to the hall of residence where we were to be billeted. I was feeling youthful, adventurous, and emancipated. On arrival, standing in the road outside the building were several coaches labelled 'Saga' filling up with old ladies. My taxi-driver's 'Where are you all off to, dear?' in the loud and careful tones reserved for those rapidly approaching deafness and senility brought me back to earth with a bump, for his remark was uncomfortably near the bone. But it was a salutary lesson. Firmly planted feet were vital if the struggles of the next two years were to bear fruit.

The course was excellent, though far too short for my eventual needs. There was so much to learn, or learn again, for student days were far behind me. The detection of harmful parasites, the control of epidemics, complex investigations made simple using basic equipment; these were just a few of the subjects that were crammed into those five days. The enormous responsibilities that we might well be called upon to bear in isolation from other medical personnel was clearly brought home to us. Our teachers, knowledgeable and inspiring, had all worked overseas, and it was good to be in the company of people to whom spending time in the third world is perfectly natural and the best thing you can do. With perspective restored, I went home more excited than ever. I was ready to go.

Chapter One

On September 7th 1991 a motley group gathered at Heathrow Airport. Our ages ranged from twenty-seven to sixty-five, and our skills from building to teaching. There were eight of us in all; two vets, a tall broad-shouldered builder and a wiry little electrician, an ex-army officer now turned teacher, an engineer from Glasgow and we two doctors. Some we had already met, but the process of fusion and interdependence, later to become so important, had not even begun. We were embarking with a group of strangers, leaving behind our children and grandchildren, all of them there to say goodbye. The departure lounge of an international airport is always a desolate place, but to us never more so than on that day.

The flight to Bangkok was uneventful from the pilot's point of view. In the cabin, however, it was a rather different matter. Our Glaswegian friend Iain had a pathological fear of flying, and we could but admire him for taking on a commitment where it was clearly unavoidable. The only way he could get himself on to that plane was by washing down tranquillisers with alcohol, dosages unspecified but effects dramatic. After an initial phase of restlessness, he finally passed out in the wrong seat, his head resting on the shoulder of an unknown but uncomplaining young lady who turned out to be a nurse. She was very pretty. He remained dead to the world; however were we going to unload him on arrival?

Our flight took us over places with golden names: Budapest, the Caspian Sea, Samarkand. It was above Burma that dawn broke after a short six-hour night, and the aeroplane windows showed us a glimpse of a lurid red sky; monsoon weather perhaps. Now we were nearly there, time and distance ridiculously compressed by man's inventiveness. We disembarked at Bangkok's busy international airport at eight a.m. My fears for Iain were unfounded, for though pale and gaunt he walked down the gangway with perfect composure and stability. His timing had been impeccable.

Our short stay in the city did nothing for our confidence. We were put up at the Comfort Inn, which lived up to its name physically but not emotionally. Hungry for information, for we were so nearly at our final destination, we appealed to those around us to fill in the yawning gaps ahead. But nothing positive was forthcoming. An English girl at the inn recently returned from Cambodia was the obvious informant. But all that we could get out of her was 'I can't possibly describe it to you; you'll just have to wait and see.' The pretty Thai receptionist behind her desk asked politely where we were going. She literally paled at our reply and said 'You're not really going to Cambodia are you? and surely not for two years?' Her concern was understandable as she enlightened us. Two of the four pioneers from our own aid agency who had gone there a few months earlier had recently returned to this very hotel, seriously ill. One had since moved away. The other, as Welsh a skinny Welshman as you could ever hope to meet, had taken to his bed in the hotel, and there he had remained, getting skinnier by the day. Friends who visited him told us later that the bed with him in it looked entirely flat, and compared him unfavourably with a stick-insect. But he made a full recovery and later became a South East Asia newspaper reporter of repute.

So what else did we learn? Only that the ordinary Thai knew nothing about Cambodia. It was a completely unknown quantity, and they turned the tables on us by their questioning, themselves interested to find out more about a country which had lost contact with the world.

As a group, we attempted sight-seeing that first morning, but events had caught up with us and an exhausted lethargy overwhelmed our little party. Abandoning the struggle, we went for lunch to a dubious street-side café, a lunch that took the blame for the first illness among us. Half of the inseparable vet partnership was to develop amoebic dysentery with remarkable speed. A river trip occupied the afternoon; foul smelling brown water sprayed in our faces as the motorised canoe, the wooden nose of its prowhead figure held disdainfully aloft, sped between the banks. On both sides of the water, busy with pleasure-boats and lines of tubby working barges, stretched shanty-towns of long-legged wooden houses, endless washing slung out to dry between them. Once we passed the bloated carcass of an animal floating on its back, its puffy neck still tethered to a pole and its four legs splayed stiffly skywards; a dog, perhaps, or a pig. On second thoughts, perhaps Caitlin did not catch her dysentery from the café after all.

A good night's sleep and another day came and went spent inhaling the stinking fumes of Bangkok's permanent traffic jam while Tim and I made fruitless attempts to visit medical contacts. His decision to take on the problems of bringing a backward country up to date had largely rested on the likelihood of a grant from the EEC. Once this had materialised, local knowledge of the best sources of equipment and drugs would be important, but by the end of the day we were none the wiser. Our search had been in vain.

Our companions too went their various ways, and it was not until we all met up in the evening that we learnt of poor Iain's loss. A packet of dollar bills had apparently been stolen from the back pocket of his jeans as he walked the streets, far more cash than any of the rest of us carried. The group was sympathetic almost to a man, with just one exception. Christopher the English teacher shocked us all by scoffing loud and long at this tale of woe. Time alone would show who was right.

At long last in the early dawn we were off on the final leg of our journey. There was a great flurry at the check-in desk for the little fifty-seater twin propeller aircraft, the only air transport ferrying between Bangkok and Phnom Penh. Our fellow-passengers were a party of journalists, large and imposing in their khaki many-pocketed jackets. Their equipment was even larger and took no note of baggage allowance rules, so half of our meagre possessions had to be left behind. We made our way across the airport through the cool morning air; the photo that I took is quite superfluous, for the image of our huddled little group boarding the tiny aircraft seems stuck on my retina for ever.

Once again, Iain was pea-green from an excess of terror and other commodities, and we did our best to divert him by chatting about our families. Knowing our profession, he thought Tim and I would be interested in his father's prowess in the field of medicine, of which he seemed exceedingly proud. He talked at length about the doctor's amazing medical achievements, tales which we did not think to question, and he positively basked in our evident admiration. We could not know what revelations lay ahead.

But for the rest of us the flight held few fears as we trundled along comfortably close to the ground. It was a relief to see crowded Thailand slipping away, and, after the blue sea of the Gulf of Bangkok, to stare down at the deserted watery plains and paddy-fields of Cambodia. News had reached us of severe flooding at the end of the rainy season. Would we be able to land? But there was no problem. We got ready to disembark. Iain had made it again. This time it was Harry the electrician who stayed snoring in his seat. Doubtless he was over-fatigued.....

A wall of heat hit us as we left the plane, the hot dusty air bouncing up off the tarmac that we walked across to reach the small airport building. A little reception party of two, James, one of our two Field Directors, and Joanna, who had set up our programme in Cambodia, awaited us. Both tall, their welcoming smiles shone out above the confusing sea of brown faces, an instant comfort to our wary little group. It was James's pink socks that made the most impression on me that first day; amazingly they were still flashing about when we left two years later.

Somehow the interminable paper-work that was delaying our fellow travellers was dealt with in double quick time and we were outside, to find the brand-new VSO truck awaiting us. It was a gleaming white, seemingly the compulsory colour for all foreign-owned four-wheeled vehicles, and proudly boasted the organisation's circular logo on its door. In we climbed and off we went on our maiden voyage into the city.

On that first day it seemed beautiful. In contrast to Bangkok's serried ranks of cars, the sun glancing off their hot metal roofs and poison pouring from their exhausts, this road was quiet. Although there were a great many small motor-bikes cars were few and far between, and the overwhelming impression was of a decrepit army of bicycles. At first we passed clusters of wooden huts, their road-side fronts busy with traders; later the road widened and houses became bigger and more substantial. But my outstanding memory of that first drive was the Frangipani trees. They lined the road on both sides, their wide-spreading branches covered with an exquisite display of large white waxy flowers. More striking still was their perfume, so delicate and yet so well able to disguise all that lay beneath its welcome presence.

As we neared our destination close to the centre of the city the roar of human living intensified, the blurred picture presenting itself to a new arrival from the West as one of frenetic activity, but of men rather than machines. Two attributes of the complex Cambodian character we learned immediately; they are gregarious, and they are noisy. Our destined hotel, enterprisingly named 'The Asie', was in a short side-road connecting the city's main street Achar Mean with the big New Market. Achar Mean (now Monivong Boulevard) is Phnom Penh's spinal column, a street of commerce and cafés, a confusion of cyclos and trucks, of cycles and motor-bikes and people, a cacophony of all human sounds imaginable and unimaginable. The rule of the road is, officially, keep to the right, but unofficially it is the law of the bully-boy. Biggest is best and woe betide you if you forget it.

But all this we discovered later, for at the moment we were simply thankful to have emerged from the initial fray without sustaining grievous bodily harm, and to be standing safe and sound in a pool of luggage outside the Asie. The exterior of the hotel did not look too daunting. Painted a dingy Cambodian yellow, and encouraging an early demise with the inevitable '555' cigarette advertisement on a vast jutting sign, it stood five storeys high sandwiched between tall buildings. The walls of the entrance hall, of the steep 'marble' staircase with gaol-worthy girders supporting its lofty, ugly central well, and of the bedrooms, had once upon a time been painted blue, but had long since faded to a dirty grey. The curtains in room 317, which was to be our home for the next two months, had started life a sunny buttercup yellow, but now, stained and grubby, they hung perilously by the skin of their sparse hooks across the big French windows which led on to a tiny balcony. This, with its chest-high barrier of chipped grey concrete, gave us a grand stand view of the activities in the street far below, or, much nearer, through open windows into the ugly apartment block opposite.

But the room was airy and spacious enough to house two double-beds with plenty of room to spare. The sheets were changed every day. One of the cupboard doors hung permanently open, but in the absence of a key the locked desk-drawer never did reveal its grisly secrets. There was even a refrigerator, which sometimes got quite cool. The electricity came and went with a speed and irregularity that puzzled us until we learnt the age of the town's generators. It was impressive that they worked at all.

To our amazement, we also had our own bathroom. The Cambodians are immensely clean; dirty bodies and clothes belong only to the real street beggars, and the sight of both men and women pouring water over themselves, though always retaining a dignified decency, is a very common one. So all Western-style buildings have at least one bathroom and often several. Ours contained a fixed headed iron-age shower, a cracked basin, and, on a lordly platform, a sit-down lavatory with a flush that worked. This was more than we had dared hope for. There were snags, of course, but one must not be selfish. The overpowering stench of other people's urine must have been enormously titillating to the resident family of cockroaches who after all had got there first, and the chips and cracks in the tiled floor made a cosy home for them. (Their friends and relations next door had a really hard time of it, attacked by our vet neighbours with such explosive vigour on our very first night that we felt sure the Khmer Rouge had arrived and all was over.) The shower, which produced a wonderful jet of surprisingly cold water, would suddenly withhold its offering, usually just after I had lathered myself all over, but this only encouraged ingenuity, an important criterion in the selection of volunteers. Another feature was the fusebox, in reality a lidless tangle of exposed wires sited immediately next to the shower and well within reach of a child.

It was fortunate that we liked the chambermaid, for she spent an increasing amount of time in our room. She kept her comb on our basin shelf and her long black hairs wandered sinuously across the off-white porcelain. Latterly, she was often to be found sitting in our easy chair when we came in. She used to invite her friends and relations, too. A half-empty bottle of rice-wine under our bed was a sure sign that her husband had been visiting, and once a well-dressed woman and child wandered into the room and made straight for the refrigerator before they realised that we were still in bed, and beat a leisurely retreat. On another occasion, something woke me in the middle of the night. Just visible in the darkness was a young Cambodian, nonchalantly and in complete silence strolling past the foot of our bed. When I called out, he gave me a long look before slowly turning on his heel and making his unhurried way back through the long room before he disappeared. I took him for a burglar, thwarted by my wakefulness. However, there is another theory. We heard much later that the hotel had been one of the buildings used for unspeakable deeds in the Pol Pot era, and that it was haunted by the lost souls of victims. Certainly the door, hidden from my sight, made no sound as he closed it after him. Perhaps after all he had had no need of it.

This shoddy hotel room was our first little home, a vital part of our life in Phnom Penh. Tim had his first bout of illness in it, lying in bed for several days smitten with severe diarrhoea and nourished with tea and soup from the café across the road. People came to visit, we read books and relaxed, learned our Khmer home-work, made pots of tea, puzzled over perplexities, laughed, cried, wrote letters, listened to music and above all enjoyed the company of the other volunteers billeted in

The Silver Pagoda in the palace complex, Phnom Penh

the rooms around us. It was rather like being back at college again, forty years on.

The Asie was our base, and from it over the next weeks we made ever more adventurous forays into the interior of this very foreign city. There was no time to breathe. We were rushed from pillar to post. There were briefings at our Field Office in subjects ranging from agency policy to Khmer politics, from malaria to the correct way to dress, interspersed with trips to the important sights of the city. One of the first of these was a tour of the Royal Palace, an opportunity not to be missed as some of its buildings would soon be closed to the public. Prince Sihanouk, in exile for over twenty years, was returning to his people, an event which in Buddhist eyes was little short of a Second Coming.

This visit took us to the most beautiful part of the city, where the fairy-tale palace, painted a glowing yellow, dominates its setting of parkland bordered by the mighty Mekong river. To the uninitiated it has a splendidly oriental look, with its red-tiled roofs topped by spiky spires and the sinuous tails of stone serpents jutting skywards, sharp like dragons' teeth. It faces east, as behoves a sacred Cambodian edifice, for Khmer kings are held by their subjects to be demigods. But it lays no claim to antiquity, for its construction started a mere one hundred and thirty years ago, soon after King Norodom moved his capital to Phnom Penh.

In the middle of the palace complex is the Throne Hall, a massive building the length of a soccer pitch and more than half its width. Round it are smaller structures, including a pavilion decorated with the letter 'N'. On our guided tour we were told that it was from this pavilion, made in Egypt, that the Empress Eugénie, wife of Napoleon III, opened the Suez Canal in 1869. It was then moved to Cambodia and presented to King Norodom. Quite why he wanted it the story does not reveal.

Inside the Throne Hall itself we saw a remarkable collection of useful Royal paraphernalia, including a pavilion each for the king and queen, their thrones, the king's chapel where the royal fortune-teller used to tell him what would happen next, some conch-shells for blowing and some bundles of sticks for beating. Further in are separate bedrooms, widely spaced, for use by their majesties during a seven-day statutory period following their coronation, and no cheating. After that, royal marital bliss could commence.

In its own compound nearby stands the Silver Pagoda. As we went round it, we were dazzled by a bewildering and stunning display of statuary, carvings, and head-dresses in gold, silver, bronze and precious stones. Its name comes from its floor, which is covered with over five thousand solid silver tiles, weighing forty-nine tons or rather more than eight elephants. We had expected to tread gingerly upon a shining sea, but found instead great tracts of dusty matting covering decades of tarnish. In any case, it would have distracted the eye from the hundreds of glorious artefacts that stood shoulder to shoulder upon it. The other name for this building is the Pagoda of the Emerald Buddha. There he sat, an exquisite translucent green, high on his pedestal. But to me he was outshone by his immediate neighbour, a life-sized replica of the holy man made in the palace workshops at the beginning of the century. Fashioned from solid gold and inset with a myriad of diamonds (nine thousand five hundred and eighty-four of them, so they say), this glittering showpiece made it difficult to concentrate on the elegant artistry of the little statue perched in its shadow. This is an Aladdin's cave of extraordinary richness and beauty, a glorious tribute to the skill of the Khmer craftsmen who created it and all the wonders within its walls.

But back to reality: we were not here on a sightseeing tour. It was time to get down to work.

Chapter Two

Our first task was to learn the Khmer language. To settle any confusion, the inhabitants of Cambodia are the Khmer people and it is only the communists among them that are notorious as the Khmer Rouge. Their language in theory should not be difficult to learn, for there is little in the way of grammar, just a multitude of words. But these are words the like of which we had never heard before. There is no comforting classical stem which forms the basis of Western speech and writings. Sleeping and waking, rank upon rank of them marched before our eyes, regiments of seemingly senseless sounds which had to be learnt by rote. There were no text-books, and in any case most of us never learnt to read or write the Cambodian script. Everything had to be written down phonetically in a series of exercise books. These were purchased in the market; covered in grey shiny paper, they bore, in English, the blue printed legend 'The Solid and Commodious Note Book that is Starched is Very Useful for Study'. That was an understatement. Our lives depended on them. If one got lost its owner was done for, as no-one else's notes would do. I filled three of them and they remain an enormously important possession, despite the persistent leakage from my brain of everything that is in them. So memory, a sadly shrivelled remnant in some of us, was all-important. Despite the use of rhymes, mnemonics and endless repetition, Khmer remained elusive to all of us, even the most nimble-brained, for many weeks, and to some for much, much longer.

The classes were small and concentration intense. Often only three of the four wooden desks would be occupied when one or other of us had succumbed to the diarrhoea that was a continuously lurking and insidious unpleasantness, something we never really learnt to live with. Our brains, like the pores of our skin, felt constantly clogged by the sticky heat, a discomfort compounded by frequent failure of the antique overhead fan. But we had enormous fun too. We laughed a great deal, at ourselves and at each other, but mainly at our comedian of a schoolmaster, whose great fat belly continuously wobbled and bounced in time to his guffaws and giggles. One facet of his linguistic ability was his skill at mimicry; he took enormous pleasure in copying with great enthusiasm and a strong Khmer flavour the various accents presented to him by the members of our group, coming as we did from all corners of Great Britain. He particularly enjoyed the Scottish Iain. His own rendering of 'therre's a wee moose aboot the hoose t'naight' was his favourite, always with a fat chuckle and an expectation of applause. We inevitably obliged, for his laughter was very infectious.

Darra was an excellent teacher, living up to his name which means 'a star', and he was also an unusual man in many respects. During the civil war, before the fateful day in 1975 when Pol Pot marched into Phnom Penh, refugee camps had been set up on the border with Thailand. Darra, a very different shape at that time I suspect, had taken refuge with his wife and family in one such camp, where he had remained until a year or so before our arrival. He had become politically active, his voice and writings increasingly heard amongst his fellow refugees, inciting opposition to the Khmer Rouge. It became correspondingly dangerous for him to stay there; even camp walls have ears. So one night he had crept away. The jungle round about was seeded with landmines, but an acquaintance who knew the locality, threading his way at night along hidden pathways, guided him out into open country. From there he was able to set out on the long walk back to Phnom Penh. Now he was busy earning money to send to his wife and children who had remained behind. One day after class he pulled out of his pocket a walletful of hard-won dollars to show us; a friend was travelling to the camp, and would take it with him. There was no postal system and he had heard nothing from his wife for nearly a year, so arrival at its destination was far from certain.

Happily, though, his life was not all work and no play, for he was comforted by another 'wife' nearby, a common situation which seemed to be socially acceptable. But even so it was easy to see that his jollity hid an inner tension, and as the stories of his sufferings gradually emerged over the weeks the reasons became obvious. He told us of the time when, after months of near starvation, he and his family had eventually arrived at the refugee camp. He was a young man then, and he had an even younger brother, still a child. On arrival they were given food but warned to eat it slowly; their stomachs, accustomed for so long to little but water with a few grains of rice floating in it to make a 'soup', would be unable to cope with a big meal. For Darra's little brother, the warning fell on deaf ears. He was a hungry child with food in front of him, and he ate. He died as a result. This background, and constant worry about his wife and children, and in particular the youngest girl upon whom he clearly doted, played on Darra's health, both physical and mental.

Our teacher had a decidedly macabre sense of humour which doubtless reflected the horrors of his past. He would write on the board sentences in English, with the Khmer translation underneath, always of course in phonetics. One such sentence ran as follows: 'two of my sons ate two of my dogs when I was not home'. He laughed so much as he wrote this that we had to stop the lesson for several minutes. His physical health continued to deteriorate while he was teaching us and increasingly often he would be off sick. Frankly, an occasional day when our poor brains could rest their bruises from the constant cudgelling was quite a relief.

The language classes and homework occupied most of our time and energy for those first two months. But other things had to be fitted in too, not least of which was to find a house to live in. This too took energy and time. Tim was determined to get settled well before he started work, a deadline that was approaching all too rapidly. The EEC grant that he had been led to expect was not after all forthcoming, a failure which made the task ahead almost impossibly difficult, and both of us needed the security of a stable background to allow us to prepare for the challenges to come. Houses that would have been comfortable and therefore easy to work from did not fall within the agency's strict financial bracket. It was a difficult time, and one that did not make for peace of mind or with our immediate authorities.

The local method of house-hunting was an unusual one. Any intermediary who made a successful introduction of client to landlord would receive the first month's rent, perhaps a year's pay by Khmer standards. So the competition was intense, and we were besieged by fortune hunters. Our most unlikely would-be agent was Prince Sihanouk's aunt, no less, but because of her lofty position dealings were carried out discreetly at Field Office level and sadly we never met her. In any case the deal failed. But it was the cyclo-drivers, that tattered band of charioteers who pedalled bicycle-driven rickshaws to make a perilous living, who headed the field. Many times we were enticed into the chair of one such contraption and driven off at high speed by a ragged and hopeful entrepreneur only to be shown some totally unsuitable dwelling. Our frequent refusals increased their desperation to the point at which, when leaving our class one day at the moment when the short tropical dusk turned suddenly to darkness, we were virtually kidnapped. Two familiar and usually friendly cyclo-drivers vehemently insisted that we climb yet again into their 'cabs' to make just one more visit. It was dark as pitch, and invisible rain slashed down with traditional tropical ferocity. Our captors pedalled like twin furies; capsize into a black, watery and polluted grave seemed inevitable and we had plenty of time to consider our fate as we were propelled through ever smaller and darker back streets. Cyclos do not sport lamps, and the only street lighting was provided by tiny paraffin-soaked wicks on the occasional roadside food stall. Suddenly and miraculously we stopped. Scared and sodden, we dismounted, and sloshing in sandalled feet through thick mud, we were finally guided up an outside staircase into the bright light of a spacious living-room, where a family sat at supper. Such normality was startling; perhaps the last fifteen minutes had been a bad dream after all. But the nightmare continued. As we were shown round, we saw that a large patch on the floor of the next room was mysteriously encrusted with dried blood. Whatever next? In a third room, the bedroom, on a hospital drip stand hung a half empty bottle of blood, its tube complete with needle hooked up beside it. But the bed was empty and neatly made. Where was the patient? or was he a victim? Had he bled to death on the next-door floor, his body hurled into the floodwaters below? Who knows? We certainly never did. In fact there was probably some perfectly innocent explanation. Later, we found that the Khmers love transfusions and give them to each other at the slightest provocation; probably the recipient had been eating at the dinner table when we arrived. But that night it seemed macabre in the extreme, and our relief was correspondingly great when our cyclo-drivers, turned back now into the kindly and gentle people that we knew, delivered us home to the Asie safe and sound.

We found our house, and not through the agency of a cyclo-driver either. A pretty little wooden building tucked away in a garden, it was built in the Khmer style on legs but with a room occupying the ground-floor space. Its separate kitchen was just a few yards away, this arrangement intentional, apparently, to keep the living quarters free of rats. These were enormous and plentiful, but we puzzled over the number seen squashed flat on the roads. This seemed to indicate a singular ratty flat-footedness; surely any self-respecting rodent would avoid death by cyclo? But as usual there was a simple explanation. These were rats that had been caught, drowned, and their corpses disposed of by throwing them out on to the road along with all the other rubbish.

Before we could move into no. 23 bis, route 334, it was necessary to make a number of alterations. Modern bathrooms (cold water only, but no great hardship in that heat), up and down, were added at our kind landlord's expense, and a concrete driveway lay through the garden to avoid paddling in the rainy season. To own a garden at all in Phnom Penh was unusual, but this was a very special one, adding enormously to the house's attraction. The site had been a banana grove, and the trees that remained, brandishing their enormous crenellated leaves like huge flapping ears, gave us a grateful reminder of the countryside where we would have liked to be. Mangoes, coconut-palms, and papayas grew in between them, and luxuriant flowering climbers looked in through our bedroom window. Best of all was the everlasting supply of limes, very handy for the occasional life-saving gin and tonic. Shady and serene, it was a welcome place of rest in the arid concrete of the city and we felt very fortunate to have found such a peaceful haven.

It was during a visit to our house to inspect the builder's progress that another little adventure befell us. The rainy season was still in full spate

Our house

and a torrential downpour had transformed our dirt-track road into a muddy canal. Its surface was smooth and innocent; gone from sight and mind were all the potholes hidden below. On our new-second-hand issue push-bikes we took to the water, our wakes rippling splendidly behind us. I was enjoying myself. But all too suddenly the scene changed. There was a bump, a cartwheel, a sense of imminent death by drowning, and an exceedingly sharp pain in my left hand. I was spreadeagled face first in the brown water, with my left arm and the front wheel of my bicycle down a very deep hole. Tim extricated me dripping with blood and filth and stood me up beside the upturned bike, its rear wheel still spinning. Kindly Khmer neighbours rushed out, and clean water from nearby water-pots was ladelled over me. A dear old lady, who later became the best-ever next-door neighbour, gave us a foretaste of her kindness by producing a tray of unlabelled bottles and dabbing a little of the contents of each on to my wound. Judging by the pain they produced they had to be good. The hole I had so unerringly found was connected to the town sewer, so it was not in a very comfortable state of mind that we cycled back to the Asie, the bicycle undamaged. How much had I swallowed? What was going to happen to my hand? Tim rushed off to buy a stomach-tube, but no such thing was to be had. Efforts to make myself sick by sticking my fingers down my throat succeeded only in making that sore as well. Frustrated, we abandoned our attempts; my immunizations were up to date, so all should be well. But within an hour, my hand began to throb and swell. Despite immediate antibiotics, by next morning my temperature was up and my head spun. There would be no Khmer lesson for me that day.

But I was lucky. Despite a few days of worry over blood-poisoning and considerable anxiety about my hand, I made a full recovery. It had not been a comfortable time. The part of it that I disliked most was keeping the wound open for drainage. This I had to do every day with a blunt embroidery needle dipped in iodine. It was the iodine that hurt. The other two daily essentials, bathing the hand and learning my Khmer vocabulary, were performed simultaneously. Half a plastic bottle cut lengthways fitted the injured member perfectly. With that and a thermos of hot water in the bathroom basin and the Solid and Commodious Notebook on the shelf above, the soaking process, grammar in and germs out, worked very nicely; a most profitable half-hour. But good as so often happens came out of bad. When, arm in sling, I went back to my language lessons and told the sad tale to our teacher, his delight knew no bounds. Apparently all that is needed to transform the teaching of prepositions is for a pupil to fall OFF a bike INTO a hole, or FROM a bike DOWN a hole, or ...... the variety, in Darra's hands, was unending. And it was all accompanied by pictures on the board of pin-men flying THROUGH the air, and of course by huge fat wobbly chuckles. However they did cover up the sewer after that, I am glad to say.

But all this of course was in preparation for our real task, to try to perform a service for the Khmer people. This is perhaps a good moment to explain the reason behind our presence and that of other aid-agencies. Why were we needed at all? Because of the existence of one man, Pol Pot, who had been responsible for the death of over a million of his fellow-countrymen.

The recent history of Cambodia is complicated, and I can only skim the surface of it. There are excellent books on the subject which go into it in far greater depth than is possible here. It is though much easier to understand the Cambodian people if you know something of what they and their immediate forebears have been through, and so in the next chapter is a brief outline of the state of affairs before and during the Pol Pot years.

Chapter Three

In 1941, King Sisowath Monivong of Cambodia died. To the university students in far-away Saigon this would suggest no major impact on their lives. His son would succeed him, and life would go on much as before. But for one of their number a rude shock was in store. Norodom Sihanouk, a minor prince and distant cousin of the king, was to be plucked from his studies and his easy pleasure-seeking life to become one of the foremost figures in modern Cambodian politics.

It was the French colonial rulers of the country who unearthed nineteen-year-old Sihanouk from obscurity to put him on the throne. They needed a puppet king, a figure-head for the people but a simpleton who would dance to their tune. Surely this young man, who by all accounts had nothing in his addled head but the pleasures of this life but was nevertheless of royal blood, was ideal for their purpose. But they could not have been further from the truth, and there is no doubt that their choice proved their undoing.

Sihanouk took his duties very seriously. Steeped in his country's traditions, he was well aware that ever since ancient Angkor times Cambodian kings have been regarded as demi-gods, and he threw himself into his new part with a will. He saw the beautiful country of Cambodia as his own earthly paradise, and he set his about task with purpose, skill, and enthusiasm. Despite his many failures, time would show that he alone understood the Cambodian people and could perhaps have given them the care they needed. But this was not to be.

In his earlier years at least, he was immensely popular with the peasants who made up the vast majority of his subjects, and in this lay his strength. He managed to combine inspiration with a close and sometimes coarse personal touch, much enjoyed by all. We are told he would rush about the countryside in a positive tornado of activity, cracking raucous jokes and stopping to chat to anyone and everyone. When at home in Phnom Penh, huge crowds would attend the 'surgeries' that he held in the palace yard. There he would listen to and try to rectify complaints, shouting orders above the noise to his officials in his shrill, penetrating voice and demanding instant attention to the problem in hand. If crossed, he would fly into a tantrum, and heaven help the unfortunate victim. He was totally feudal in his outlook, accepting no criticism or disagreement, and enfolding his subjects in a comforting web of myth and legend to protect them from the wicked world outside. Side by side with all this went his personal dedication to the good things of life, the whole package wound about by a silken thread of charm and bulging with a ferocious intelligence and extraordinary political skill.

Cambodia had been a French Protectorate for roughly a hundred years, and Sihanouk's first ambition was to rid his country of the foreigners' unwelcome presence. But already he was in trouble, for strong opposition to the way in which he was handling the French had arisen among certain young people who were eventually to alter the course of their country's history. Their origin was the Sisowath School for the children of the elite, of which they were all past or present pupils; all, that is, but one. His name was Saloth Sar, later to adopt the nom de guerre Pol Pot and become the most notorious tyrant of his generation.

Saloth Sar was different, both in background and scholarship. Born into a farming family, his school-days did not run smoothly. It seems that academic skills were beyond him, so at the age of nineteen he signed on at a technical college in Phnom Penh to learn carpentry. Under the care of an older brother, he kept himself out of trouble, working hard and showing no interest in politics. But things were to change dramatically, and it was the acceptance by the elite of the Sisowath School Alumni of this pleasant but unremarkable young man that was to transform not just his life but that of many thousands of his fellow Cambodians.

Slowly Saloth Sar emerged from the shadows. He was the first of his colleagues to win a government scholarship to Paris, where he spent three years studying radio-electricity. A number of his fellow students soon followed him, and it was in Paris, in the heady atmosphere where almost all the workers were openly communist, that these young people were transformed from student democrats to militant Marxists. But in one respect, Saloth Sar had not changed at all. No doubt because of the time taken up by his political activities, he once again failed his examinations, his scholarship was suspended, and he returned to Phnom Penh. But although his academic life seemed at an end, his political career was only just beginning, and it was through him and his Paris friends that the Cambodian communist party came into being.

Meanwhile in 1953, twelve years after coming to the throne, King Sihanouk finally rid his country of its French overlords. Now he could concentrate on problems at home. Feudal as ever and desperate to remain in power, he found himself faced with an insurmountable difficulty. There was to be an election, and it seemed inevitable that his right-wing government would be overwhelmingly defeated by the ever-increasing numbers of left-wing intellectuals whose origin lay in the Sisowath school. As king, he was not allowed to play a direct part and there seemed only one solution to this dilemma. He renounced his kingship in favour of his father and became a politician. Having abdicated and reverted to prince, he formed his own political party just in time. By dint of military suppression of his opponents combined with his enormous personal charm, he swept the board and won every single seat. The infant communist party, well and truly beaten, ran for its life.

Then in 1960 came the Vietnam war. Sihanouk was determined to keep his beloved country out of this struggle between the North Vietnamese communists on the one hand, and South Vietnam backed by the USA on the other. But as the war dragged on, America's President Nixon, unbeknown to the US Congress, took this out of his hands. The White House secretly sanctioned the clandestine bombing of Cambodia along its border with Vietnam in an attempt to stop the movement southwards of communist Vietnamese troops. Night after night for fourteen months American B52s bombed Cambodian territory, killing unknown numbers of innocent peasants.

Sihanouk found himself in increasing political difficulties. Playing his opponents off against each other, he tried to balance himself between the US and their Vietnamese enemies. Disapproving of America, he felt bound to appear friendly towards their communist opponents while at the same time redoubling his witch-hunt against the left wing in his own country. Saloth Sar and his enlarging band of followers were pushed further and further into the jungle. There, as they nursed their hatred in isolation of mind and body, their ideals began to fester and their philosophy to harden. The Khmer Rouge had been born.

But there was trouble too much nearer home. One of the most influential members of Sihanouk's government was Lon Nol, holding the dual role of Prime Minister and Military Adviser. Although outwardly supporting the prince, the conservative Lon Nol was secretly totally opposed to his master's apparent alliance with the Vietnamese communists. As Sihanouk's policies became more inconsistent and jumbled in his attempts to steer a middle way, mysterious rumors began to spread, no doubt planted by clever men but nevertheless holding mystical appeal for peasants still steeped in their country's traditions. The White Crocodile was seen again in the land. Tradition has it that this legendary beast, present at the birth of Cambodia, always appears at times of important change. No-one could say where and when the manifestations started, but in March 1970, as whispers of some mighty happening became ever louder, Lon Nol moved in for the kill. As soon as Sihanouk's back was turned on a visit abroad the general pounced, carrying out a military coup against the prince who, in his absence in China, was tried, found guilty of high treason, and condemned to death. Cambodia was now a republic for the first time in its long history. Queen Osama, Sihanouk's mother, drew a sacred weapon from its scabbard, a magic sword which would predict the fate of her son. Alas, its usually gleaming blade had tarnished a deep black. This was the worst possible omen, and a fitting confirmation of the predictions of the White Crocodile, which had already sunk once more beneath the muddy waters of mythology.

And so began an even more bizarre chapter in the history of the country, now in the hands of Lon Nol. His early years had had much in common with those of Saloth Sar. He was born of peasant parents and, like Sar, showed little sign of talent in his youth. Both had the same goal: to restore Cambodia to its former glory. But whereas Sar chose the forward-looking route of communism, Lon Nol, steeped in the occult and in mysticism, attempted the same ends by putting back the clock and re-igniting religious fervour.

His was perhaps the weirdest route of all. This little man, his skin so dark that he liked to be known as 'Black Papa' by his troops to underline the peasant origins of which he was so proud, actually believed himself to be the saviour of Buddhism, the leader chosen by Buddha to wage war against the foreign infidels. His troops were directed not for reasons of military strategy but by his own powers of divination, aided by his astrologers. Because Lon Nol believed that the occult would lose its power if made manifest, Prince Sihanouk had been kept in total ignorance of his general's delusions.

To keep himself from harm, he carried with him battered talismans given to him as a child. And he was just as careful to protect his troops. He taught them how to cut their skin to allow Buddha to enter their bodies and bring them strength, and what to inscribe on their clothing. He encouraged them to go into battle sucking holy amulets and wearing magic scarves and vests to ward off bullets, and would postpone battle engagements until he was satisfied that these precautions had been properly taken. His objectives were often holy monuments rather than enemy positions. In short, he quickly displayed a total lack of military acumen and an obsession to turn the war into a crusade against the Vietnamese infidels and to reassert the glory of Buddhism.

So Lon Nol struggled on, fighting and failing in his own version of the war. His rag-bag army of ill trained and ill disciplined men and boys dressed up as soldiers was no match for the strong Vietnamese troops, and battle after battle was lost. There was little doubt that he was a political pawn in the hands of the Americans, who in return for his attempts to subdue their mutual enemy, the communist Vietnamese, poured dollars into his coffers. His officers became ever more corrupt, debauched, and dissolute. To uncaring outside observers, the whole thing smacked of farce. The world laughed at t0his tiny general, who had tiny furniture built to make him look tall by comparison. They laughed at the name of his military spokesman, Am Rong. The tears would come all too soon.

But on he went, despite suffering a severe stroke from which he only partially recovered. He lost battle after battle against the powerful Vietnamese communists, now moving westwards across the country. Only by dint of increasing American intervention and aid was it possible for Lon Nol and his army to survive and to continue to fight a war which was to last for five years.

Meanwhile, what of Saloth Sar, and what of Sihanouk? Saloth Sar was still in hiding in the jungle. In exile for so long, the communists' philosophy had turned in upon itself, fermenting in its hatred of corrupt authority. Loyalty to Anka, 'the organization', so called to disguise its communist roots, was now becoming one of its central tenets, frightening in its extremism. For Sihanouk, too, matters had not stood still. In exile in Peking, unable to return because of the death sentence imposed on him at the time of the military coup, he turned a complete political somersault and allied himself, in absentia, with the Khmer Rouge against his former colleague Lon Nol. The acronym of this new alliance was FUNK.

Finally, in 1973, the American war in Vietnam was over. The Americans went thankfully home, and so did the Vietnamese fighting Lon Nol in Cambodia. Now it was time for the Khmer Rouge to come out of their jungle hide-out. They hated Lon Nol and all he stood for, and now that the Vietnamese were no longer there to oppose him it was their turn to take up the battle. But America had not finished with Lon Nol either. Although officially out of the war, the US still needed their Cambodian ally to continue 'their' war against the communists. The Nixon administration sanctioned the bombing of the Khmer Rouge, and for two hundred days and nights a fleet of B52s dropped another 250,000 tons of bombs on Cambodian soil. Available maps were far from accurate, and both Cambodian civilians and Lon Nil's army suffered large numbers of casualties from 'friendly fire'.

Saloth Sir's surprising response was to set up the first co-operatives, agricultural areas sealed off and guarded by wide booby-trapped tracts of land. On the face of it, the purpose of these was for the intensive production of rice, the work scheduled to take place between the American bombing raids. Covertly, they were the earliest centres for the indoctrination of the peasants with Maoist principles. Brain-washing had begun. This was the beginning of the end of family life and the sanctity of the people's religious philosophy, Buddhism. Pol Pot's time was almost ripe.

At last, in response to increasing pressure from the US Congress, the American pounding stopped. Now Lon Nol was on his own. His troops were starving and terrified. Corruption had reached unplumbed depths, with senior officers maintaining their own lifestyle by selling off American weapons to the enemy, and food prices were soaring on the black market. In the eyes of the government troops, the Khmer Rouge, driven mercilessly by their officers and nourished on rice from the co-operatives, was possessed of miraculous strength. Little by little the communists advanced on Phnom Penh, now overflowing with over a million refugees from the countryside. Lon Nol's troops, demoralised and exhausted, were finally defeated and on April 17th 1975 the Khmer Rouge, dressed in black from top to toe, marched into the capital. Every living soul was forcibly removed and driven out into the countryside. The sick were literally dragged from their hospital beds and many of them left to die in the gutters. There was no mercy and no quarter; the old and the very young, the frail, the dying, all had to leave immediately.

Out into the fields they went and were put to work, planting rice, creating irrigation systems, and tending vegetables, back-breaking tasks which, to many who were old or unused to physical work, were a sheer impossibility. Saloth Sar's metamorphosis was complete. Pol Pot and Angka had arrived.

From that very day, Pol Pot made his overriding ambition clear. His country was to become the miracle of the twentieth century. In just fifteen years it was to be transformed into Asia's leading example of a modern nation, its new-found wealth based on a programme of intensive agriculture followed rapidly by industrialisation. This achievement was to be realised in a total vacuum, sealed off from all outside help, for after all had not the interference of countries both east and west provided nothing but grief? It must have been an intensely exciting moment for Pol Pot when he realised that at long last he could put into practice the plans which had gradually evolved in his mind over so many years. But no longer was this the mind of a normal man, perhaps in part because of the many persecutions and privations that he and his beloved party had suffered since their student days. The result of the stresses and strains to which they had been subjected is clearly illustrated in a photograph of his wife, a lively fellow student to whom he had become engaged in Paris, and who had later been a teacher at the French lycee in Phnom Penh. Taken towards the end of the long period of enforced hiding in the jungle, the picture shows a white-haired woman, aged almost beyond recognition, the suffering of her mind reflected in her strange stance and expression. By the time the Khmer Rouge finally reached Phnom Penh she is reputed to have gone mad, and was thereafter kept in a special house set aside for her use.

It seems that Pol Pot had reckoned with the bodies of his people but without their minds and spirit. His whole idea was based on an ethic of work, work that was relentless and without respite. He argued that, given a land of such plenty, it was only a matter of intensive labour to bring it to its full potential. But there must be no distractions for the labourers. Family life must be sacrificed to the god of productivity. So the commune scheme was set up throughout the whole country, the children snatched away from their parents to live a separate existence, arid and loveless. There was to be no more time squandered on the simple joys that were the fabric of Khmer society. Dancing and music, idle conversation, even lovemaking were banned. Husbands could visit their wives at certain fertile times of the month simply to provide the increase in population needed to grow rice and yet more rice. Bright colours, beloved of the Khmer, were frowned upon. Happiness was a sacrilege, and cleanliness paramount. The leaders, denying themselves cigarettes and drinking little, spoke very softly and cultivated a habit of calm, always slow and deliberate in their bearing and movements. And perhaps worst of all, Buddhism was outlawed. Monks, the revered elders of the people, were killed and the pagodas destroyed or used for secular purposes. It may have been the chopping of these spiritual roots as well as of all family ties that left the children so defenceless and allowed their crippled growth into the pitiless teen-age butchers of the Khmer Rouge who tortured and killed with such ruthlessness.

There was total and absolute severance from the outside world. The borders with all surrounding countries were closed and guarded with landmines. All services were cut off. There were no telephones or telegraph, and all planes were grounded. The country was turned into one huge labour camp, peopled by workers who had lost touch with families and friends and who had no idea what was happening nor any means of finding out. But still in many of their minds, the omnipotent Angka, the 'Organisation', cloaked in mystery and secrecy in order to hide its own failings, remained a power in which they could have ultimate trust. To others, passive acceptance of these new miseries was an article of their Buddhist faith, for could this not be the beginning of the end of the world that had been predicted from earliest times? In any case, they had no choice but to obey. The alternative was certain death.

Phnom Penh was the centre where Pol Pot and his henchmen lived in comfort. The rest of the country was divided into zones, each with its leader responsible only to the Centre. After settling three million people in the countryside, the new government set to work on the elimination of its enemies. First came the hierarchy of Lon Nol's regime. Next on the list were the bourgeoisie, tracked down by secret police. From this wholesale disappearance of everyone with any education arose the legend that those who wore glasses or a watch were doomed. The killing was always covert; people simply vanished, never to be seen again. But ample evidence of it remains. We visited the prison in Phnom Penh where many of these victims had been incarcerated. Its name is Tuol Sleng, and it is now kept as a museum, a horrifying memorial to the deaths of all those who, had they lived, might well have brought peace and prosperity to their country. In this building, ironically once a school, were tortured over seventeen thousand people, doubtless including some of its former pupils; those that died in the process were buried in the grounds, but most were finally taken outside the city to the ill famed 'Killing Fields' and executed there. Captured too on camera, row upon row of terrified faces, eyes wide with horror, look out upon the visitor from the walls of the prison, entire rooms lined with this record of prisoners facing a cruel death. Several smaller rooms are kept as they were when the regime ended in 1979; the corpses that had been shackled to the iron bedsteads are no longer there, but their blood is still spattered on the walls, and near life-size photographs leave nothing to the imagination. But what most brought home to me its awful reality was a row of tiny individual cells, too small to lie down in, and roughly built of modern air-bricks. These were not copies but original, and made us realise yet again just how recent it had all been, ending a mere twelve years before we had arrived.

Pot Pot's ideals had become obsessions and his natural fears paranoia. He had turned from a gifted leader to a tyrant of unprecedented proportions, ruling through unmitigated terror. He began to suspect all those around him. If the output of rice from one particular zone did not come up to expectations, always in any case set impossibly high, it was the fault of its leaders who duly 'disappeared' in an orgy of wholesale torture and killing. Purge followed purge, as enemies were seen everywhere. The definition of 'enemy' changed so constantly that even the lives of faithful followers hung by a thread. Had its leaders but realised it, Angka was already destroying itself.

Pol Pot had another mission: the destruction of Cambodia's age-old enemy, Vietnam. Such a victory would unite the whole nation behind him, a nation that was confused and baffled by the events of recent years. This at least would be something that everybody could understand. The beginning of the end came with a border raid on Vietnam by the general in command of the eastern zone. His defeat came as a bitter blow to Pol Pot, who ordered ruthless reprisals on the officers commanding the troops, a few of whom managed to escape over the border. There, in order to save their skins they changed sides, and eventually were to play a vital part in the defeat of the Khmer Rouge to which they had so recently belonged. The purge of the eastern zone was widened to include no less than one hundred thousand people, the biggest yet, and culminated in the murder by Pol Pot of his astonished general, faithful to the end. In his next breath, Pol Pot declared the revolution a success to date and launched the beginning of phase two, an ambitious programme of educational and industrial reform.

Its failure was inevitable. The workers were dying in their thousands, not just from murder but from widespread malnutrition and disease. The immaculate records kept at the extermination centre at Tuol Sleng show that during this last year it was the industrialists' turn to become victims of wholesale slaughter, men who in all good faith were trying but failing to scale the impossible heights set by Pol Pot. The cycle of destruction over the four year revolution was carefully set down in these death lists; in the early months, the leaders of the Lon Nol regime, next the bourgeoisie, then Khmer Rouge officials themselves of ever more elevated rank, and now finally those who were to have lead the country into its wondrous industrial future.

Pol Pot's aspirations were in ruins. Perhaps he still had hopes that he would become the saviour of his nation by a military defeat of Vietnam. But it was not to be. When Vietnam invaded Cambodia on Christmas Day 1978, it took that country precisely thirteen days to march into Phnom Penh and declare the end of the reign of terror. But it was not initially in their own name that they came, but under the banner of the group of Khmer Rouge army officers who had fled the country in fear of their lives during the purge of the eastern zone. They called themselves the Kampuchean National United Front for National Salvation, and one of their leaders was Hun Sen, prime minister of Cambodia to this day. Of course they had the backing of not just the strong Vietnamese army, but of the might of the Soviet Union too. But it does seem that there has to be a twist in every Cambodian tale. Where else could there be such a turnabout?

Events do not stand still, and much has changed, and is still changing, since that day. After ten years, in 1989 the Vietnamese finally withdrew their troops, but left behind them a puppet government in the guise of the Cambodian People's Party with Hun Sen as its leader. The Khmer Rouge thrived in the Vietnamese army's absence, and two other political parties, the Royalists and the Monks' party, completed the quartet of warring groups all at each others' throats. The international community offered a solution. The four parties were to sign a peace-treaty and demobilise their troops. The UN would move in and, forming a coalition with representatives from each group, would run the country for eighteen months while preparing for 'free and fair' elections. All references to 'policies and practices of the recent past' were to be dropped. In other words, in exchange for their co-operation, Pol Pot and the Khmer Rouge were to be acquitted of their sins.

So, on October 23rd 1991, just six weeks after our arrival, the Paris Peace Accords were signed by all four parties. Now, as a result of the amnesty, all sorts of things could happen; and they did. The result for us, in our unique positions as neither tourist nor local, made for an extraordinary period packed so full of events and experiences that it was difficult to absorb so much. There was no respite for us if we wanted to keep abreast of events. We were right in the middle of history in the making, and we were determined to make the most of it.

Chapter Four

The enormity of the horrors that befell Cambodia following Pol Pot's victory was to be thrust upon us very soon, but first we had more of our own little problems to tackle.

It was still early days, and the period of 'orientation' laid down by our organization had some time to run. In theory, these two months put aside for acclimatization to so much that was new seemed sensible. But in practice we would have preferred the familiarity of work to give us some stability. And in any case, this was why we had come, why we were putting up with heat, sweat, mosquitoes, infected sores, diarrhoea, and emotional slaughter, not to mention predatory pirates of the cyclo brigade.

But it cut both ways, for all play and no work gave time for a great deal of fun as well. The happiness that comes from close contact with a small group of like-minded people, thrown by force of circumstance into one another's company, goes very deep. The differences which would normally loom large of age, background and career become insignificant; we were all in it together, for better and not for worse. We talked and laughed and drank canned beer in ever increasing variety as more and more Western goods became available. As time went on, we had picnics of the Khmer kind, we played tennis and football, and we took part in wonderful musical evenings and amateur dramatics. We even went on several magical occasions to the seaside, a tropical paradise and a dream come true. And all the time, over the whole two years, our horizons were enlarging as we made Khmer friends too, got to know our neighbours, and slowly realized that life was not so very strange after all.

One of the best things about those early days was the fascinating people we met. The Asie hotel had no restaurant, so for every meal we went to the Baryon cafe opposite. This was popular and a great meeting-place. To reach it we had to cross a busy street, a microcosm of Phnom Penh activity. Monks were constantly passing singly or in groups with their orange robes and shaven heads, each followed by a small boy carrying a three-tiered tin food container, the modern equivalent of a begging bowl. Frequently, an amputee would swing past on his crutch, empty trouser-leg proof of his encounter with a mine; there are still thought to be about ten million landmines scattered about the country, more than one each for every man, woman and child. Little boys scuttled by, the six-foot pole across their shoulders blazing with the colors of feather dusters suspended from it in a row. These are no luxury, but an indispensable aid to the housewife. The dust in the dry season covers everything with a thick blanket that would rapidly grow up into an eiderdown if left undisturbed. All sorts of wares were on mobile sale. There was the ice-cream van, a handcart pushed by its owner, the bell on its shaft struck regularly in time to his step. Long rolls of rush matting glided along, five feet up on the heads of the craftswomen who made them. Bread-sellers mounted on bicycles declared their wares, the mournful 'Noon-pang' sending people hurrying to their doors to make their selection from the big basket covered with a grubby grey canvas cloth. But my favourites were the noodle-sellers, in early mornings and late evenings. A young boy would stroll down the street, tapping a stick on a flute-sized bamboo.

An amputee crossing the road

The rhythm was intricate and the site of impact wandered up and down the bamboo, creating different notes. The result was a wistful almost-tune that to all of us came to encapsulate the whole scene. Following several minutes later came the hand-pushed trolley, hot Chinese noodles aboard.

Three times a day we wove our way through the throng to the pavement opposite, negotiating en route a gutter full of filthy water awash with flotsam. Two more obstacles followed: the snake cage and the dustbin. The amazing thing about the dustbin was that it was there at all, for most garbage sat in sheets and piles in the streets. But an occasional large square metal dustbin overflowed at the edge of a road, always with its sad entourage scrounging for scraps. Even more surprising was the system for refuse collection. There was actually a huge dustbin lorry with mechanically-worked jaws to do the job, and labelled 'Made in Paris'. The problem was that when it broke down there was nothing to take its place. The snake-cage contained delicacies for the gourmet, not to mention something very special for local Lotharios. Cobra blood, so they say, is an aphrodisiac of remarkable properties. To obtain it, you must 'milk' the length of its owner with finger and thumb, and only then can the depleted reptile be chopped up and put in the soup.

The dustbin outside the Bayon restaurant

The Bayon was a cheerful place, presided over by 'Papa', a grey-haired Cambodian who got to know us all and made us feel very much at home. The food on the whole was good, served at small Formica-topped tables by waiters and waitresses, clean and smart. The same phrase could not, however, be applied to the kitchen. We never dared to take a really good look at it, but as its entire front opened on to the pavement it was difficult to avoid a frequent sidelong glance which was far from reassuring. It looked like a scene from Dante's Inferno, a cavern in Hell where men, stripped to the waist, wielded huge implements over blazing charcoal burners. It must have been from this kitchen that most of our health problems arose, for every one of us succumbed to diarrhoea and sickness during our first few weeks.

It was in the Bayon, in those days one of the best restaurants in town, that we began to meet others unconnected with our group. While at lunch one day, a Khmer lady got up from her table, came across and greeted Tim with great warmth. But it was a case of mistaken identity. Puzzled at first by his lack of response, she explained that he was the double of a film producer with whom she had been working on a documentary about Cambodia starring Hang S Ngor (later tragically murdered in Los Angeles) who took the lead part in the 'Killing Fields'. Her name was Vanna Owme, and she told us a little of her history. She, with her mother and three sisters, had left Cambodia before the Pol Pot era to work in the States for the UN. Although her immediate family was safe, she had lost a number of relatives to the Khmer Rouge, and had set herself to champion the cause of the Cambodian people. Her moment of terrifying glory came when in 1987 she went to a big peace conference in Bangkok attended by the leaders of the various warring factions in Cambodia. Prominent among these was Khieu Sampan, the acting head of the Khmer Rouge under Pol Pot's nominal leadership. In response to Khieu Sampan's claim to be the representative of the Cambodian people, she had forced herself on to her feet and with shaking knees had confronted him with the words 'You are not the representative of the Khmer people. You are a liar. You are a murderer.' She had then literally run from the room, overtaken by emotion at her own temerity, and had hidden herself away in her hotel. Next day, almost too frightened to show her face, she found she had become an overnight celebrity. Her challenging remarks had achieved newspaper and television head-lines; her message had reached the world at last. Since that day, she has interviewed Lon Nol on American television, and has toured Europe with the film produced by Tim's look-alike. No wonder Sihanouk christened her 'Cambodia's Joan of Arc.' Vanna's husband's name was Ed. He was a large, phlegmatic American of few words, a perfect springboard for her restless energy. The couple planned to come and live in Phnom Penh, hoping to find a house big enough to accommodate some of the homeless children sleeping rough on the streets. Their opinion of the government orphanages was scathing.

A few days later, Vanna invited us to a party. October 31st is Sihanouk's birthday. Although at the moment he was still in exile in China, this was to be a very special anniversary in eager anticipation of his return the following month and there was to be a party at a huge and elegant hotel near the Royal Palace, the only one of its kind at that time and totally out of tune with the rest of the city. And, wonder of wonders, there was to be a birthday cake. Even now, my mouth waters at the thought of that invitation to eat cake in the Cambodiana. After two months on an Asian diet, you can forget six of the deadly sins, but the seventh becomes an obsession: GLUTTONY. We scarcely took in that there was to be a press conference as well. We accepted, of course, for ourselves and for our two vet friends Caitlin and Bill, our Khmer language classmates. The four of us arrived at the appointed time, but were kept waiting for over an hour, told that a government minister who was to attend had been delayed on matters of national importance. It seemed that a surprising number of uniformed police had also been invited. Finally, our little party and an army of journalists, notebooks in hand, were herded into a small room, and Vanna appeared. Standing in front of a vast, square pale yellow birthday cake, she read out a letter from the hotel manager. It was, he said, forbidden to hold political meetings on the premises, so please would we just celebrate the birthday. The truth dawned; clearly we were here under false pretences, but what were they? 'So that's all' said Vanna, and proceeded to cut the cake amidst stony silence. Journalists began to ask questions. 'No comment' and 'It's a sad day for Cambodia' were her only replies, and suddenly she burst into tears. This time the silence was absolute, broken only by the squeak of knife on plate as Vanna vented her feelings on that beautiful cake, viciously dissecting it into smaller and smaller pieces. The atmosphere was electric with even the most intrepid media-men struck dumb, an unprecedented event. After what seemed an eternity, a quavering bass voice started singing, and gradually everyone else joined in. That ragged and tuneless rendering of 'happy birthday dear Sihanouk' as the assembled Western newsmen finally found their voices must surely rank amongst the oddest ever.

The spell was broken, and a few more questions followed. Could we not move outside, and have the press conference there? No, for imprisonment would inevitably follow. And all this was being recorded on a huge video camera, carried round on the shoulder of an impassive Khmer. Each one of us was photographed full-face for several seconds. When we learnt later that Vanna's objective had been the launch of a new anti-government political party, we rather wished that caution had overcome greed. We were surely now on file as enemies of the state, and anyway the piece of cake we were eventually given was so small that it served only to whet our appetites. Our dejection was complete when we were told that the large chunk of cake remaining was to go to the poor of the city. We reckoned we qualified anyway.

Vanna disappeared back to America after that and we have no more news of her. And as time went on and no armed police arrived on the Asie's doorstep, our apprehension faded and eventually vanished. But nevertheless all of us were under surveillance, though we did not know it at the time. An unsmiling blue-uniformed official sat permanently at a desk just inside the hotel door. We took him to be the porter, but learnt later that he was a government official, put there to keep a strict eye on the comings and goings of us Westerners. We were, after all, in a country under communist rule.

Rumour had it that spies numbered amongst the cyclo drivers, too. They would have fitted the bill perfectly for ferrying us hither and thither they were constantly in our company, but there were never any facts to support this theory. One day, we were approached by a group of them. Their spokesman, pushed forward by the rest, asked us for help for one of their number, a youngster called Ret S'mai who was known to us all by his engaging grin. What we did not know was that he had an artificial leg hidden under his trousers. To drive a cyclo at all is hard work for even unloaded they are heavy and cumbersome. But to do so one-legged without complaint is admirable; no wonder the poor fellow sweated when he went up hill. His colleagues told us that his leg was a bad fit and giving pain, and please would we write to England for a new one for him? These lads had become our friends, so something had to be done and automatically anything concerned with health fell to the lot of Tim and myself.

A few days later Ret S'mai and I had an assignation at the local Rehabilitation Centre. This was a fascinating place, a showpiece that we had already visited as part of our orientation but ironically whose existence was unknown to Ret. Set up in the grounds of an old tumbledown pagoda or wat and dealing almost entirely with the limbless, it was the product of the co-operation of three separate non-government organisations (NGOs), from Ireland, America and France. That in itself was an achievement, for NGOs are notorious for their inability to work together, at best from inefficiency and thoughtlessness, at worst from sheer rivalry. To newcomers, still with rose-coloured spectacles perched firmly on their noses, this came as a rude shock, and it was a relief to find that here was a notable exception.

Although some of the patients at the centre were farmers, most of them women, the majority had been soldiers. Ret had joined the army to avenge the death of a brother killed by the Khmer Rouge. Then he himself had trodden on a mine. Usually it was necessary for a patient to get government permission to attend the centre entailing up to six visits to the right people, too much for a man disabled and in pain. Fortunately the presence of an elderly white woman oiled wheels which grudgingly began to turn, but it was clear that my protégé on his own would have had

Construction of a wooden above-knee prosthesis at Wat Than

short shrift from the Khmer officials. We were shown round, and looked through the unglazed windows of the large dark dormitory closely hung with hammocks where patients attending from the provinces could stay. We saw the workshop where the prostheses were made. This was in the charge of two prosthetists, an Indian and a Dane, who after four years of training were teaching a team of Khmers to produce light plastic below-knee artificial limbs. The above-knee prostheses were still literally wooden legs, the joint a simple hinge. This was not a popular job, and I found the reason a surprising one. To the Cambodian, the man who has lost part of his body has also lost part of his mind. This makes him not only an object of fun, but also unemployable in any situation remotely intellectual. To work with or on behalf of such people casts a slur on the technician. The salary, too, is only about eight dollars a month; but then that is much the same for anyone employed by the government, be he soldier, teacher or doctor.

In the second section we visited we met Father Jim, a delightful Irish-American priest full of enthusiasm for the work. Here there were workshops for retraining in carpentry and metal-work, in typing, and in machine-sewing. Later, Tim and I were to buy a cupboard there for our house, but on this visit I simply marvelled at their achievement.

Lastly came the physiotherapy department where treatment was being carried out on a number of couches in a new purpose-built room, big and airy and painted a pretty turquoise blue. I talked to Patrice, a French physiotherapist, working with three Khmer colleagues who had recently graduated from their three-year statutory training, and with a number of students. It all seemed very efficient and modern apart from their use of kaolin poultices, old fashioned but very comforting for backache sufferers. It was their method of heating them that brought us sharply down to earth as we walked out through the back door, for there in the garden was an old lady, boiling them up in a huge witches' cauldron over an open fire.

Outside, too, we watched two youngsters being taught to walk again between a pair of parallel bars. Sitting waiting for attention was a silent, withdrawn man, his pinched young face reflecting a lifetime of trouble. He had made his own false leg from beer-cans, a remarkable feat of DIY. He had even produced ankle movement by fixing the foot to the leg with rubber.

Ret S'mai was given an appointment for a fitting the following day, and we both went home happy. But very quickly the first hint of trouble made its appearance. My protégé turned up at the hotel, demanding six dollars to pay for his 'free' leg, as this would reduce his waiting-time from six weeks to four days. Clearly corruption was creeping in, but whose? and what should I do? I consulted Father Jim at the centre. On his advice I paid up and Ret S'mai got his leg, but that was not the end of the story. Far from it. Fate had clearly decreed that our lives should become increasingly tangled. Over the next few weeks, Ret S'mai's credibility and my credulity were to be stretched ever tighter until the final rupture, but that is looking too far ahead. In the meantime, he continued on his winning way. I shall long remember the gift of green coconuts he shyly brought us to thank us for his new leg, and the song he sang to us. A natural musician, there he sat, strumming a borrowed guitar and singing a long Khmer lilt in a light falsetto voice, the hauntingly beautiful cadences rising and falling in an age-old melody.

Music was everywhere. All Cambodian ceremonial events have their own accompaniment, seemingly played as loudly as possible. A marriage or a death celebrated in a residential street, sometimes for days on end, can literally drive neighbours out of house and home, particularly those of us coming from elsewhere. The heat makes it impossible to shut windows and in any case most of them have no glass, so there is no alternative if sanity is to be saved. Unhappily the traditional Khmer musical celebration of these events, particularly of weddings, is rapidly being replaced by pop music, occasionally live and vigorously rendered by local artistes but more often recorded and blaring from speakers set at full blast.

But fortunately some Cambodian families evidently still preferred the music passed down to them by their forebears. On these occasions, we would have the privilege of watching and listening to the Khmer traditional musicians seated outside on the pavement, blowing and bowing and plucking and drumming their beautifully crafted instruments. Somehow this art had survived the Pol Pot years, still handed down from father to son despite the forced disintegration of families during that time.

It was not only the fathers that were teaching their sons, however. One of the institutions to make a startling recovery at the end of the Pol Pot era was the College of Fine Arts, housed in buildings set in open ground at the edge of the suburb of Tuol Kork. Little did I realise then just how familiar this area was to become, for it was here that my Cambodian medical colleague and I were eventually destined to buy our brothel. I was merely aware that it was an undesirable district where young ladies should not be seen at night and marvelled that the College nearby seemed so crucial to the recovery of the Khmer people. That this should be so in the face of such devastation is surely a measure of their love of music in all its forms. All through the ages song and dance have been intrinsic parts of their being, their stay in time of trouble and the expression of their relief when rescue comes.

Relief came to me, too, from this source, for here worked two important people in my life, Alice and Catherine. They were the only two Western teachers in the College, both English and both violinists. I met Alice first. She was a tall, dignified lady in her fifties, quietly spoken and with fluent Khmer, who had been out in the east for over thirty years. Somewhat incongruously, she buzzed about the city on a small motor-bike, violin tied on behind. At least, it would have been incongruous anywhere else, but here everything was turned upside down and it was only the unexpected that happened. Lewis Carroll would have loved it. I too had taken a violin with me, a sturdy country-bumpkin of a fiddle, made in Romania and assembled with a modern glue that would resist the unsticking properties of a humid climate. Within a few days of our arrival, Alice invited me to attend her regular Tuesday evening session, and this was to be the first of many such occasions. Would-be musicians assembled in all shapes, sizes, ages and nationalities, bringing with them an ever-changing array of instruments and causing Alice to delve yet again in her big tin trunk to find some music that could be played by us all. Invariably, she gave the exciting parts to her visitors, myself included, and played along with the most inexperienced to give us confidence. Usually the music was Mozart or Telemann, and the show must go on, come what may. The unexpected lurked constantly. One night the German consul arrived in a great fluster. On his way to collect his son who was playing his flute with us that evening he had been bitten by a dog. There are occasional rabid dogs in Phnom Penh, and the consul had not been immunised. In my capacity as 'the doctor' should I rush out into the night to search for vaccine? Hospitals could immediately be discounted, for it was certain that none of them would have any. There were no telephones, and anyway all the aid-agency offices would be locked up. I had only my pink push-bike and it was pouring with rain. As the bite was on the foot, the furthest point from the brain, and the rabies virus is a slow mover, I decided that the next day would do just as well. As happens so often, it was all a fuss about nothing for in the end the animal proved to be just a bad tempered bitch.

More common were the inevitable power cuts, and we would have to play by the light of oil lamps. The heat was intense, both from the lamps and the lack of fan-power, and spectacles slithered relentlessly down slippery noses. Alternatively, a sudden spurt of electricity would set fans whirring overtime sending music scuttering across the room, and we quickly learnt that the coloured plastic clothes-pegs on sale in the market were essential equipment.

To me, those evenings were magical, and I shall always be grateful to Alice for them. It might seem incongruous to be playing Corelli in Cambodia, but for a short time it transported us to a known and much-loved world, blocking out the mass of imponderable situations lying in wait outside.

Chapter Five

Throughout the whole of this early period, a worry was gnawing away at the back of my mind. What work was I actually going to do? Other things were getting under way. We had learnt enough geography to find our way about, and enough Khmer to go shopping in the market. Our bodies were settling down; there was less enmity between our stomachs and the diet, less florid reaction to the mosquito bites, and the humid heat was becoming less overwhelming. We had made friends with the geckos, little lizards that ornament walls and ceilings everywhere, and cockroaches and rats were becoming a little more tolerable. We had bicycles now, and could dispense with importunate cyclo-drivers. Our trials of house-hunting were over. The end of our two-month period of orientation was approaching, but still I had no job, nor even the likelihood of one.

This was an unusual situation. Almost always, a volunteer is sent out at the request of the host country to fulfil a specific task, and each of the other members of our group had a job to look forward to. Bill and Caitlin were off to Battambang in the north east of the country, to work in a veterinary college there. Iain and Harry were to pass on their respective skills of mechanical and electrical engineering in the local technical school, Christopher would be teaching English to a class of prospective interpreters, and Peter was to oversee and train a group of builders. Tim's brief was to work alongside the twenty-five Cambodian doctors in the country's main referral hospital for women, and to try to bring them up to date. This was no small task as he was to discover to his cost, but at least he had work to go to, whereas I had none; there had not been time to do the necessary research before our departure. But fortunately, before leaving London, I had been given the opportunity of talking to a senior member of ODA, the Overseas Development Administration, a doctor who had worked in Cambodia during the civil war right up to the moment of Pol Pot's march into Phnom Penh and had shown a great deal of personal courage at that time. When she heard our plans combined with our total lack of overseas experience, this redoubtable lady, later to become a good friend, gave us a look I shall never forget. A long appraising gaze from a pair of bright blue eyes penetrated our very souls, and I suspect revealed a couple of mugs who had not the faintest idea of what they were about, which was of course perfectly true. But she put it very kindly: 'You're very brave' was her only comment. This was followed, as always, by immensely practical advice, and I left armed with a list of important people in Phnom Penh who might be helpful in my search for the right job.

So within a week or two of arrival and clutching my list, I set off to try to find work. An abortive quest in the impressive and wonderfully cool offices of UNDP, the UN Development Project, led on to a visit to the doctor in charge of WHO, a big friendly American who gave me a great welcome. He and a newly-arrived AIDS epidemiologist were starting to plan an AIDS prevention programme. Here in Cambodia, in stark contrast to neighbouring Thailand, the HIV virus was almost unknown. To keep it that way was a huge and very exciting challenge in which I was invited to take part. At first sight this seemed a unique opportunity; what could be more useful than helping to prevent yet another wave of genocide? But how was it to be done? This was the problem, for no-one knew. Ignorant of everything that was going on round me, what could I possibly achieve? So, perhaps mistakenly, I said no. By chance this was the exact field in which I would eventually be working, but from a very different approach and after the passage of nearly two years, two years in which the HIV virus took an invisible but ineradicable hold.

With AIDS and HIV now in the forefront of my mind, I called on Anne-Marie, an experienced French nurse who had been working with prostitutes for several years. These poor girls had a bad time of it. In regular police raids on the brothels, they were rounded up and initially confined in a house known as 'the orphanage'. From there, they were transferred to an island in the middle of the Mekong, where they were virtually imprisoned. It was here that Anne-Marie and a nursing colleague worked, doing their best to diagnose and treat the wide variety of sexually-transmitted diseases (STDs) that they found. They had no doctor and no laboratory back-up, an almost impossible task. Eventually, treated and hopefully cured of both the disease and the trade they plied, the girls were released back into the community. One can only speculate on what happened next.

Anne-Marie was not welcoming. Although she became more friendly, the CV that she asked me to submit to the director of her organisation produced no results, and I was still unemployed. Protocol was part of the problem. I was not allowed to visit hospitals and offer my services unless I had been invited by the authorities to do so, and no such invitations seemed to be forthcoming. The reason for this may have been that I was not a 'specialist'. There was no shortage of Cambodian doctors, although through no fault of their own quality and quantity were not in perfect balance. Yet another doctor with no money behind her for equipment and drugs was far down on the priority list. (VSO provides only personnel, with no routine funding for work that they undertake). A fellow volunteer called Tom came to my rescue. He was a nurse, twenty-seven years old and six foot four, his height a source of wonder to the smaller Cambodians. He and his wife, an English teacher, had arrived a few weeks before and had quickly settled in. His job was to upgrade the nursing in the Municipality Hospital, a one hundred and fifty bedded hospital for the very poor. This was no mean task, for nursing in Cambodia bore little relation to nursing in Britain as it was practised then and he was the only member of staff who was not a Khmer. It was his plan that I should join the medical staff, and that the two of us working together would try to make an impact.

This seemed a good, if somewhat alarming, idea to someone whose last employment in a hospital had been over thirty years ago. But after all I had been foolish enough to turn down the easy options, and so, after gaining permission from the hospital director, I was taken round. This was another rude awakening, and that first day I was appalled. It seems strange now, for in the end I came truly to love that place. But not then, nor for a long time to come.

The hospital was a jumble of buildings, the main concrete block looking across a wide boulevard to a beautiful lake, clad with pink lotuses. Although there was no air-conditioning, somehow this building never felt really hot; it must have faced the right way for the prevailing wind to waft through its unglazed windows and long wards, doing its utmost to overcome the lavatories' terrible stench. The upper floor was reached by a stone staircase with an iron balustrade that would have done justice to a prison. This climbed up from a narrow open court yard, where bikes, both motor and pedal, would be neatly parked in rows until late afternoon. Then any that remained would be pushed out of the way, a net strung across, and the area transformed into a badminton court. Many a time I had to interrupt a game ducking under the net to cross the yard, my doctor friends, stripped to the waist, grinning their greetings. First-class players some of them were too.

There was no badminton in the yard on my first visit. In fact the whole hospital held nothing but the barest necessities. I saw row upon row of rusty iron bedsteads without mattresses or bed-clothes, each with its drip stand supporting a virulent yellow infusion bag, the contents coloured by a mixture of useless vitamins. Drips are an obsession, to every Cambodian an essential part of treatment on admission to hospital. That such 'remedies' could do far more harm than good was a very hard lesson for the Khmer doctors to learn.

But that day I was not there to criticise but to observe. There the patients lay, often two or more people to a bed if visiting families happened to feel weary. All were fully clothed, and had only a thin rush mat to protect them from the ancient springs. The floors and walls were concrete; there had once been paint, but only patches remained, mingling with the stains of spills and of an insalubrious assortment of bodily rejects. From the filthy walls sprouted bare electric wires, some ending in strip-lights, others in a forked tongue of live current, when there was any.

I was conducted on a ward-round by respectful Cambodian doctors who stood back and expected me to work instant miracles just by standing at the foot of each bed. What did I think about a thirty-three-year-old woman who had been unconscious for three weeks, her slight frame already comma-shaped as the paralysed muscles of her right side contracted relentlessly. There had not even been a proper examination, let alone any useful investigations. I could do no more than make a few wild guesses. Several young men were there, forest workers, unconscious from cerebral malaria, and a pregnant woman with the same condition. This was a disease that I was to get to know only too well over the ensuing months, but about which I knew next to nothing then. At the end of the ward was a body-shaped pile of white muslin. I went to peel back the covers, but Tom stopped me. 'I wouldn't do that' he said. What or who was underneath? An old man had been found lying on the hospital steps. Covered with sores and tormented by flies, he had been left to die; none of the doctors or nurses would touch him. It was Tom who had come along, cleaned him up and carried him to the bed. There he lay breathing his last, but at least the flies could not get at him.

This, though daunting, was real and exciting, and perhaps at last my search was over. A number of formalities still had to be gone through, of course. Clearly to cover the whole hospital was impossible. Choices must be made, and mine did not entirely concur with those of Dr Veng Thai, the hospital director. I do not think he really knew what to do with me still, and pointed me in the direction of the ante-natal clinic. This was run by a fearsome female medical assistant of the old school, who clearly knew a great deal about the subject already. I had the feeling that I should simply be an extra pair of hands, and that this was a move merely to keep me out of mischief. My years in practice had given me strong leanings towards general medicine, so why could I not work in the medical wards? This was not welcomed, and once again it was Tom who found the answer. Even in the short time he had been there, he had discovered that the Khmers love lists and tables. He suggested that I draw up my own timetable, make a neat copy with sections and sub-sections, systematically laid out between straight lines, and present it to the hospital director. So I set out exactly what I wanted to do, including a somewhat vague Saturday morning (normally very much part of the working week) and it was accepted with apparent eagerness. But Veng Thai was no fool; probably he just wanted to get the thing settled as much as I did.

Meanwhile, fitness was becoming a problem for like everyone else we were finding the enforced confinement to the city difficult, both mentally and physically. The government ruled that no one must travel more than fifteen kilometres (ten miles) outside Phnom Penh without a permit, for their own protection. In any case, there was no public transport to carry you, and nowhere to go when you got there. The countryside was heavily mined, making it essential to keep to roads or well-worn paths. So we had to find ways of exercising within the confines of the city. An unexpected feature of the town was the Olympic stadium for we had been unaware that in 1966 Cambodia had applied to host the Olympic Games. The bid had failed, but this tumbledown legacy still remains as a useful playground for the citizens of Phnom Penh. It has fallen into disrepair, grass grows up through cracks in the concrete stands, and the bright green algae-covered rainwater that half fills the swimming pool is a temptation only to street urchins. But it does boast four blue concrete tennis courts and a thriving tennis club, presided over in our time by a shrivelled monkey-like figure who for a few riels sold us a small crumpled piece of grubby paper inscribed in the Khmer script, our membership card for a month. There was a coach and a number of his hangers-on, young Cambodians who were good players and would sell their services to give us a game. We enjoyed ourselves there until the weather became too hot and the importunity of the acolytes too wearing.

Near the tennis courts was a football field where on Saturday afternoons several of our young English friends joined the locals for a game. On one occasion, Iain, nothing if not sociable but known by this time more for his drinking skills than his sporting ones, took part, and halfway through the game collapsed unconscious. When he came round, he announced for the first time that he was diabetic. He had, he said, been given a bottle of insulin by his practice nurse at home, with instructions to inject himself in an emergency, and as he had not felt too good before the game he had drawn up what seemed to him a reasonable measure and pressed the plunger. On the face of it he was lucky to be alive, but as tests were carried out and his medical records traced, it gradually became clear that neither now or at any time past did he have diabetes, and that the entire story, insulin and all, was the product of an imagination which we were only now discovering was limitless. Iain-watching, with his activities both real and imagined hopelessly intertwined, became an ever more intriguing pastime. By now, we had discovered that his father, far from being the eminent medical man described to us on the journey out, was an out-of-work shipbuilder. Iain's enthusiasm for life knew no bounds, and we were all apprehensive about his fate, the end to which his flights of fantasy seemed bound to lead him.

An appealing way of taking exercise as well as a blessed relief from the heat was the swimming pool at the Cambodiana, that big hotel where we had eaten cake. It was a beautiful blue pool, surrounded by sun-loungers under the shade of big umbrellas. Smiling Khmer waiters, wearing shorts and bearing aloft cold drinks on little trays, busied about. It was quintessential Graham Greene, the White Man's Club but with a difference. Gone were the alcoholic tea-planters and the district officers, and in their place little clusters of aid-workers, intense and earnest, sitting in swimming costumes deep in collective consideration of some weighty problem. It was a quiet place then, before the UN came and drove us out. But that was later.

One of the Cambodiana's greatest assets is its position. It overlooks the

Mekong river, an immense and awe-inspiring stretch of water, always a turgid milk chocolate brown and speckled with picturesque fishing boats. But the lives of the fishermen who use them are anything but picturesque. The newcomer has only to stand beside the swimming-pool, aloof and secure in his Western-ness, and look over the dividing wall; there, right in front of him and providing a colourful foreground to the waters beyond, are the shacks where they live. Tumbledown shanties built of palm leaves may raise cries of pleasure at their quaintness from visiting wealthy Americans (for already tour agencies were starting up) but to the younger and more idealistic volunteers the comparison produced a huge philosophical dilemma. We were not here as tourists. We were here to work alongside the fishermen as part of their own community. To us old ones, hardened to the ways of the world, this posed little problem, I regret to say, and our weekend visits to the pool provided both exercise and a welcome relief to all five senses. But some could never bring themselves to go there. The contrast was too great.

Gazing out from swimming pool level, one unbroken stretch of water meets the eye. But flying over Phnom Penh gives a different perspective, a spectacular aerial view of not one but four rivers forming a capital X. The upper limbs are the Mekong (east) and the Tonle Sap (west); the lower, the Mekong still to the east, and the smaller Bassac on the west. The city is tucked into the western angle of this cross, and straggles mainly northwards along the Tonle Sap. This, despite its appearance, is no ordinary river. Regularly every year it turns round and runs the other way; but after all, what else can you expect in this country of contradictions? As always, there is a sensible explanation. In the rainy season the Mekong rises. When its waters reach a certain height, the Tonle Sap acts as a flood-relief channel, and the surplus water from the Mekong flows up it to a great lake at its northern end, some seventy kilometres north of Phnom Penh. As the waters subside, so the direction of the channel changes, and all four arms of the cross once again flow south. The lake is enormously important. It supports a huge fishing industry, vital to the country's economy, though sadly, as many of the fishermen are Vietnamese, it is also a site of Khmer Rouge activity. And of course the land round about it, once the waters go down again, is very fertile.

Standing beside the smooth, flat, slow-moving Mekong as it flows past the palace in Phnom Penh and trying to picture it at its source,

I could almost believe in the White Crocodile. Tradition holds that it is this mythical beast that makes the Tonle Sap turn in its tracks. That the real cause is the melting snows of the Himalayas in far-off Tibet where the Mekong rises seems almost as unlikely. It is a mighty river. Flowing south and gaining strength all the way, it separates Laos first from Burma and then from Thailand before it runs straight down the middle of Cambodia and out into the South China Sea. The vital ports of the delta were captured with the southerm tip of the country by Vietnam in one of the many scuffles between the two countries. But the Mekong still remains a vital waterway, and during our two years, more and more big ships from many countries were arriving and mooring at the wharves of the city.

The wharves were fascinating. They occupied a long stretch of the river bank in one of the most squalid areas of Phnom Penh, north of the exclusive surroundings of the Royal Palace. There was constant loading and unloading as trading boats pulled in and out. We watched as one such craft discharged its cargo, the emerging life-sized Buddhas laid out in rows on the dock and gazing woodenly up at their creators with a benign expression on their brightly painted faces. On the next pitch, men were struggling with huge bundles of sugar-cane, the sagging ten foot long stems making them an awkward burden. Futher on still, it was difficult to find a passage between stacks of charcoal, neatly bundled. And so it went on. There was always something to watch; standing on the banks of the Mekong was never dull.

Chapter Six

In a hot country, water assumes immense importance. The river was a very popular place. At weekends and in early evening, young people dressed in their best would stroll along beside it, enjoying the coolness reflected from its surface. But there are other inland waters too, notably a beautiful lake some fifteen kilometres south of Phnom Penh at a place called Chong Eik. We were told that in the old days well-to-do families would travel out from the city to picnic there on a low hillock overlooking the water. It was for this reason that Pol Pot chose it as the site of his main extermination camp, for these were the very people that he wanted to eliminate. These are the Killing Fields.

No picnicking goes on there now. It is a place of pilgrimage, and there can be few foreign visitors to Phnom Penh who do not feel bound to visit it. The drive from the city is a bumpy one, along narrow earth roads through attractive countryside. Then comes the left turn down a straight track, and, at the point of arrival, a big notice which I quote verbatim:

PRESENTATION OF THE EXTERMINATION CAMP
CHOEUNG EK.
THE EXTERMINATION CAMP CHOEUNG EK IS ABOUT 15 KM FROM PHNOM PENH IN THE SOUTH-WEST. IT IS IMPLICATED IN THE ORGANISATION OF THE BIGGEST SECURITY CENTRE OF KAMPUCHEA DEMOCRATIC IN POL POT REGIME UNDER THE NAME S21. S21 HAD ITS HEAD-QUARTER AT TUOL SLENG PRISON. ALL THE VICTIMS (PEASANTS, WORKING, INTELLECTUALS, MINISTERS, KHMER DIPLOMATS, FOREIGNERS, WOMEN, CHILDREN...) DETAINED AND TORTURED DURING INTERROGATING AT TUOL SLENG WERE LATER SENT TO CHOEUNG EK FOR LIQUIDATION. A LOT OF POPULATION AND POL POT SOLDIERS OF THE EASTERN ZONE WERE ALSO SENT

THERE SINCE MAY 1976. TOWARDS THE END OF 1980,
86 OUT OF 129 MASS GRAVES WERE UNEARTHED IN
THE EXTERMINATION CAMP AND 8985 CORPSES WERE
FOUND.
A STUPA HAS BEEN ERECTED TO PRESERVE THEIR
REMAINS AND ALSO TO COMMEMORATE THE DEATH OF
THE KAMPUCHEA PEOPLE UNDER POL POT REGIME.

This English translation, in capital letters which diminish in size in order to fit it all in, occupies the lower half, with the original in Khmer script above it. In a further effort to accommodate the English words in the space available the sign-writer was evidently forced to split on to two lines the word 'peasants'. So now the sentence reads 'ALL THE VICTIMS, PEAS, ANTS, WORKING, INTELLECTUALS,...'etc.

To me these adaptations add greatly to its pathos.

The stupa mentioned on the placard is built in traditional pagoda style, striking in its tall narrow shape and bright white, grey and yellow paint. As the visitor approaches, his eye is drawn to the long windows which occupy each of its four sides, but it is not until he is almost on top of it that its purpose becomes clear. It is entirely full of skulls, neatly stacked on shelves and sorted and labelled according to sex and age. Many of them have gaping holes at the back where they were struck in life with a hoe. There is a small gap in the otherwise uninterrupted terracing where those belonging to Westerners have been removed.

From the stupa, which is on slightly higher ground, there is a marvellously peaceful view of the lake beyond; it is not surprising that it had been a popular beauty spot. On the near bank is a pastoral scene where cows wander, finding grazing in this well-watered patch of countryside. Despite its truly gruesome connotations, this is a place of stillness and of rest, permeated by a strange tranquillity.

On this our first visit, some of the cattle had strayed closer and, tails swinging, were casually treading the paths between a number of large pits in the ground beyond the stupa. These are the mass graves, now opened, each one having held between twenty-five and fifty people, some buried headless and many of them children. As we followed the cows along the narrow paths, hastily skipping over a snake that suddenly slithered across in front of us, we could see shafts of bones still protruding from the earth walls; on one of these sat a beautiful dragon-fly, the sun catching

Skulls at Choeung Ek: the 'killing fields'

Open Graves at Choeung Ek

its shimmering wings. But it was the half-buried strips of clothing, their still-bright colours drawing our attention as they fluttered in the pleasant breeze, that made us realise the enormity of it all, and once again served as a reminder of just how recently this had been a place of unimaginable horror. They say it smelt of blood for two years afterwards.

Kem, the Cambodian secretary from our office, came with us on that first visit. Pretty and smiling, she too walked round and looked at the stupa and the graves, and it seemed at first that it was only the snake that upset her. Then she led us unassumingly to the shady side of the stupa, where we all sat down on its steps to recover from what, even to outsiders like ourselves, had been a gruelling experience. She rested with us, and it was then that she began to speak. In a low voice and in excellent English, she told us her story, a story typifying the suffering of every Cambodian during that terrible time. She told it quietly and without drama. Simple and understated, its starkness conveyed utter despair.

There had been ten brothers and sisters in her family, two of whom were murdered and three who starved to death. She described to us the deaths first of a brother, then of a sister. Her brother, on the point of exhaustion from hunger, had managed to capture and eat a lizard. But he was so weak that he fell and was unable to get up again. He implored his companions to find more food, but when they eventually succeeded he was too near the end. He was unable to eat it, and he died. The sister's tale was sadder still. Emaciated already from starvation, she developed copious diarrhoea, so Kem and a third sister were nursing her naked, for frequently soiled clothing was more than they could cope with. One night, the indignity became too much, and she implored them to dress her. Gentle Kem would have complied, but was overruled by her companion, obviously a tougher proposition altogether or perhaps simply too exhausted herself to act. That night, their sister died. For her at least the shame and sadness were over, but for poor Kem, guilt at denying her this simple request remains to this day.

But she herself had to go on. She had been put to work to build a dam. Slight in build, she nevertheless became very strong, and was able to carry forty kilograms of mud at a time on her frail shoulders. Backwards and forwards she went, on and on, and finally the task was finished. Because she was such a good worker, and because she had been cunning enough to pretend to be married (for it was not expected of married women to be as strong as single ones) she had so far been spared. Her job done

Kem

and with marks for good behaviour, she was allowed to go and search for her parents. At last she found their work place, but alas, her mother had gone the same way as her brother and sister, and only her father remained alive.

Throughout this time, she like all her companions was wearing the one set of clothes that she had been given at the beginning. This was a pair of black 'pyjamas' and she told us how, as time went on, the upper part of the trousers became thicker and thicker and the legs shorter and shorter as they cut off the bottoms to patch the top.

And then at last it seemed that her own end had finally come. She and others had actually been put to work to dig their own graves when a miracle happened. The Vietnamese arrived and set them free. Their gruesome task thankfully abandoned, she and her friends slowly made their way back to Phnom Penh. It was a distance of a hundred and seventy kilometres, and weak as they were, they had to walk the whole way and with no shoes on their feet, for four years of hard labour had long since worn out their one pair of sandals.

She told us that, for ten years afterwards, the horrors never left her mind, and that even now not a day went by without memories.

Within moments of the end of her story, Kem's cap was back on her head at a jaunty angle and her radiant smile shone through her tears. In that instant, she became to me the absolute embodiment of the courage and resilience of her people.

She had given us much food for thought. Her simple eloquence could not fail to colour and deepen our own perception of the intensity of anguish to which the kindly smiling people round us had been subjected. Going home in the back of the truck, as our bodies were thrown this way and that by pot-holes, so our minds were jolted into a deeper reflection on what had gone before. We had been drawn here by duty and curiosity, but we were leaving with an overwhelming sense of desolation. Having seen with our own eyes the splintered skulls we had no choice but to believe eye-witnesses' accounts of the atrocities that they themselves had seen. We had read of the unconcerned smiles on the soldiers' faces as they went about their gruesome tasks, carelessly gossiping amongst themselves. We had read about the murder of children by the simple expedient of swinging their heads against a tree. We had read of the typical case of the mother lashed to a tree-trunk, watching her new baby laid on the ground to die of heat stroke, carefully placed just outside her reach. Her own lingering death must have come as a huge relief. We had read and heard all these things and more. But sitting book in hand in a comfortable chair in a comfortable English home, such stories, though doubtless true, had seemed so disconnected from our own lives that their reality could be shirked. Now we could no longer avoid confronting the undeniable truth that these things had actually happened, here by the steps on which we sat.

.

Chapter Seven

The very day of our visit to the Killing Fields was the eve of Prince Sihanouk's return from exile. He had been away from his country for the last twenty years, and the excitement was intense. To the older people, this his second coming was little short of miraculous. They remembered back to the good old days, when the demi-god Sihanouk had been in his half-heaven, and all was right with the world. During the preceding weeks, gangs of workmen had been hammering and sawing, planting and painting. The palace and its encompassing walls turned back to their original sunny yellow. The surrounding streets and parks, usually clotted with squatters, were miraculously cleared, the poor people driven out of the city in a fervour of cleansing for the great man. It all looked stunningly beautiful; presumably this was a return to how it once had been.

So, on the evening of that same day, four of us unlocked our bicycles and rode through the dilapidated, poverty-stricken streets round the Asie Hotel, past familiar rubbish-heaps and families camping out on the pavements, to reach the purified air of the palace precincts. To our surprise, there was almost no-one about. We were dominated by a colossal portrait of the Prince, depicting him as a young man; as everyone knew he was in his seventieth year, what was the point? There were strings of coloured lights outlining the contours of all the buildings, a splendidly reckless outpouring of electricity which was to last all of three days and which we were to pay for later by ever-increasing power-cuts. But it was worth it. It felt rather like Christmas Eve. There was that expectant hush, when the hard work of preparation is finished, the Christmas Tree lights are switched on, and we children are waiting with bated breath for Father Christmas to arrive.

The only people to share this with us were a couple of French girls, aid-workers like ourselves, and the Palace Guard. The soldiers had pitched a tent on the grass in front of the gates, and were squatting in circles on the pavement, playing cards. They were very friendly and seemed to welcome our presence. We probably relieved their boredom.

The great day dawned. Khmer classes had finished at last and we should have been free to join in the general mood of festivity. But we had one piece of business to attend to first. Burglaries were rife in the city, and our future landlord, Pay Hayleng, was insistent that we should take on his son to guard us in our new house, apparently a common custom. But we had other ideas. Ret S'mai, the young cyclo-driver who had been fitted with a new leg, wanted to better himself, and we needed someone to keep the burglars at bay. We had some misgivings, for once or twice Ret had shown aspects of his character which we did not care for. However, putting these aside as aberrations, we decided that he and no-one else was the man for us.

So early that morning, standing in our future garden, we argued it out with Pay Hayleng in our best French. We were not entirely worsted, but had to be content with a reluctant 'we'll see'. Disappointed, we went off to join the revellers in a far from holiday mood. But it was a beautiful sparkling morning, and our ill-humour soon evaporated. The sun shone, and a cool breeze brought relief from its heat. The crowds were out, and the flags were flying. Buses were still disgorging their loads of scrubbed school-girls and boys, all in uniform and each carrying a small paper Cambodian flag. They looked very spruce. Perhaps it is the uniformity of colour not just of shirts but of hair too that makes massed Asian school-children look so much smarter than their European counterparts. Certainly the black-and-white effect in the bright light was quite dazzling. They settled themselves along the edges of the long straight road leading to the palace, the boys squatting and the girls sitting with legs tucked decorously under them. Enormous care had been taken with the girls' coiffures, and despite the breeze not a hair escaped from their intricately plaited tresses. No one seemed to know when the Prince was expected, and no one seemed to care. Some had already been there for six or seven hours. But within minutes of our arrival, there was a stirring and a buzzing in the crowd. He was coming!

We ran for a better position. Rearing up in front of us was an ideal vantage point, the Independence Monument. Not exactly a jewel in Phnom Penh's crown, this enormous tiered edifice, liberally sprinkled with concrete Nagas, the ubiquitous Hindu serpent-god, was erected in 1958 to celebrate the departure of the French. Its steps are a great meeting-place; for young men on Saturday nights, for monks, for the white clad elderly religious matriarchs, and now a perfect lookout. I was clearly about to make the journalistic scoop of scoops. With a good camera in hand, a perfect view, and a rapidly advancing royal procession, how could I fail? The cavalcade approached down the long, straight boulevard, first the motor cycles, and then a stream of white limousines. Now we could see the open state car, distant figures standing in it and waving to the crowds. Suddenly it was upon us. Captured dead-centre of the view-finder, I took the perfect picture, the fairy tale Prince returned at last to his tropical kingdom. But I had reckoned without the tremor I get when excited. Life is, without doubt, full of bitter disappointments. We followed the crowds who followed the prince to his palace. But he had disappeared inside, and there was no more to see. Neither did he appear later in the day to address his subjects, as had been rumoured. But it had been a memorable occasion, and we even had a re-run on television in the squalid café where we ate our supper.

The famous and the infamous made their reappearance within a few days of each other, and as always it was the infamous who captured the attention of the world. The front page headline of the Times of Thursday November 28th 1991 reads 'Lynch mob attacks Cambodian leader', and alongside it is a photograph of the gory profile of an elderly man, blood streaming down his face, entitled 'Revenge'. This was Khieu Samphan, now nominal head of the Khmer Rouge despite Pol Pot's continued covert leadership, who under the terms of the Paris Peace Accords felt entitled for the first time since 1979 to enter the country. In the event, public opinion decreed otherwise.

That morning, I went shopping in the big New Market. Evidently some demonstration was afoot, for the pavements round about were thronged with people holding posters depicting a white-haired man, his face disfigured by a vast X. On my way home I cycled past a large and orderly crowd marching in the same direction as myself, many bearing the same poster. Two lorry loads of green-clad police with riot shields drove by. Soon my path was almost blocked by yet more crowds and, attempting to escape down a side turning, I found it cordoned off by anxious police. The reason was alarmingly clear, for a hundred yards off, swirling above the heads of a solid mass of people was a dense cloud of flame-flecked black smoke. The conflagration, the throngs of men and women, the almost tangible tension in the air, all combined to dispel any further aspirations I might have had to become reporter of the year.

Discretion suddenly seemed eminently the better part of valour, and I rode inconspicuously on my way. (There were, in fact, five good reasons why I was about as inconspicuous as a dinosaur. I was old, tall, pale, female and one-handed, the other hand being in constant use holding down my voluminous cotton skirt. Released, this would have produced a sixth reason that beggared all the rest. But to-day, people had something better to think about).

It was not until I had heard the World Service News, crackly on the short-wave band of the radio we had bought in that same market, had tried to understand local gossip, and later had read the *Times* cutting sent from home, that I was able to put the story together. Khieu Samphan had flown into Phnom Penh that morning, announcing to the world that he was 'very happy' to be back. He went straight to the house of a fellow-politician, Son San, and some four hours later the leaders of a mob of several thousand people shouting 'KR assassin' broke into the house and forced their way up the stairs. It seems that Khieu Samphan, rising from his arm-chair and facing the mob with courage and dignity, momentarily moved his enemies to pity and stopped them in their tracks. But there was one exception. One man, stepping forward from the crowd, hit the Khmer Rouge leader on the head with an iron bar. Khieu Samphan fell to the ground, clutching an attaché case to his chest, with a member of his bodyguard crushing him in a bear-hug for protection. Then the mob surged forward, punching and kicking him. Some say that the police acting as a buffer had to sit on him; others that the crowd tried to string him up and hang him from the light fitting. Somehow, the police got him outside where a second picture in the Times shows him clambering up a ladder into an armoured personnel carrier. Meantime the mob had pulled off doors and window frames, enlarging the pile with furniture, and had made a huge bonfire in the street, sending high into the sky the black smoke and flames that I had seen. Khieu Samphan beat an ignominious retreat to the airport, and Russian pilots in a government aircraft flew him back to Bangkok. His visit had lasted just seven hours.

By chance we knew the journalist who had captured that moment of history, reminding the world of the bitter tensions still warping the country. To the gratification of our friend, his picture of a bloodied Khieu Samphan had appeared on the front page of most major newspapers. Like so many people we came into contact with, he was a character with a capital C, the sort of man we would never have met in the normal way.

Corsican by birth, his trademark was his moustache, a simply enormous walrus affair suspended beneath a totally bald pate. He had some strange stories to tell. In his early life he had been a member of a gun-toting gang in Corsica. Disenchanted with his blood-thirsty way of life, he had travelled the world, and chance had finally brought about this unlikely encounter with a pair of English doctors. He popped up in the most unexpected places, and always, sweeping his moustache aside, with a gallant flourish kissed my hand. On one of our rare visits to the coast, over three hours by car from Phnom Penh, I was relaxing in the warm water in a magical world of my own. Suddenly there was a splash beside me, and out of the sea erupted a familiar figure. There can be few who have suffered a damp and near-naked embrace by a Corsican bandit in the languid waters of the South China Sea.

The final event before work started was our house-move. November 15th was our last night in the Asie Hotel, just ten weeks since we had arrived. Anxious though we were to settle in our own little house and garden, suddenly the prospect of the responsibilities of home ownership seemed daunting, and the shabby old Asie correspondingly friendly and secure. But we had scored one victory. Our landlord had given in, and Ret S'mai was to be our guard.

Early the next morning Peter arrived to move us. Peter was the builder, one of our original groups of eight, and as he had already started work had the use of a big white truck. A great crowd gathered round it as we staggered out of the hotel with more and more luggage, and willing hands helped us across the few feet of pavement. Before going 'home' we had to do some shopping. Our landlord had provided us with a bed, a mock-marble melamine affair, more suited he thought to our Western taste than the pleasing plain wooden ones in common use. But we had no mattress. The markets sold almost everything, from fly-blown meat to electric table-lamps ornamented with little plastic dogs that glowed in the dark. But for large furniture we had to look elsewhere. Certain streets were dedicated to selling certain goods, and our first stop was in a road lined with tiny open shops piled high with mattresses and hard pink over-stuffed pillows. The mattresses were all foam rubber and the only choice lay in thickness and quality. Left to ourselves, we would probably have taken the easy way out and bought the top one. There surely could be very little difference, and in any case our agency budget was tight. But we were reckoning without Peter. Not for nothing did his muscles bulge and the hair spill out from the neck of his T-shirt. He stood over us as the little stall-holder pulled out each mattress in turn for us to lie on. For this I shall be eternally grateful, for the hard floor seemed to jump up through every one of them. In despair, the owner took my arm and led me through a curtain at the back into a tiny cubby-hole, where she invited me to lie down on her own grubby bed. It was blissful. Back we went, and out came a mattress from the very bottom of the pile. Expensive or no, this was the one for us. We actually bought two. We were expecting friends from England, and so excited were we at the prospect that half a month's allowance seemed a small price to pay.

Next came the street of furniture shops. This was a fascinating place. Each had its own workshop where wood was of good quality and plentiful, but the workmanship often poor with frequent use of unseasoned timber. Foreigners were coming in, and goods must be supplied in a hurry. Our Field Office had not yet come up with a final figure for our budget, and there had been dark mumblings about keeping our clothes in cardboard boxes, to us not a practical long-term proposition. Our eye fell on a second-hand filing cabinet, a large solid wooden cupboard with rows of little hatches. What better for filing away our socks and knickers? It was handsome and cheap. After a good scrub, it served its purpose admirably, and stored everything from sheets to sea-shells.

Perhaps we did not sleep so very well that first night. Our bed with new white cotton sheets and mosquito net was perfect. The city hubbub had gone, but this quiet street brought its own surprises. Next door was a smallholding where doves cooed and an anxious trainee cockerel practised all night for his morning alarm call. There were other stranger noises too. What sounded like a clockwork toy erupted spasmodically in the garden. First would come the winding-up process, cog-wheels clicking to the turn of an imaginary key. Then came a rasping treble-bass double-creak, a 'tock-eye' repeated always four or five times, loud and vigorous at first, then dying slowly in volume, tempo and pitch. The whole process would be repeated several times, the wind-up evidently essential to the final proclamation. Try it. We discovered that it was made by a senior member of the gecko family, a Tokay of evil repute. It was said that if it landed on your scalp, it dug its talons in so deep that it had to be surgically removed. We have no positive evidence to support this claim, I am glad to say, but we did see the creature more than once. The first time it had just shed its tail, giving us quite the wrong impression.

The most spine-chilling and exciting new noise was the howling of the wolves, or at least that is what it sounded like. They must have been dogs, but dogs reverting to the habits of their ancestors, always at the time of full moon. One would start to bark, another and then another would join in, until suddenly the staccato reports would coalesce into a weird and mighty siren of sound, as all over the city they sang together for perhaps a minute. Then, as if at some given signal, the unearthly chorus would fragment again and die. It was an uncanny experience, lying in a strange bed in this strange country, gazing at palm trees silhouetted against a great disc of moon and listening to the banshee wailing of lost souls.

The entry in my diary a few days later is a shocking one, even in this land of the unexpected. We were going shopping, to buy more necessities for our new home. My nursing colleague Tom and K. his wife had lent us their cook for a few days, to help us to get straight. Her name was Samut, and she lived with the numerous members of her extended family in a wooden house no bigger than our own. Unmarried, the joy of her life was Kling, a chubby baby boy put into her arms the previous year by his penniless young mother who could not make a home for him. (Tragically, four-year-old Kling has since died from a sudden illness.) Samut and I had squeezed ourselves into one cyclo, a usual habit among friends, and were heading for the market, when we were forced to a halt by a crowd of people. I assumed there had been a road accident, for motor-bikes were always running into something, usually each other, and people loved to gawp. But Samut, pale and shaken, nudged me and pointed upwards. There, in the middle of a huge tree, some fifty feet up, was a girl. Her long white night-gown stood out starkly against the dark green of the leaves; standing stiff and straight, legs a little apart, she seemed in a trance. With her big eyes and her mouth opened in a round 'o' she looked transfixed, hypnotised into a state of ultimate stillness. I remember wondering if she could have climbed out of a near-by upstairs window in her sleep. And then, my eyes moving down to her bare feet, I realised that she was standing on air. At last I saw the rope and the truth dawned. She had hanged herself. It was all so melodramatic, so clean and tidy, so much more like a stage-set than real life, and somehow this made it all the more horrible. Already there had been four hours of daylight, and it had happened last night. Why had they not cut her down? A love affair was behind it. That was all I ever heard.

Taking a breather

We celebrated the end of our two month initiation with a picnic on the river. Khmer picnics, a favourite family relaxation, are complex events. A great deal of trouble is taken with the preparation of all sorts of delicacies, salads and fruit. Floor mats are spread and covered with pretty little dishes, the company sits round the edge, and the feast begins. This one was less exotic for it was a poor English copy of the Cambodian original, but there were enough victuals and enough beer, and it was a good day out. We had hired a double-decker motor boat for the occasion and lazed about on the open top deck, spreading ourselves between the pot-plants and finding some shelter from the sun under a big umbrella. Our numbers were swelled from time to time by inquisitive children, visitors from their living quarters on the enclosed lower deck where the owner-driver made fruitless efforts to confine his family.

It was enormously peaceful pottering up the Mekong for an hour or two. The wide vista of water, its colour and sheen changing with the light, rested the eye. We passed fishing boats, some brightly painted, others merely functional, their owners, often identifiable as Vietnamese by the conical shape of their hats, casting and re-casting their big nets. The banks slid by, brownish-yellow mud topped by the green of banana trees. We passed a woman washing herself, fully dressed, long black hair dripping as she stood waist-deep. Shouts across the water warned us of children swimming. Sure enough, round the next bend was a group of little boys camouflaged against the muddy bank, whooping and somersaulting as its steep slippery incline shot them into the water. The smallest ones waved, their elder brothers, approaching puberty, decorously used both hands to cover themselves as we went by. Off-white humped cattle, most of them skin and bone ('worms', pronounced Bill) picked their way down familiar paths to a drinking place. On a beach a small crowd had gathered to launch a new fishing boat. Nearby, a group of squatting women did the family wash.

Our destination was Koh Aknyatai, a village famous for its silk-weaving. As we approached, the empty sky began to fill with swooping shapes. Small birds, their paths describing perfect arcs through the ever more crowded air, drew intricate patterns as they dipped and dived all around us. These were bee-eaters, spectacular little birds conspicuous by their immensely long spiky central tail feather and their plunging flight. The colours of their plumage, an exotic blend of soft brown with an almost fluorescent green, matched perfectly with their surroundings. Their homes were the scores of holes in the steep bank which we had to scramble up to reach the village. The boatman beached the boat, and up we went, on to a dirt track which took us to a tiny hamlet. A jumble of wooden and palm leaf homes stood on their long legs, with tall mango trees growing up between them and chickens scratching about on the dusty ground. Within seconds of our arrival, we had a bodyguard of dirty ragged children, swelling in numbers as the bush telegraph signalled our appearance.

Cambodia's children must be amongst the world's most appealing. Tugging at our heart strings, they gazed up at us with huge brown eyes, shy but standing their ground in the face of this extraordinary invasion of tall pale people with strange coloured hair. Most were solemn, though the more extrovert managed a winning gap-toothed smile. The hems of voluminous grubby T-shirts hung inches from the ground, skinny shoulders escaping from sagging necklines. Bare tops, bare bottoms, or bare all over; nobody cared. A little girl wore a spotless muslin dress. A small boy sported a shirt covered with badges and bearing the legend of an English cub-scout group. There were no shorts underneath. These children looked well fed. Some were still small enough to be barrel-shaped, but none had the telltale pot belly of the malnourished, their extra rations stemming from their mothers' weaving skills, no doubt.

One little girl came up and grabbed my hand. Surprised at her boldness, I realised from her funny little face that she was mentally defective. A small boy appointed himself our guide, and it was some minutes before we realised he was deaf and dumb. By signs, he made himself perfectly clear both to us and his friends, who involved him naturally in their games. These children, who would certainly be given labels in the West, fitted with no obvious difficulty into this uncomplicated community.

Under several of the homes were looms of the most basic design. It must have been a good place to work, for the house acted as umbrella and sunshade, and the area was cool and spacious. Despite the dim light, the colours of the silk threads stretched on the long frames shone out in rich reds, blues and purples. At the end of each frame sat a young woman, working with feet and hands in an intricate sequence of movements too rapid to follow. As if by magic the length of material grew, inch by inch, and an extraordinarily complex frieze was woven into the end of each length with silver thread. It was sad to realise that these beautiful girls would themselves never be bedecked in their own shining silk, for they were paid a tiny fraction of the market price. And it is hard to imagine that those whom it finally adorned gave a single thought to its humble origins, presided over by scurfy pigs and scabby chickens.

They dyed their own yarn. I saw skeins in a truly royal purple hung out to dry on a line slung between two posts. An old bicycle wheel turned by a man squatting beside it wound thread from skein to bobbin, the silk he was working on glowing a rich ruby-red in the strong sunshine. Before Pol Pot, the raw silk had been locally produced, but now it had to be imported. The mulberry groves which used to feed the silk-worms were destroyed by the Khmer Rouge and have not yet been replaced.

Soon it was time to turn back. Darkness would fall with little warning, always at about six p.m., and our boatman was anxious to get home. We settled down on board to sleep or read or day-dream. But not for long. Ahead of us, in the middle of the river, came a splashing and a shouting. Binoculars brought into focus a most unusual craft leading us down the river at great speed, and slowly we gained on it and drew alongside. Here was something else we had not seen before. No less than forty oarsmen, twenty on each side, were standing precariously balanced in their long low canoe and paddling for all they were worth. The air was filled with yells of encouragement and cascades of water. Under a large umbrella in the brilliantly decorated bow stood a gyrating figure, swaying a prayer to propitiate the spirits and to bring success to his boat. Behind him, drum between his knees, squatted the time-keeper, bare hands beating out a frenzied rhythm, goading on the crew to even greater efforts. They were a motley lot, every one of them adorned over some part of his anatomy with a kroma, that bit of check cloth that no Khmer can ever be without. Variously turban, scarf, or loin-cloth on this occasion, its other functions are legion and its possession indispensable. The slender boat was filled to capacity with a crescendo of activity as the men pitted their strength against our diesel engine, and indeed for a while muscle did outdo machine. Finally they dropped behind, as we literally sailed off into the sunset. And what a sunset. Often it is a contrast that focuses the mind and senses, and this was no exception. A glowing red sky is beautiful, and so are the jet-black spiky silhouettes of pagoda and palace. But put one against the other, and add a handful of brightening stars, and what do you get? A moment that can only be left to the imagination or the memory.

The end of our day came quickly. Through the sudden silence that fell as, docking, we cut our engine, the shouts of the battling boatmen still reached us faintly across the water. They were practising for the inter province boat races that were to take place in a few days time. An annual affair, the Water Festival is one of the main events of the Cambodian calendar, coinciding with and celebrating the turn-about of the Tonle Sap. It is officially a three day holiday, but nothing could be taken for granted. It took us some time to realise that, though fixed holidays are frequent, whether they are actually to take place is only announced the preceding evening on television and radio. As we could understand neither we usually got it wrong. I would turn up to work to find the hospital almost deserted, or else, staying away so as not to be caught a second time, I would be greeted with 'Where were you yesterday, Yea?' (Yea means grandmother. Nobody ever called me anything else, except occasionally 'Loke Yea', sticking a 'Madam' on the front).

It seems that during the Water Festival the whole world turns out to watch the races and show off their best clothes. There are eighteen provinces in the country, most of them entering a boat for the great race, some teams smartly turned out in their team colours, the poorer ones wearing whatever they can muster. Only two boats race at a time, so it is a slow business. The banks of the river are thronged with a cheering audience of literally thousands and thousands of people, all in their

Sunday best and many bedecked in the funny hats that are on sale everywhere. The little girls are encased in frilly nylon frocks. The heat is intense. Stalls, set up higgledy-piggledy all over the place, do a brisk trade in food and drink. The more agile spectators clamber up anything that will give them a better view, where some even get excited or hot enough to jump off their vantage point into the water. The mud churns up underfoot. It is a tremendous occasion.

And then, on that first night of our first Boat Race Day, came the crowning glory, a totally unexpected and crazily extravagant firework display. The town's children had never seen fireworks before, and the gasps and whoops of sheer incredulous wonderment that greeted each explosion of fragmenting brilliance in the huge night sky were the best part of the whole crowded day. The money had been well spent after all.

Chapter Eight

It is always good to have something to look forward to, and throughout those unfamiliar early days we were sustained by an exciting prospect; close friends from home were coming to stay with us. The post was unreliable and telephones few and far between, so the proposed visit took on a great importance. Time plays curious tricks; though it seemed like half a lifetime, we had only been in Cambodia for a few weeks so there could be very little preparation. However, we did what we could. Our visitors already had the mattress for their bed, but their room needed brightening. Where could we buy paint? The faithful Samut took me to the market. We had decided on pale turquoise. The obliging girl at the paint stall went about her business, elegantly clad in the traditional sombot or skirt which, though flatteringly figure-clinging, gives ample room for movement with its deep lengthwise pleat. First came a big drum half full of white emulsion paint. Next I had to choose from an assortment of coloured powders, sold by the gram. A wild guess at a pinch of blue and another of green sent her kicking off her shoes and scrambling up on to the table, the powders were sprinkled into the drum of white paint on the floor, and she set to work, stirring vigorously with a long stick. A little adjustment of colour, and hey presto! it was done. The drum was lifted on to one cyclo, Samut and I clambered into another, and we were on our way.

It was Ret S'mai's first day at work. He had arrived exactly at seven, and had spent the morning vigorously digging. We congratulated ourselves on our choice of guard-cum-odd-job-man. But now he seemed at a loose end, so could he perhaps paint the spare room? Oh yes, he was very good at painting; he had much experience. So I gave him the brush and paint pot and left him to it. Alas, a few hours later all there was to see were a few greasy looking sea-green daubs scattered round the walls. It seemed the paint would not 'take', and upon enquiry Ret simply shook his head mournfully.

Our landlord appeared. Annoyed, he explained that the paint needed dilution; he would send in his own workman. In a couple of days the job was done. His fee was £1.50.

The day before our visitors were due to arrive was the day of Khieu Sampan's clash with local residents. The news of the battle and his ignominious retreat had spread rapidly round Bangkok where they were staying and had reached their ears late that evening. Should they or should they not come on to Cambodia as planned? Their safety was in question, but they did not want to let us down. Their plane to Phnom Penh was due to leave in the early hours of the following morning and it was beyond the capacity of the answer phone that took their night call to the British Embassy to help them. There was no way in which they could contact us. What should they do?

We too were in doubt as to whether they would brave the situation, so as we went to the airport to meet them we tried to prepare ourselves for the worst. But we should have known better. There they were, large as life. It would take more than a civil war to put them off. They took one look at us, refrained from critical comment, and made a shopping-list. On it were tinned butter, long-life milk (fresh dairy products were not available) and any other Western luxuries that might be found. Our sturdy group of eight had visibly withered; all of us had lost weight, some a great deal, but we looked at each other so often that we had scarcely noticed. Tim in particular was suffering with frequent bouts of diarrhoea and sickness, and as a result his mood and energy level, along with his weight, were disappearing into his boots. Our friends kept their dismay to themselves, but did all they could to put things right. A change was what was needed. In any case they could not visit Cambodia without a glimpse of Angkor.

'Go to Angkor, my friend, to its ruins and its dreams'.[1] The only way to obey this command in the time available was to travel by air, and it was with great excitement that the four of us booked ourselves on to the next day's early-morning flight. The little Russian plane was very old and gave us a few nasty moments. We had not long been airborne when clouds of smoke began to billow from the luggage lockers. Our ruminations on an inevitable death were cut short when a more seasoned traveller kindly explained that this was not smoke but merely condensation as the air temperature changed.

I am not archaeologically literate, so I knew almost nothing about this legendary city when we set out for our half-day visit. To spend fewer than six hours looking at buildings that have survived six centuries and that took eight hundred years to erect is an insult, but even so it opened our eyes and the beginning of our understanding to a world which does much to explain present-day Cambodia. For Angkor is not just an awe-inspiring collection of monuments; it is an extraordinary record of ancient history, mythology, religion and customs that still keeps the minds and pens of scholars busy, and will doubtless do so for a long time to come. To explore it in any detail is again not within the scope of this book, nor was it physically possible in the few hours that we spent there. But to talk about Cambodia without including Angkor would be to miss the point, for the kingdom of Cambodia was founded both physically and spiritually on the glories of that ancient city.

So, for the beginner like me, what is Angkor? It is the remains of a huge collection of ancient buildings, covering one hundred and twenty square miles and built over a period of eight hundred years, beginning in 802 AD. It was the centre of a vast empire, which at the height of its power covered not only present day Cambodia, but parts of all three of its neighbours, Thailand, Laos and Vietnam. In it lived a large community, and its richness depended on the natural elements that surrounded it; water and an endless supply of good building material. But it was the vision, pride and skill of its successive kings and the craftsmen they employed that made it what it was. Its site is the Kulen plateau which overlooks the Tonle Sap lake and the large area of fertile plain surrounding it, watered by tributaries of the Mekong. Here was huge potential for the growth of crops in the fertile top-soil, and a rich underlying supply of sandstone and iron-ore. The surrounding forest provided a seemingly limitless source of timber.

And so in 802, inspired by King Jayavarman 11, began the building of this mighty empire. Each ruler added to the glories of his predecessor, and gradually the kingdom grew in wealth and power. Physically, water was its underlying strength. Lakes and canals were constructed to store and carry it to vast paddy-fields, where armies of workers grew rice in quantity sufficient to nourish king and commoner alike. The homes and palaces of the people were built from the wood of the jungle, for although tiled roofs distinguished the houses of kings from the thatched huts of their servants, nothing more permanent than timber was used for the walls of either. So if this had been all, we would have no lasting monuments to marvel at today. But the temples were built from stone, which in the finite view of man is indestructible. Kings and their palaces come and go, but their gods go on for ever.

An abundance of rice and raw materials may have been the physical basis of Angkor's strength, but it was the intensity of belief in their gods that inspired its rulers to such heights. Perhaps it was the desire for personal power or perhaps the belief that the king was truly the link between god and man that induced Jayarvan 11 to proclaim himself a 'god-king', and to initiate a new religious belief, the devaraja cult. In any case, from then on it was accepted that every Khmer king was the earthly representative of a deity.

He could choose his own god. In the earlier part of the Angkor period, the religion was Hindu, as in much of India today. This lays down that its followers should worship, amongst a multitude of lesser gods, the deities of the Trinity; Brahma, Siva and Vishnu. So the new king had to choose one of these, his decision marked by a temple ceremony and the erection of a symbol or linga, usually made from polished stone. The symbol for the god Siva, whose cult was uppermost in the early kings' rule, was shaped like an erect phallus. Later, the shaft was sometimes divided into three parts, the base representing Brahma, the middle section Visnu, and the upper portion and tip still associated with Siva.

Later still, Buddhism was added to the choice. It too had spread from India, where it had begun as a reform movement against Hinduism. I hope a brief version of the story of Buddha will not come amiss, for the Buddhist religion has had a profound influence on the Cambodian people, steeped in it as they have been for more than a thousand years.

Buddha 'the Enlightened One' was born in 623 BC to a royal couple of noble lineage, the Sakyas, living in the Himalayas. He was a very special child, gentle and loving, quite unspoilt by all the palace luxuries that were showered upon him. At sixteen he married a beautiful princess, and the young couple stayed on within the confines of the palace, blissfully unaware of the world outside. In any proper fable they would have lived happily ever after, and that would be the end of it. But this story had a different ending and all because the young prince went for a ride. He and his horse strayed outside the palace grounds, and there for the first time he came face to face with reality, an experience that was to revolutionise his whole world and influence mankind for centuries to come. The story goes that he saw four things; a Hindu priest, a sick man, a beggar and a corpse. Horrified, there and then he made the momentous decision that he would give up everything to help the suffering world.

So one night when he was twenty nine years old, leaving behind his wife and new-born son whom he knew would be well cared for, he abandoned all that was familiar and went away, accompanied by his faithful groom. Also with him went four guardians of the world, each holding in his hand one of the horse's hooves to muffle the noise of galloping and so avoid discovery. This event became known as 'The Great Renunciation'. He rode until he found a resting place in the forest. There he cut off his long hair with one stroke of his sword, symbolising the renunciation of the world. For six years he lived the life of an ascetic, studying Hindu teachings and subduing all bodily wants. Indeed, so rigorous was his self-denial that he nearly died. But despite this physical mortification, he was not achieving his spiritual goal of self-enlightenment and at last decided to try a different course. Feeding and clothing himself, he continued to meditate, but this time in a state of reasonable comfort. And thus he achieved his ends. One night, as he was seated under a Bodhi tree on the banks of a river in Bodh-Gaya, his mind became perfectly pure and free from evil, and the innermost nature of all things was revealed to him. He had reached his Enlightenment, or Nirvana.

Then it started to rain. A tropical downpour cascaded from the heavens, but so deeply unaware was he that he failed to notice. A snake called Mucilinda came to his rescue. Coiling himself up he made a raised seat for the Buddha, keeping him out of the puddles; his multiple raised heads were a perfect umbrella, and thus is Buddha often depicted in Khmer art.

Buddha was thirty-five when he attained enlightenment. From then on, for the next forty-five years, he travelled far and wide, tirelessly devoting his time to reading and preaching. He lived simply with the disciples that were joining him in increasing numbers. With love in his heart and infinite compassion for the sorrows of the world, he led a life of total self-sacrifice in his efforts to guide people into the way of truth as he saw it. And then in 543 came the Great Demise when at the age of eighty, surrounded by many of his devoted followers, he died. Legend has it that all the trees around him burst into flower to do him honour.

So what of Angkor? Its earlier kings were steeped in Hinduism; later, there was a grafting on of Buddhism. By as early as the seventh century there was a unique amalgamation of these religions, and a combination

The Bayon Temple, Angkor

of Hinduism and Buddhism gradually evolved to suit the particular needs of Cambodia. Architecture and art reflected the religious and mythical beliefs of the period. Certain tenets had to be incorporated into the buildings; the ordinary and the spiritual and magical worlds were to be linked by physical structures. To marry the details of architectural construction with its underlying legend and belief must be a fascinating study.

Thus, the construction of temples was based on the image of Mount Meru. In far-off times, the world was believed to be a single continent, in the exact centre of which stood Mount Meru, holding up the heavens. Mount Meru was the axis of the world, and round it were seven concentric rings of mountains, signifying successive stages of knowledge. Finally came a stone wall, and outside this again a moat, to represent the Oceans. Mount Meru is the dwelling-place of gods and rulers, the sanctuary for ascetics and thinkers; above it are layers of heaven, with Nirvana, the ultimate goal, soaring over all. This concept was faithfully portrayed by the early builders of Angkor. Each temple represented Mount Meru, built on either a natural or an artificial mound. Round it was a stone wall, and round that the Ocean-moat. Often a causeway was built to it, representing the link between man and gods. Endless details of sculpture and carving furthered the theme. The direction in which the temple faced was important, too. As east represents the rising sun, life and masculine sexual prowess, most temples are built to face in that direction; west is the sign of death, and inevitably of womankind.

Unfortunately, we knew almost none of this when the four of us set out for Siem Reap, the nearest town to the temple complex. We had neither time nor energy to do our homework, and in any case, the visit came as a total surprise, a generous gift from our visitors. Once again we had been extremely lucky with our timing. Because of the civil war, the temples had been closed to tourists for over twenty years. Their reopening just five weeks earlier was yet another sequel to the signing of the Paris Peace Accords.

Our lack of knowledge did not spoil our trip. It was a brief but unforgettable vision of great majesty and beauty, of towering blocks of weathered sandstone carved into fantastic shapes, of a bewildering intricacy of chambers, galleries, columns and steps, their pinkish colour glowing in the soft light from an overcast sky. The water of moats and lakes mirrored in its stillness soaring towers and the dark green foliage of giant trees. Contrasting with all this grandeur, tiny wild-flowers, delicate and insubstantial, half hid their blooms behind rugged fragments of stone. Behind and beyond it all lay the forest.

Imagine what it must have been like for explorers through the centuries who, struggling to cut a passage in the thick jungle, came upon all this. After 1432, when the city was sacked by neighbouring Thailand, it fell into disuse. From then until the middle of the last century there are recordings of occasional sightings of Angkor by missionaries and travellers of several different nationalities, but there are no detailed accounts of it until that of one Henri Mouhot, who is traditionally but wrongly accepted as the first foreigner to discover the ruins. He was a naturalist, a Frenchman with an English wife, who lived in England. He set off for South East Asia in 1859 under the patronage of the Royal Geographical Society, rediscovered Angkor, and made and recorded a detailed survey of its ruins. Five years later he died of a fever in Laos without ever returning home. His work was published posthumously.

On our flying visit we had time to visit only two of the monuments. The first of these was the Bayon temple, a weird and fascinating complex, not a place where I would choose to be after dark. The visitor is surrounded on every side by enormous identical faces carved in stone. They do not look at you, for their eyes are almost closed, but the mysterious half-smile on their thick lips does not exude welcome. Escape from them is impossible, for their hooded gaze looks out north, south, east and west from a confusion of different heights. They are carved on towers, fifty-four lofty blocks of rugged sandstone, every one hoisting aloft its proclamation of four impenetrable faces, one cut into each of its four sides. There is still mystery surrounding this temple, but it is thought that the faces represent the bodhisavatta Avalokitesvara. To become a bodhisavatta was the Buddhist religious ideal; the title implies the achievement of Nirvana, but its renunciation in favour of returning to earth to help human suffering. The name Avalokitesvara means 'The Lord who looks down in compassion', and the endless repetition of his likeness in the Bayon temple is thought to signify the omnipresence of the king presumably exercising his right as devaraja.

This particular king was Jayavarman VII, a mighty ruler who reigned towards the end of Angkor's period of greatness. It was he who built Angkor Thom, the last capital of the Khmer empire, and it was in the exact centre of this that the Bayon stood, an allegory of Mount Meru, a temple-mountain linking heaven and earth. Angkor Thom was a city on an immense scale. Square and enclosed by eight miles of stone wall nearly thirty feet high, it contained palaces, barracks, offices and houses, both noble and humble, and gave refuge to nearly a million people. Its walls, entry towers and causeways guarded by stone gods and demons still stand, but the wooden dwellings have long since gone the way of the kings and commoners who lived in them.

King Suryavarman 11 lies buried in Angkor Wat, the only other monument that we had time to visit. It is the best known and best preserved of all the temples, and unlike nearly all the rest, because it is a burial place its entrance is in the west, the direction of death and the dying sun. The portrait of its five towers is the national symbol; you see it everywhere on the national flag. (From some angles, it is only possible to see three of the five. The present flag, as during the Pol Pot era, shows only three of the towers.) Architecturally overwhelming in its splendour and complexity, it is almost a relief to turn to something the eye can encompass more readily, the intricate detail of the wall carvings, to which a whole gallery in the temple is devoted. Lengthways these carvings cover more than six hundred yards, and are over six feet high. They are a remarkable demonstration of the skill of their craftsmen who by chiselling out the background and leaving the design in low relief have created the effect of a three-dimensional painting.

They depict Indian epics and legend, as well as scenes of history and warfare. My favourite was the Churning of the Ocean of Milk, a legend from Hindu mythology. The story goes that for a thousand years gods and demons struggle against each other, both hard at work churning the Ocean of Milk in order to extract the elixir of life which would render them immortal and incorruptible. Defeated and exhausted, the gods go to Vishnu, one of the Hindu Trinity, for help. He encourages them to continue but suggests that to achieve their goal they work with the demons rather than against them. So they start again, this time working in concert. But Mount Mandara, the pivotal point of the churning, starts to sink. Once again Vishnu comes to the rescue. He descends to earth as a tortoise, offering the back of his shell to the mountain for support. Enter Vasuki, a serpent. He curls himself round the pivot, and, stretching himself out into a rope, offers his tail to the gods and his head to the devils. The gods and devils alternate in a tug of war, pulling first one way and then the other; the mountain rotates backwards and forwards, and thus the churning continues for another thousand years. Finally their efforts are rewarded, and the elixir of life appears. All this and more is depicted in perfect detail, the ninety-two demons, their eyes bulging, pitting their strength against eighty-eight gods. The workmanship is extraordinary, and the whole tapestry in stone as fresh as if it had just been carved.

Sightseeing is hard work, and we were ready for our lunch in the one and only hotel. But this was to be poor Tim's undoing. He had developed an allergy to some unidentifiable ingredient in local cooking which as soon as it reached his stomach produced first pain and then violent vomiting. The lunch that day must have contained an overdose, not helped by the speed at which we had to gobble it in order to catch our plane. By the time we reached the airport, he was distinctly green, but we comforted him and ourselves with the thought that the flight was short and we would soon be home. We had reckoned without our two celebrities, Prince Sihanouk and Khieu Sampan. They had arranged to meet each other in Bangkok. The Prince's plane had just taken off from Phnom Penh and was on its way there. There was no radar, so the entire Cambodian sky had to be kept clear of flying objects in case of collision. Although Siem Reap and Bangkok are in diametrically opposite directions from Phnom Penh, there we had to sit for two solid hours closeted in the tiny uncomfortable departure lounge, waiting until the coast was clear. Tim went a curious shade of grey and sat entirely still and silent. Our visitors said afterwards that they thought his last hour had come.

At last we were on the plane for the short hop back to Phnom Penh, and a taxi took us home from the airport. Now Tim could be sick in peace. He well and truly availed himself of the opportunity, and a miraculous cure resulted. It was not after all a case of 'See Angkor and die'. Of course his illness had cast a shadow on the day, but it had been a great experience and a more important visit than we realised at the time. Two years still stretched ahead and we thought we would surely have another opportunity to go back and see more of the celebrated temples. But because of increasing pressure of work and the danger of travel from civil unrest this turned out to be our only opportunity. Thank goodness we made the most of that short visit.

Chapter Nine

The departure of our friends two days later marked a milestone in our journey. Playtime was finally over, and work was to begin in earnest. Tim had already penetrated the unfamiliar world of January 7th Hospital, named after the date of Pol Pot's final defeat by the Vietnamese. If anything, 'his' hospital was even more decrepit than mine, a stark contrast to the cool cleanliness of the clinical surroundings that he was used to. The discovery of just how stark was not long in coming. He was demonstrating one day a particular operation for the treatment of cancer of the neck of the womb by a method that, though common here, was unknown to his Cambodian colleagues. A successful outcome was particularly important, to prove that here was a life-saving operation that could be safely added to their repertoire. All was going well. Two bottles of blood had been supplied by the excellent blood-bank, run by a team of Cambodians under the guidance of a French medical organisation. The first one had emptied itself into the patient's arm when Tim began to suspect that something was seriously wrong. The colour of the blood oozing from the operation site had changed from a healthy red to black. Glancing up he saw that the drip-stand was empty; there was no second bottle hanging on its hook. What were the assistants thinking of? The lady was losing blood, and urgently needed it to be replaced.

But this apparent lapse was intentional, for only now had it dawned on the staff that not just the second bottle but the first one too was three months out of date. This situation could well have the direst of results. Blood for transfusion must be both fresh and matched directly to its recipient, and a messenger had been sent that very morning to the blood-bank to fetch carefully prepared supplies. So where were they, and how had this dreadful mistake been made? How had stale blood, cross-matched long ago for a different patient, come to be in the theatre at all? Somewhere between the blood-bank and the operating theatre, old blood had been substituted for the new. There could surely be only one explanation; someone had succumbed to temptation and had sold the fresh supplies. A patient's life had been put at serious risk for the sake of a few pence.

For the next two days, the fate of the surgeon and that of his patient hung together in the balance. If she lived on, so would his reputation; if not, it was unlikely that any excuse, however overwhelming, would be acceptable. Her death was almost inevitable and took just two days in coming. But somehow Tim survived. Slowly and with infinite patience, he chipped away at torpor born of resignation, at ignorance and prejudice, and was eventually rewarded by a new enthusiasm and hope amongst his colleagues. But not for a long time to come.

Our Field Director, James, was of course closely involved in setting up my project at the Municipal Hospital. At 7.30 in the morning of Wednesday the 4th December 1991, he drove me to the hospital in the agency truck and escorted me to the bottom of the grim staircase leading to General Medicine where I was to be initiated. I remember very clearly his parting avuncular blessing. I had my hand on the iron bannister. He patted it, and said 'You don't know how much I envy you'. I could scarcely believe my ears, for the only thing that was stopping me from turning tail and running away as fast as I could go was my hold on the rail. But that I could appear even remotely enviable was a crumb of comfort, as it must mean that my nervousness was well camouflaged. Maybe I could even hoodwink other people too.

Everybody knows the sensation of forcing yourself to do something you do not want to do in order to achieve a worthwhile result, like going to the dentist. Having taken the first step of making the appointment, there is an inevitability about the final surrender in that awful chair. So it was that day. All the plans and preparations had brought me remorselessly and inevitably to the foot of this particular staircase. What happened at the top of it and afterwards would determine the outcome of my whole venture.

At the top of it that first day I arrived in a gallery overlooking the narrow courtyard where the staff played badminton. An iron footbridge at this level straddled the yard, bridging the gap between two tall blocks, the upper storeys of which still towered above me. The building on the near side housed the out-patient consulting room, a small ward for one or two private patients and my medical colleague's office. They were dark rooms with small windows and more often than not there was no electricity, so the bright daylight of the gallery and footbridge took on an unexpected importance as an X-ray viewing platform, as I was soon to find out. But not quite yet, for the investigations on that first day were limited to the bare bones of the enterprise. My initial operation was merely exploratory. I had to find out as much as I possibly could about the internal workings of the hospital and all its systems. I already knew that it had an extremely poor money supply, but I had yet to discover how this debilitating anaemia affected its vital parts. Before I could even think about treatment, a prolonged period of careful observation was essential. Hand in hand with this went the importance of developing a good relationship with my Cambodian colleagues. There was no hurry. Our agency's choice of two years as the usual length of contract is a sensible one, as it does away with the necessity for instant action. The doctors with whom I was to work had managed perfectly well without me before I came, and would manage perfectly well without me after I had left. In any case, the most I could hope to achieve for them was to graft on Western medical methods to the already considerable skills of many of them. But I could do nothing without first gaining their confidence and if possible their respect. In this I was handicapped by two factors, my status and my sex. I was not a 'specialist' and so not the ultimate source of knowledge in any one field. They wanted someone who could give them all the answers instantly, and the fact that sometimes I had to look things up in textbooks did nothing for my reputation, at least at first. That I am female was not such a disadvantage as it would be in many countries, but it certainly did not help. My age on the other hand did. Asians have great respect for the wisdom and experience that are supposed to come with the years and to the Cambodians, with their average life expectancy of only forty-eight, that I could still be working was a constant source of amazement.

Of course I knew little of all this at the beginning, but in any case I was much too apprehensive to have any tendency to bossiness. The only way to arrive at feeling comfortable in these new surroundings was to become familiar with them, and now was the moment to start.

This was Dr Long Ky's domain, and I turned off the gallery to which my staircase had led me into his dark office in search of him. But the room was empty. It seemed he had already started work, and a smiling nurse led me over the footbridge into the opposite building which housed the male and female wards, decorously separated by a dental surgery. We went first to the women's ward, and there he was, a small slight man in a white overall, standing beside a patient's bed. He had kicked off one sandal and, with leg bent and bare brown toes clutching the bed's metal edge, he wrote in the notes that were resting on his knee. This attitude was to become very familiar; repeated in every ward all over the hospital, it was as much part of the doctor's image as the inevitable stethoscope. With him stood the senior nurse carrying a pile of patients' folders, a pattern so familiar from ward-rounds in hospitals at home that I immediately began to feel better. He greeted me with his lovely shy smile, gold fillings gleaming, and a quiet 'Bonjour, Madame'. He was the only one of my three counterparts who would not even attempt to speak English. This had not worried me greatly, as I thought I spoke French adequately. By coincidence and long before I knew of our plans, I had attended a course in French conversation at our local College of Further Education at home and seemed to have reached a reasonable standard. But Odette, our teacher, had spoken with a beautiful Parisian accent, the musical lilt of her voice a joy to listen to. My English variation and Long Ky's Cambodian one, both equally ugly, were at opposite ends of the spectrum and to hear us trying to talk to each other would have made her weep. I was near to despair on that first day that we would ever be able to communicate, particularly as he also spoke very quietly. But fortunately the ear accommodates itself, and we came to manage very well.

All Khmer doctors can speak some French, for it is the language in which they are taught their medicine. This is a legacy from the period in which the country was a French protectorate. In those days, all educated Cambodians spoke it fluently, but as it was mainly this section of the population that was wiped out by Pol Pot, it is now spoken less and less. The exception to this is in the medical college, for there all lectures are in French, and the students if not already fluent must attend language classes to be able to understand their teachers. This will presumably continue for the foreseeable future, for the Faculty of Medicine in Phnom Penh, the only medical school in the whole country, has recently been restored to its former glory by the French government in return for a promise to that effect.

Fortunately for me, my initiation in Dr Long Ky's medical wards was a gentle one, as many of the beds were empty. We progressed slowly down the long narrow ward, my colleague's loose sandals slopping on the rough concrete floor, and stopped at the foot of each occupied iron bedstead. None of the patients seemed very ill, and once again I was puzzled by the fact that each one had a drip running into her arm. With the mumbled explanation in unintelligible French and the frighteningly inadequate notes, I was none the wiser as to the purpose of these transfusions when we came to the end, but erring on the side of discretion I decided to bide my time.

Several of the beds were the centre of a little focus of social activity. Sometimes it was only possible to distinguish the patient by his intravenous drip, for patient and visitors alike were dressed in ordinary clothes, and all lay or sat on the rush mat which was the only form of bed covering. At the head of the bed there would often be a little pile of personal belongings, perhaps a bright cushion or a folded blanket and a metal food container. Beside these lay one or two small plastic bags, a translucent pink or green in colour, or sometimes a screw of cheap paper. These proved to contain a mixed assortment of tablets and capsules, the patient's prescribed medication, which the relatives or even the patient if well enough had been out to the market to buy. A list was made by the doctor on a scrap of paper and handed to a husband or mother who then went out shopping. The drugs were not labelled and it was up to the patient and his family to distinguish them by colour and size, and to remember which was which and when they should be taken. The purchases must be made a day at a time, for tomorrow the medication might be changed.

We came to a bed where the patient lay all by himself, with no family round him. Gaunt and thin, he looked as if he had not eaten properly for a very long time. Neglected in appearance too, his grimy face and hands and grubby clothes showed clearly that he was past caring about cleanliness, normally so dear to a Cambodian's heart. Beside him lay a small bundle wrapped in a dirty kroma or check scarf, which probably contained all his worldly goods. There was no food container, nor pills in plastic bags. I gradually found out the reasons for his sorry plight. First of all, why was he not washed and made more comfortable? There were nurses in plenty, sitting around in clean white overalls, chatting to each other. Why did they not do some nursing? By devious means and still determined not to appear critical, I found out the answer. These nurses were in a different category altogether from our own, at least as I used to know them in my hospital days. They were adept technicians, putting up drips, taking blood samples and giving injections with great aplomb. But they did not regard it as part of their duties to care for the patient's needs in any way. I discovered that it is the family who do the caring. It is a relative who guides her charge to the smelly bathroom or on to the metal chamber pot beside the bed, who steers the head of her vomiting loved one towards that same pot on the floor, and who administers pills and potions at the right time. Later as things advanced it was the relative who measured the quantity of urine and made sure that her charge did not become dehydrated. One husband regularly washed out his wife's chest cavity with a syringe and tube. Food, too, was supplied by the family. There was a hospital kitchen, its rafters open to the skies as there was no money available to mend the roof, but at that time the free meal of poorly-cooked rice that it supplied was minimal and to a sick person inedible. So for our poor lonely sufferer not only was there a total neglect of hygiene but of nourishment too.

I asked about drugs. This patient was clearly penniless, and so had to rely entirely on the hospital pharmacy, which issued a free supply of a few basic medicines only. Penicillin tablets were always available, and so were aspirin and paracetamol, and the inevitable vitamins. Two other injectable antibiotics were sometimes but not always on the list, as were a handful of other remedies. But such a meagre choice did not bode well for the recovery of these victims of extreme poverty. The men and women in this situation, without money, family, or friends, were usually in a state of chronic malnutrition that was often the basis of the illness that brought them in. So they were a bad risk anyway, and with no proper food or medicine to offer them their hospital stay did little to help. Even when I was able to supply them with drugs from a fund kindly donated by my own family and friends, often it was too late. They died in any case.

We finished our ward-round, and recrossing the footbridge went back to Long Ky's office. This was furnished with a desk and chair, a cupboard, a group of wicker chairs set round a small circular table and in the corner a bed where he slept when on call, and which doubled as an examination couch for extra special patients. The table was decorated with a vase of plastic flowers and a little tray which held a teapot and two upturned glasses. For the first of many many times I was invited to sit at the table and a drink was poured for me from the pot. That day it was cold tea, but more often than not it would be boiled water, for tea cost money. In either case it was a welcome necessity, for frequent drinking was essential in that heat. My 'host', always the soul of politeness, would then help himself, and we would discuss together the patients we had just seen.

Dr Long Ky was avid for knowledge and sucked it up like a sponge. Medical textbooks were few and far between and more often than not seriously out-of-date. He had a small store of them in his cupboard and when we got stuck on a particular problem he would jump up and pull one out, and together we would pore over the French pages. There are many differences between French and English medicine, so I would often go scuttling back home at lunchtime to the one textbook I had brought with me from England to sort out my own ideas on the disputed point. How I longed for the expertise of my specialist colleagues at home, for here there was no higher authority to call upon and it was up to us to do the best we could. This of course made it all the more exciting and challenging, but inevitably there were tragedies too.

After our break, there were often outpatients to examine in the room next door, though I do not remember seeing any that first day. And so my first morning came to an end. Dr Long Ky and I said goodbye to each other in our best French, and with mutual assurances that we would meet again on Friday I returned down the stairs that had seemed so nearly insurmountable just a few hours before. To say that the ice had been broken conjures up an impossibly wrong image in that humid heat. But at last I had made a start, one that had been so fascinating and had opened up so many possibilities that, with hindsight, perhaps James' remark had not been so ludicrous after all. Perhaps it would even prove possible in the end that he had been right to envy me.

Accustomed by this time to getting around town, I went outside the hospital entrance where there was always a waiting group of cyclo-drivers. I was not yet wise to the fact that if I ignored their clamorous offers and walked round the next corner, the price of the ride home in a casually passing chariot would be halved. But I was learning fast. Next to the clutch of cyclos was a roadside stall selling such vital hospital necessities as cold drinks and babies' woolly hats. I stopped beside it for a moment to watch a young couple leaving the maternity unit, brand new baby in its mother's arms, and grandmother bustling along behind. Even in the hottest weather, a thick double-knit bobble hat seemed to be compulsory wear for every self-respecting infant, and this one was no exception. I watched intrigued as the family prepared to mount the father's waiting motor-bike. He got on first, followed by his wife who settled herself side-saddle on the pillion, one foot on a convenient support, the other dangling nonchalantly. Her arms were occupied by the baby, but in any case she would not have held on. It was not done for men and women to touch each other in the street, and the women, to whom riding astride would have been unthinkable, had such natural grace and poise that their slender bodies seemed to weld themselves to the machine and its movement. The baby on her lap was obviously in grave danger but, though I witnessed a number of motorbike accidents, I never actually saw one involving a child. For an awful moment I thought that Grandma was going to get on too, for it was fairly common to see two women sidesaddle on the same pillion, legs turned to right and left respectively. But greatly to my relief she settled herself in a cyclo. She was portly for a Khmer, and in any case was burdened with the rolled bed mat and various bits of extraneous luggage. They obviously knew their limits and set off down the road in tandem. I hoped they would arrive safe and sound.

Now it was my turn to scramble into a cyclo. There was a variety of gesticulating drivers to choose from and as usual I picked out one of the older ones, who were generally farmers come into town to try to supplement their meagre income. They always seemed grateful for the fare, agreed upon anew each time, and were rarely aggressive and demanding as some of the young men could be. After the ceremonial dusting off of the grubby plastic seat with the driver's filthy kroma, we set off at a steady pace, his sinewy old legs driving the heavy machine with surprising strength. I stopped him for a moment at the baker's, which was on my way home. There were two of them, side by side, both selling delicious fresh bread baked in the French style. There were plenty of street breadsellers too, but the weevil count in their rolls tended to be unacceptably high. Sometimes I bought flour there as well, but it had to be used up quickly. Weevils flourish in a hot wet climate, and flour kept for more than a week or two looked when the tin was opened as if someone had chucked in a handful of agitated coffee grounds.

Back in my cyclo, the driver set off again, cramming on a battered straw hat and grinning all over his wrinkled face as I tried to give him instructions in Khmer. It was no use telling the cyclo-drivers the address of your destination. They had no idea of road names or numbers, and it was entirely up to the passenger to guide them.

Arriving home with my new bread for lunch, I was struck again by Tim's appearance. His face was very thin and edgeways on he looked like a piece of cardboard. He was dwindling away, and suddenly I got frightened. I turned him sideways to the mirror and made him look at his reflection and at last he understood why I had been complaining for weeks about his loss of manly beauty. We both realised it was time to take action before he disappeared beyond recall.

It was not sensible to be ill in Cambodia. There was no health clinic to which we could turn in time of need, and no hospital that any of us could bear to be in. The few Western doctors scattered about the various non-government organisations (NGOs) were all prepared to see sick colleagues out of working hours when they could, but there were no formal arrangements. Our agency established contact with a French group who took on our health needs for a while, but it was all very haphazard and unsatisfactory. Laboratory tests were a problem too. Although there were one or two good pathologists working at the city laboratory, the Pasteur Institute, its results were unreliable to say the least. Tim with his constant diarrhoea had already had tests carried out by them and nothing abnormal had been found. In short, if you were really ill, it was necessary to leave the country.

Chapter Ten

The following morning we both knew that poor Tim, unwell though he was, would have to struggle alone to the agency office to report sick. I had only just started work and to miss my second day at a time when my reputation was far from established would not have made a very favourable impression. We did not of course know what the outcome would be, but our hopes for Tim lay in the direction of the Bangkok Nursing Home. This was an establishment which seemed to belong to a different era. A pleasant house set in a large garden in the centre of Bangkok, with a lake in which turtles disported themselves and where all kinds of birds gathered to drink, it made a wonderful haven for the sick who could afford to go there, and we were protected by an excellent health policy. One of its two senior physicians was an English doctor trained at St. Thomas's Hospital in London who went to Thailand twenty-five years ago, married a beautiful Thai girl and has lived there happily ever since, and it had and still has an excellent reputation. Bangkok is famous for its tropical diseases hospital and skilled specialists in all fields of medicine, any of whom the Nursing Home could call upon. Another of the Home's great assets was its Scottish matron, a nurse of the old school who combined strict discipline and high standards with the kindest of hearts and who supervised an excellent kitchen. All in all, it sounded too good to be true, and in any case, as we told each other in a desperate attempt to avert disappointment, it would almost certainly be full.

But that morning I had to put all these hopes and fears out of my mind as I concentrated first on my hazardous journey to work and then on my inaugural day in gynaecology outpatients. The hospital was about three miles from our little house. To get there, I had to ride my bicycle along a short section of unmade roads, dirt tracks whose pot-holes grew ever bigger as the months went by, and then to turn right on to the city's main highway. Traffic arrangements were basic, but there was a very definite pecking order. At the edge of the road were pedestrians on what passed for a pavement if any, picking their way between a variety of mantraps ranging from portly pigs to the gaping portals of the city sewer. Next came the push-bikes and cyclos, then the motor cycles, and lastly in the centre of the road cars and trucks. Push-bikes were the victims of all other wheeled traffic in that they were totally vulnerable. Their advantage lay in their manoeuvrability, and the fact that they did little damage to others in a collision. But this was cold comfort when you were on one, a pathetic little rabbit in this mechanical jungle, a prey to the confusion of roaring honking beasts that encompassed you on every side. The cyclo-drivers were definitely cock of the roost of the leg-driven traffic. Their machines were heavy with a sturdy bumper on the front, which the more carefree drivers were inclined to use as a battering ram. They had no bells, but made a loud and somewhat sinister click with their questionable brakes as a warning of attack from the rear. But it was the motor bikes that posed the greatest number of problems. First there was the invasion of the visiting cyclist's own personal space. I would often become aware of a mechanical presence travelling alongside, accommodating its speed to my own slower one. Efforts to ignore it, to continue to pedal sternly ahead, eyes front and head in air, would finally be overcome by curiosity. Why was someone keeping such close company? Eventually I would be forced into a sideways glance, and a flashing smile and barrage of questions would erupt. 'What is your age? What country do you come from? What is your name?' The Khmer desire to speak English to a Westerner was overwhelming, and this would be the prelude to a language lesson on wheels. Occasionally I became so desperate that I would try to shake off pursuit by stopping at a roadside stall on the pretext of buying something, only to find my pupil standing beside his motor bike, quietly and politely waiting until I was ready to continue the lesson.

As the main means of mechanical transport, motorcycles were employed in all sorts of improbable ways. Whole families would ride on them, three or even four children sandwiched between their parents seated fore and aft. Young daredevils used them to show off their virility, swooping and weaving in and out of the traffic at terrifying speed. Angled right over, disaster was never far away, and yet another victim of head-injury would join the hospital ranks, for crash helmets were virtually unknown. But it was the versatility of these machines as transporters, their engine capacity in most cases only 75 cc, that never

My cycle ride to the hospital

ceased to amaze me. I have seen a pillion passenger holding not just one but several six foot by four foot sheets of plate glass upright between himself and the driver, who unconcernedly piloted his way through the traffic. I have seen bundles of thin metal rods, of the kind used for reinforcing concrete, tied transversely on the pillion seat, and sticking out at least three feet on each side. One such gladiator neatly opened the left knee-joint of a fellow volunteer travelling in the opposite direction, himself a pillion passenger. He arrived at our house late one evening to be stitched up, sheet white and with one blood-soaked trouser leg, having travelled several hours since the injury. It does not often fall to gynaecologists to repair knees, particularly male ones, but fortunately both surgeon and patient did well. The victim later enrolled in one of the NGOs involved in de-mining. Huge cylinders of bottled gas, crates big and heavy enough to tip the bike over on to its side when forced to stop at traffic lights, baskets and bundles of every shape and size became a normal part of the workaday scene. But I was baffled for a long time by what looked just like a medical drip set complete with bag and tube suspended over the engines of motor bikes that were harnessed to laden trailers. I eventually discovered that this was exactly what it was. The little engines, overheated by both climate and load, needed a constant cooling spray of water to keep them from seizing up.

So this was the traffic that was lying in wait for me as I left the house that morning, abandoning Tim to wend his wobbly way alone to the office. I had a sick husband, it was the first time I had tackled the journey on a bicycle, and it would be my first session with a different colleague in a different department of the hospital. None of these things produced great ease of mind. Perhaps it was at that very moment that I made the conscious decision to tackle each day's problems as they came, no matter what. Hobson's choice, no doubt, but somehow to define it helped, and it was a decision that was to stand me in good stead, at least for most of the time.

The journey was painless and even pleasant. At seven in the morning it is still cool, and I enjoyed the exercise and independence. Nobody accosted me, rammed me, or cut my knees open. Journey accomplished and bike securely locked against the multitude of thieves, I made my way to gynaecology outpatients, where I was to work for two mornings a week. This consisted of two tiny interconnecting rooms leading off a wide corridor. Neither room had a window. In the first was a desk and three chairs, and in the second two basins, an old hat stand on which surgical gloves were draped to dry, and a shelf with a steriliser and a surprisingly modern binocular microscope. The rest of the narrow space was almost entirely occupied by an ancient examination couch, only half the length to which we are accustomed here, which accommodated the lady patient's upper body. Her legs would be immediately and unceremoniously strung up and apart, her feet in stirrups hanging from two vertical poles, one on either side of the near end of the couch. At its foot stood a stool and a gruesome bucket. The walls had once, a long time ago, been white. The basins were encrusted with deposit from the town's filthy water. And over and above all, hanging from the ceiling, was an electric fan, its three two-foot blades winding their rackety way remorselessly through the long hot hours. The noise it made was overwhelming. Normal conversation was impossible. Sensitive personal questions and answers had to be shouted from one end of the couch to the other, the patient's head rearing up from her poor body suspended in a position of exposed humiliation. There were many times of course when the fan hung silent, the electricity that turned it and that illuminated the tiny windowless rooms cut off yet again. On these days I would arrive to find a big padlock on the door, or else patients and staff sitting placidly side by side on the bench outside, waiting for better times. Sometimes my colleague would be fumbling about inside one of the dark little cells, sorting notes by the flickering light of a candle. For some reason the candles in gynaecology were always red. Equally inexplicably, there seemed to be no such thing in Cambodia as candlesticks. Somebody could have made a fortune.

That first day I could hardly bear the indignity of it all. Cambodian women are no less modest then any others. Rather they are much more so, their culture dictating the decent covering of even arms and legs by suitable clothing. A Khmer lady would never be seen in a swimming costume in the sea or river. She would modestly wind herself up in a length of cotton print with a skill that I never mastered (luckily I had the foresight to wear a costume underneath in my practice runs), so that she was covered from head to foot even in the water. Of course the patients must be examined, but surely more privacy could be arranged. The history could be taken first before undressing, sitting with the doctor or nurse. All sorts of ideas buzzed round my head in time with that awful fan. But once again caution must prevail. I was here to watch, listen, and learn.

And once again, the redeeming feature of this macabre scene was my colleague. The Khmer people look much younger than their years, and I was astonished to hear that Dr.Vathiny was not only married but had two school-age children. I had thought it surprising that she was old enough to be qualified. Small, attractive and a little plump (she loved her food) she had that vivacious bubbliness which endears, and not only a good grasp of medicine but a sympathy for and tact with her patients which was sadly lacking among many of her colleagues.

How had she learnt her medicine? She was too young to have started her training by 1975 when in common with everyone else she had been driven out of Phnom Penh by Pol Pot to work in the fields. I gradually found out some of her history, though many gaps still remain. She was one of the first intake in the Faculty of Medicine when it was opened again in 1980. To set in motion a new medical course when so much had been destroyed was an extraordinary feat. Later I saw pictures of medical students who had been wiped out en masse, typical formal college photographs with long rows of smiling white-coated undergraduates, now almost all dead. Of the applicants for the first medical courses after Pol Pot only the best had been accepted, among them Vathiny and several others of the doctors I came to know well. It seems that right from the start it had been a well-organised training, despite the mass destruction by the Khmer Rouge of almost all textbooks. With the help of old notes, the few remaining books, and guided by some of the forty surviving doctors and others coming in from Vietnam, the five year course had got rapidly under way. Later, help came from East Germany and from other countries behind the iron curtain such as Cuba and in particular Russia. Considering the difficulties, the early products of the Faculty were quite remarkable, and must have shown great application as students in addition to their natural ability and intelligence. I was fortunate to have found them.

Vathiny's financial reward for all this effort was a poor one. She earned, like all the doctors, between ten and fifteen American dollars a month, enough for her family to live on for a few days. Her husband, a handsome young army surgeon working for the same salary at the military hospital, had no time for private practice as his unusual skill and dedication made him much in demand on the public side. So to support their own children and her husband's extended family who were dependent on them, Vathiny in common with most other doctors took on as much private practice as possible. She was constantly at the beck and call of a member of the royal family, Prince Sihanouk's sister, who had been a famous Apsara dancer in her youth and now suffered from a chronic disease which needed constant supervision, and for which she travelled to Paris from time to time to visit her French specialist physician. Vathiny gained much kudos but no money for this honour. However she was devoted to 'The Princess' as she called her, and in all fairness did receive handsome presents from her from time to time which she showed me with great pride. The bread and butter of her private practice came from friends and neighbours who lived round about the Military Hospital residents' quarters in which the family had an apartment. For some reason I had expected these to be clean and faintly clinical when I visited the first time. Instead, they were an overcrowded slum.

But despite all these difficulties, and despite the fact that she seemed doomed to spend every day of her working life incarcerated in those two hot dark closets, for there is no career structure in the Cambodian medical hierarchy, almost always she was bright and cheerful, exuding *joie de vivre*. I once asked her about this. When you have spent four years of your life near to starvation, she said, when you have been watching family and friends die around you and anticipating your own end at any moment, the answer is simple. It is just wonderful to be alive, to expect to remain alive, and to have enough rice for you and your loved ones to eat. What more can anyone want?

I heard little about her own sufferings in the Pol Pot time. I knew that she was very hungry like everyone else, eating grass, lizards, and virtually anything that could be scavenged. (I suspect that this was the explanation for her present self-confessed greed. Often she would come into work clutching her stomach, suffering from acute indigestion or profuse diarrhoea from eating the wrong things or far too much of the right ones.) But she told me one appealing story. She was working at that time about seventeen kilometres from Angkor, and surprisingly every now and again managed to steal a day off from her labours in the fields. On these days, somehow she would glean enough fragments of food to pack up a picnic and would set off all by herself in the cool of the early morning to walk the long distance to the temples. There she would spend the day resting in the shadow of Angkor's glorious monuments, soothed by their serenity and eating her meagre meal. At dusk, she would walk back again. This seemed quite out of keeping with the busy bustling little lady that I knew, but clearly it had meant a great deal to her.

Our routine in the clinic was a simple one. As Vathiny attacked the patient from the rear, I squeezed up beside the couch to the head end, and attempted to talk to the sufferer. My colleague spoke English quite well and in the early days had to interpret for me, but as time went on and my medical Khmer vocabulary increased, some direct communication became possible. History-taking from the patient is a skill held by Western doctors to play a vital role in diagnosis. I suspect this had not been part of the limited Cambodian medical curriculum, for it was notable for its absence in all departments of the hospital, though there were exceptions with individual doctors.

For the first few weeks, I examined every patient after Vathiny had finished. An ancient surgical glove, which had been carefully washed in the filthy tap water, rolled up, placed in a smart stainless steel instrument drum, and finally cooked in a steriliser that did not work, would be handed to me by a nurse, fished out of its container with long forceps. I am right-handed. Often it would be a left glove. There followed manoeuvres to turn it inside out from a left glove to a right one, and finally the start of a long struggle to get it on to my hand. The gloves were old, fragile and small, and my hand large, hot and sweaty. It was a near impossibility. A good sprinkling of talcum powder would have eased its passage but talc is expensive. Suddenly one day a big tin of it appeared and my troubles were over. Looking back, I suspect Vathiny had bought it herself. I cannot think why I had not thought of supplying my own.

After the examination, the patient was unstrung and allowed to dress while we conferred as to diagnosis and treatment. Then my colleague would take her back to the room with the desk, and patient and doctor would sit down for the final consultation. The patients loved her. They loved her kindness and the trouble she took, and I feel sure her pretty face and attractive personality did much to make her clinic a popular one despite the indignities involved. And she delivered results.

The end of the morning came, and I was not sorry to escape from the noise and heat of that confined space. It was a relief to get back on my bicycle and thread my way home again, my mind busy with what I would find. Would Tim be there? Would he have left for Bangkok already? There was no telephone in the hospital, so no one could have contacted me. However there he was, standing on the balcony, certain proof that he was neither dead nor departed. But departure was imminent. He was to catch the afternoon flight to Bangkok, and, joy of joys, was destined for the famous Nursing Home. The worst of our worries were lifted, and I was able to see him off for the airport with a much lighter heart.

It seemed as if mosquitoes must carry messages as well as malaria, for no sooner had Tim left than sympathetic friends were calling with offers of help. It was apparently unthinkable that a lone lady remain lone for long. The faithful Samut who had been so helpful to us with shopping and cooking in the early days pressed me to let her stay in the house and keep me company. But I needed space and in the end as usual got my own selfish way. I had Ret S'mai to guard me by day, and locked and double-locked myself in at night. Samut did not stay, and I enjoyed company when I wanted it and wriggled out of it when I did not. With hind-sight the decision was unwise, but no harm came of it.

The week of Tim's absence went quickly. There was a telephone in our agency office just round the corner and unreliable though it was I was still able to ring him up a couple of times. Although the sound of his weak voice was far from reassuring, his news was fairly promising. Examinations and tests, set up immediately, had revealed no less than three possible problems all of which had been missed by our own Pasteur Institute. The two separate parasites that were attacking his intestine could be treated and killed. But there was the possibility of a third illness; tropical sprue. This is an odd disease, mainly occurring in South East Asia, where the body fails to absorb fat in the diet. Weight loss is progressive and can reach dangerous levels. If the initial treatment of a long course of antibiotics fails as it sometimes does, the only thing to do is to go home.

Tim was discharged from hospital the moment he put on half an ounce in weight. The roast beef and Yorkshire pudding had done their job well. (Purists among any doctors who may be reading this might well say that such a diet is highly unsuitable for sprue). But he was only allowed 'home' with the strict proviso that any reversal must result in return to Bangkok first and then probably to England for good. We both felt fairly confident that this would not happen.

Chapter Eleven

While Tim was being fattened up in Bangkok I was still breaking fresh ground at work. Introductions have already been made to Dr Long Ky, the physician in charge of general medicine, and Dr Vathiny, whose help and support were to be the mainstay of my later efforts outside the hospital. Dr Chuoy was the third in this remarkable trio, and it was he who, within the hospital confines, became perhaps my greatest mentor and friend. He was tall for a Khmer, approaching six foot. But then he was half Chinese, a frequent combination in Cambodia. Perhaps this had something to do with his personality, too. His attitude and outlook were different from any of the other doctors I met and seemed much more Western. His dedication to hospital work was total. Despite the fact that his salary at fifteen dollars a month if he was lucky was no higher than anyone else's, somehow he managed to avoid devoting time to private practice and so could spend longer in the wards. He must I think have had some private means for he surely could not escape at least partial payment towards his children's extra schooling. But he was certainly very far from rich. His wife sold cigarettes at a street-side stall, and they never invited me to their home for they were probably ashamed to have me there. When times got hard and the bottom fell out of the value of the local currency, the riel, he could no longer afford to break his morning's work by having breakfast at the local street café which doubled as the hospital canteen. Instead, he had to eat a dollop of last night's cold left-over rice before he came to work at seven a.m. The theft of his precious motorbike from inside the hospital ward where he had momentarily left it unlocked was a major tragedy in his life. He wanted to replace it with a push-bike, but his wife would not let him. If wealthy Westerners chose to pedal dilapidated bicycles through the heat of the day, that was their own bizarre business, as incomprehensible as their desire to be here in the first place. But for her own husband, a clever and much respected doctor, so to demean himself, why, that was unthinkable. He eventually settled for wrapping his tall frame around the tiny motor-scooter on which his daughter had ridden to school. She walked.

Chuoy, which means in English 'help', his kind bespectacled face permanently creased by a little furrow between his brows, was an obsessional worker. He rose at four a.m., pulled his twelve-year-old daughter out of bed and gave her an hour's English lesson. At five, he went off to his own English class for a couple of hours. Then back home for his cold rice and into the hospital by half-past seven. At the end of a full day in the ward, he would go back to school for another hour's English lesson, finishing at six. In the middle of the morning, before the value of the riel fell so disastrously, he would take a break at the hospital canteen often courteously inviting me to join him. We would pick our way along the rough mud track that led from 'Intensive Care' where he worked, and which was housed in a separate single-storey building. In the wet season there would be huge puddles to circumvent as we slithered across the slippery reddish mud, littered with hospital refuse. This path led to the boulevard fronting the hospital, where plastic tables and chairs were set out on the pavement. Behind them yawned the uninviting mouth of a typical dark street-side café in which we had to take refuge on a rainy day. It was filthy. There were flies everywhere. I was too cowardly to order anything except hot tea without milk, the delicious jasmine tea on sale everywhere. But when times were good, the doctors seated with us round the table would embark on a substantial meal, usually of a soup in

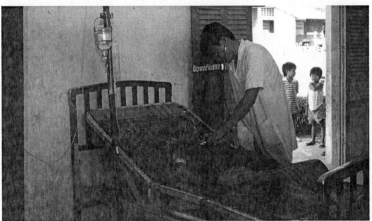

Dr Chuoy examining a patient in intensive care

which long thin Chinese noodles lay draped like the corpses of drowned worms over meaty chunks of bone. I never saw any of the women doctors or nurses there, even such emancipated ones as Vathiny, and I certainly would never have ventured there alone. But I felt it a great privilege to be invited. For a long time I was not allowed to pay for my tea. Apparently etiquette laid down that one member of the group paid the bill for his friends. Once I had learnt the rules I was able to 'treat' them all.

I mentioned that the English meaning of my colleague's name is 'help', and hearby hangs a cautionary tale. Fortunately it had been recounted to us early on by Darra, our English teacher, for otherwise it might well have been me that fell into the trap. A visiting Western dignitary made a speech to the suffering people of Cambodia. He had taken immense pains to learn enough Khmer for the occasion, but had evidently not had a friendly Darra to guide him. His eloquent dissertation ended with the words 'and it is my dearest wish to help you all.' Imagine his surprise when his entire audience, sitting until then in polite silence, erupted in an explosion of mirth or shocked distress. No-one had warned him that 'help' in Khmer is a difficult word for an Englishman to pronounce. 'Chewy' means help; but lean it just a little towards 'Choy' and it is instantly transformed into an all too common four-letter word. His final phrase, so carefully chosen, had not given quite the message he had intended.

Intensive Care was my greatest medical challenge. Clinging still to the French nomenclature, it was known as 'Réanimation' or 'Ré-a' for short. To reanimate is to restore to life and Chuoy and his staff certainly did their best despite formidably awful working conditions. Ré-a was housed on one side of a large square patch of grass behind the main hospital. The other three sides were formed by a collection of buildings containing wards for paediatrics and infectious diseases, the roofless kitchen, a small laboratory, and hospital offices. It was a long single-storey building, made of concrete and with a red tiled roof. Down each side unglazed windows with slatted shutters let in the elements and the mosquitoes. The doorless doorway led straight into the main ward, with seven beds on each side and at each end a partial screen dividing off a separate small 'room'. Beyond the right hand screen were twin beds for private patients and several motor-bikes belonging to the staff. Beyond that again were Dr.Chuoy's office and the bathroom and lavatories. On the concrete floor of the bathroom, with its open gutter and drainage hole, stood a vast concrete water tank, a yellow plastic bailer balanced on the edge. The technique was simple; the patient or his relative scooped water out of the tank over his head. There were two 'squat' lavatories, one for the patients and the other, always kept padlocked, for the staff. It was an embarrassing moment when I arrived home one day to find the only key in my pocket, but I am afraid I left the staff to their own devices until the next day, when, coward that I am, I slipped it back unseen on to its hook. Unlike the state of affairs in the rest of the hospital, that department was spotless with no smell of urine. A cheerful smiling cleaner came daily, but quite often I would catch Dr Chuoy scrubbing away for all he was worth, the other members of staff languidly following his example.

Behind the screen at the opposite end of the ward was the office with table and chairs, where every sort of activity took place from note-filling through chess and snack meals to homework by Chuoy's children. Here too was a huge autoclave in which articles were affectionately placed in pious hope, though everyone knew it did not really work. But the main use to which I put this particular cubby hole was for the hand washing ceremony. There were no basins or taps in Intensive Care. There was no question of washing your hands after examining each case. But at the end of every ward round Chuoy politely but firmly escorted me here. He and I together would go out of the back door on to the doorstep. Standing side by side on the step, we would hold out our cupped hands over the grass, for all the world as if we were taking Holy Communion. An attendant nurse would bail a little water from a bucket over them, and then tip on a few grains of detergent from a plastic bag. After a suitable period of cleansing, the soap would be rinsed off by several bailersful of water, followed, with a little bow, by the presentation of a towel, always to me first and always clean. This indicated the end of the morning's work. Once, going back down the ward, I found a patient had come in whom I had not seen. I went to examine him, but was stopped by a horrified doctor. 'But you've already washed your hands' he said. At my leaving party, to which all staff were invited, one nurse who was usually shy and tongue-tied and with I thought few words of English to my astonishment got up and said in front of everybody 'What shall I do now I haven't got Yea's hands to wash?'

So what sort of cases did we see in Intensive Care? There were all kinds of weird and wonderful diseases, some that I was familiar with and many others that were strange to me. But in both numbers and severity, it was the malaria sufferers that predominated, nearly all of them young men. Here was yet another conundrum. Malaria is not particular as to its victims, so why this apparent prejudice against normally healthy men in the prime of life? Chuoy explained that these were all forest workers, and that it is in the jungle where they work and where mosquitoes are in their hot, damp element that the main danger from malaria lurks. These boys were employed in felling trees for the often illicit timber trade.

Part of the fascination of medicine lies in the hidden dramas that go on behind the scenes, and the story of malaria is no exception. There is a cast of four; two human victims, old and new, a female Anopheles mosquito, and a microscopic single-celled organism or protozoon of the Plasmodium group. Anopheles mosquitoes are entirely responsible for the spread of malaria from one person to another. The female bites a malaria sufferer, and, contained in the blood that she needs for her own nutrition, sucks in both the male and female forms of the protozoon that are circulating in his body. Inside her stomach, these join forces and multiply, surely one of nature's quirkier arrangements. For a new meal, the mosquito attacks a new victim, sucking his blood after injecting him through her proboscis with a now strong contingent of parasites and thus passing on the disease. There are four species of Plasmodium causing four different forms of malaria which vary considerably in their severity. The only one that need concern us here is Plasmodium falciparum, the cause of cerebral malaria, the most dangerous form and the one most often seen in Cambodian hospitals.

Phnom Penh was full of mosquitoes, biting bare arms and legs and causing a great deal of discomfort. It was impossible to get a good night's sleep without a net over the bed. But there was no malaria in the city, for the simple reason that these were not Anopheles mosquitoes. All the cases that came into the hospital had travelled from outside, many of them coming long distances. I remember one such patient on my first ward-round with Chuoy. He had been brought here from the north-west of Cambodia, the area from which much of the timber is illegally exported over the border with Thailand. There he lay half way down the ward on one of the battered old iron bedsteads, his only protection from its flat spring base a thin straw mat. He had no pillow and no bedclothes, his limp unconscious body covered with his check kroma. It was very hot, and a plastic bag of roughly chopped ice had been dumped on his chest. The inevitable intravenous drip ran into his outstretched arm. Next to him sat his mother, her restless hands constantly adjusting his kroma, lines of deep anxiety etched into her face. As we approached the bed, she stood up and gave me the traditional greeting of respect, hands held palms together in front of her body, with a little bow. Because I was white I was assumed to have magic powers and to be able to achieve miracles. She poured out a flow of Khmer, far beyond anything I had learned at school, but in an obvious and desperate plea that I would save her son's life.

It seemed to me hopeless. He had already been unconscious for four days, suffering the severe cerebral form of the disease where the organism attacks the brain. He had arrived severely dehydrated, unable to drink in his unconscious state, and was now being kept alive by the fluids running into his vein, this time an essential part of his treatment. Too little fluid would mean the accumulation of waste products in his body which would poison him. Too much would waterlog his lungs and he would drown. And as well as quantity, quality was vital too. The delicately balanced chemical content of blood and body tissues cannot be maintained by giving whatever solution comes most readily to hand, as many of the medical staff seemed to think. Selecting the correct one is vital, and even where there are sophisticated laboratory tests to monitor this, as in the West, it can be difficult. But in our little hospital no such tests existed, and results had to be achieved by experience and guesswork alone.

No wonder I felt gloomy. But unlike me Dr Chuoy had had plenty of experience, both of working unaided by modern methods and of malaria. Coming from the northwest himself, he too had suffered severely from the cerebral form of the disease, I suspect in the Pol Pot era, although he never talked about that time to me. He had already worked in this hospital for several years and must have treated hundreds of patients. His training had included a year in Vietnam, learning about intensive care in a hospital with better amenities than this one, but that must still have fallen well below Western standards. Using his expertise, his practised eye, ears, and hands, he achieved quite remarkable results, and this case was no exception. To my amazement, when I arrived in the ward a few days later, the patient was up on one elbow, his ever attendant mother helping him to eat a bowl of rice. A week after that he went home.

Of course there is more to the cure of malaria than simply maintaining the status quo. Active treatment must be given, and the drug at present favoured by WHO in this part of Asia is that age-old remedy, quinine. Quinine comes from the bark of the Cinchona tree, which originated in the Andes mountains of South America. This family of trees was called after the Duchess of Cinchon, the wife of the governor of Peru. I imagine that her sufferings as she lay ill three hundred and fifty years ago were much the same as those of today's patients, and it must have seemed nothing short of miraculous when, after drinking a simple infusion of a chunk of tree bark in water, she made a full recovery. The Jesuits are said to have spread the glad tidings about Cinchona's healing properties all round Europe, and so for a time it became known as Jesuits' bark. In the dense jungle of South America, even to locate and fell the Cinchona trees, let alone to strip, dry, pack and transport their bark must have been well-nigh impossible. It soon became obvious that this was impractical and trees were becoming scarce. So attempts were made to introduce the species to Asian countries, and now, after many failures, there are plantations of them in most parts of the tropics.

Other drugs for the treatment of malaria come and go; some are excellent but are limited in their general use by price and other factors. It does seem, though, that the prize must go to the herbalists of old. The South American Indians of the seventeenth century may have been ahead of their time, but thirteen centuries earlier still, in the year 341 AD, a textbook was published in China that was to have startling repercussions nearly two thousand years later. It was a work on the treatment of medical emergencies written by a Mr Ge Heng, and entitled 'Zhou Hon Bei Ji Fang'. In this, he recommends the use of a medicinal herb quing hao (annual or sweet wormwood) for the treatment of fevers. Probably used in country areas of China ever since, it re-emerged in 1972, when Chinese scientists extracted from it an active principle with considerable anti-malarial activity. This they called quinghaosu (literally the active principle of quing hao). Its Western name is artimesinin. From early trials it seems extremely promising. The result of more major ones is awaited with eagerness.

But the world of scientific trials was far removed from our grubby little ward in the middle of Phnom Penh. Here what mattered was not statistics but whether So Peap, father of seven, would ever work again. We did not think so. He had been unconscious for days, and we had done all we could. Quinine had failed. We knew that to use artimesinin, the Chinese wonder-herb, would be to incur the wrath of WHO, who quite rightly (I suppose) were biding their time until there was positive proof of its efficacy and safety. We also knew that it was So Peap's last hope, for he was dying before our eyes. In any case, we had no quinghaosu, although it was occasionally available in the market. There was no telephone, but by now my bicycle had become a familiar friend, and off I pedalled to seek the help of another doctor from our own agency, seconded to WHO to work specifically on malaria. Without further ado, he and I and of course the faithful Chuoy visited the patient again together. Principles went to the wind, and in no time we had managed to lay our hands on a course of tablets of the extract, administered down a stomach tube. By the next day So Peap was conscious and it was not long before he too went home to join his family.

These were some of our success stories. But there were dismal failures too. Plasmodium falciparum does not just attack the brain, though that is bad enough. It is when the kidneys are severely affected that the worst of the troubles come. If the kidneys fail, the patient dies, killed by the poisons that accumulate from his own bodily processes. If these poisons can be washed out of the body artificially for a limited period until the anti-malarial drugs have had time to work, then his life can be saved. Otherwise there is little hope. This cleansing process is known as dialysis, of which there are two main kinds. The only relevant one here is peritoneal dialysis, for this is theoretically an easy procedure which can be carried out with the minimum of equipment. It involves running fluid into the patient's abdominal cavity, leaving it there for two hours and then letting it out again, taking with it any poisons that the kidneys have not been able to expel by normal means. The process can be repeated several times. The abdomen is lined with a thin transparent membrane called the peritoneum, rather like a sheet of permeable cling-film. Fluid in contact with it can suck out chemicals from the body tissues on its other side, thus purifying the blood running through them. It sounds as if nothing could be simpler, but sadly there are great difficulties, such as the danger of infection and the cost of the large quantities of sterile fluid required. Often the patient is already severely ill from other malarial complications, and is in no fit state for even a simple procedure. In short we dared not attempt it. On several occasions, Chuoy and I were forced to stand beside a young man's bed, helplessly watching the empty bag attached by catheter to his bladder and willing it to show some signs of filling. But the ominously few drops of urine that appeared were almost certain proof that he would not be with us much longer, and there was absolutely nothing that we could do to save him.

Angus, our World Health ally who had come to our rescue with artimesinin, was doing his best to persuade WHO to set up dialysis units in certain centres where patients could go for treatment. This would gladden Dr Chuoy's kind heart beyond measure. He suffered greatly whenever a patient died.

Chapter Twelve

Tim came back from Bangkok just in time for Christmas, burdened with parcels. The biggest was a large square box which proved to contain, of all things, a microwave oven. He was determined to stop the charade which had so nearly been his downfall, the pretence that his British-made stomach had turned Cambodian overnight. For everyday nourishment Khmer food would have to do, but at the weekends when we did our own cooking the microwave opened up magical possibilities.

To reach our kitchen, we went down the outside flight of concrete steps from our living quarters and walked a few yards into a separate single-storey building. Inside, let into holes in the white-tiled working surface, were three braziers in diminishing sizes. Made of earthenware, these pots were on sale very cheaply everywhere for use in the kitchen or simply on the ground, as means allowed. Bits of dried coconut shell were used as kindling, and filled with charcoal they made a very efficient method of cooking. But this was a slow process, so one of our first purchases had been a double gas burner. Calor gas had just arrived in Phnom Penh. This was all very fine until the gas ran out without warning, invariably when preparing a meal for friends. The shop was on the other side of town and the long cycle-ride that this entailed gave waiting guests a welcome chance to drink rather more beer than was good for them. The service itself was excellent. In no time at all, a new two-foot ton-weight canister would be strapped on to the back of a motorbike, and delivered and connected well before the weary cyclist returned to resume her cooking. We soon came to our senses and invested more of our grant in a second canister.

Gas ovens were unavailable, but never mind; we had a microwave. Such a thing was unheard of in Phnom Penh, and we were the laughing stock of our English colleagues. That a humble volunteer should own such a thing was unthinkable. But when fish pie, apple crumble and shortbread began to appear on the menu they soon changed their tune.

It was too precious a possession to keep in the kitchen, so we vaunted its presence in our sitting-room, mouth watering in its shiny black and white glory. But alas, there were bitter disappointments in store. Even we had realised that without electricity it would not function, a frequent occurrence. What we had not reckoned with was the lowering of power every evening just when we needed it. Darkness fell at about six all the year round. Then everyone turned on their lights and their television, and the lucky ones their air conditioners. The poor little oven's light and turntable obediently responded to the switch, but that was as much as it could manage. There is a woeful lamentation in my diary upon the first fish that emerged as raw as when it had entered.

The vagaries of the electricity supply led to another discovery. Tim, always an outdoor man who has cooked on many a camp fire over the years, decided that we could make our own oven out of a biscuit tin and heat it over the charcoal burner. Inwardly scoffing, I went along with the idea, certain in my own mind that we were in for another inedible meal. Not a bit of it. It was one of the best roast chickens I have ever tasted.

We must have been lucky that time for as a rule the chickens were too tough to eat. They were brought into town from the countryside, often by boat. One day on a visit to the wharves we came across an untidy pyramid of ruffled brown feathers with beaks and legs and scrawny necks sticking out at all angles. It was not a pleasant sight, but when at the top of the three-foot pile a bleary eye opened or a parched beak gasped for air, the decision to become a vegetarian was instant and inevitable, even if doomed by greed to failure. With their legs tied in bundles and the breath crushed out of their pathetic bodies by the weight above, what hope had the birds at the bottom of the pile?

From the wharf, bunches of these chickens would be carried round the city, suspended by their legs from bicycle handlebars. The dead ones hung straight down; just a few who were clinging to life managed to raise their heads. I could never get used to that sight, nor to seeing two pigs tied together sitting up in a cyclo, for all the world like a couple of housewives on their way to market. Though clearly destined for the slaughter-house, these had been happy pigs, rooting about in the streets and snoozing contentedly in the gutters. Their misery in the cyclo would be short-lived, and as pork was the only edible meat we could not feel too sympathetic. It was illegal to kill cows for food until they had done ten years hard labour, and the stories that our vet friends told us of cattle killed by such mortal sicknesses as anthrax being cut up for meat almost before they were dead somehow made beef lose its attraction.

By that first Christmas, we had two members of staff, Ret S'mai and a cook called Cha. Cha was Samut's brother-in-law, of course. ('Of course' because employment was in very short supply, and must be kept in the family wherever possible). It was unusual to have a male cook, but Cha assured us that he did all the cooking at home because the food that his now pregnant wife produced was inedible. Verification of this fact came all too soon when the two of them changed places; Tira's initial efforts were catastrophic, but she is a lovely girl and I will hear nothing against her. Cha not only cooked but washed up, cleaned the house, and did the laundry. There was a lot of laundry, for the heat meant a fresh set of clothes at least once a day. Clothes were washed in two of the biggest plastic bowls I have ever seen, at least three feet across, one red and one blue. Everything was scrubbed, rinsed, and then hung over the washing line to dry. The line stretched from the mangy mango tree at the foot of our outside stairs to a second one further up the garden, and was a motorway for enormous ants whose one aim in life seemed to be to cross, recross, and cross again. If I forgot to shake my shirt with sufficient vigour when taking it in at night, voracious insects took a formidable revenge when I put it on again in the morning. Ants excreta have never preoccupied my mind, but there is no doubt that they exist, for often white clothes would have a dotted line of brown spots as if to say 'fold here' where they had hung across the line. There were certain garments, too, which were obviously very tasty. Lacework was never my favourite at the best of times.

It was good having Cha around. He was always cheerful, and managed a few words of English. He appointed himself our odd job man. A little bit of carpentry here, the replacement of a burnt-out lead there, part of the makeshift wiring that threatened to turn the wooden house into a bonfire at any minute; he could turn his hand to almost anything. When it was coconut-picking time it was he who, barefoot and stripped of almost everything, shinned up the immensely tall tree at the bottom of our garden with a knife between his teeth and threw down the green head-sized fruits. He worked from seven to half past ten in the morning, and then went home after sternly locking the house against Ret S'mai. He and Samut disapproved of Ret. They said he was 'not a good boy' and we were just beginning to wonder secretly if we were wrong and everyone else was right. Some dollars had disappeared when it seemed that only he could be the culprit. And he was lazy, there was no doubt. But he still charmed us with his good humour and his great big happy grin, and the garden did benefit from his ministrations in fits and starts, when he felt like it.

Cha came back again after lunch on weekdays and cooked our supper, the main meal of the day. Cambodian food involves a great deal of chopping, and he would squat on the concrete floor, the chopping board cut from a tree-trunk on the ground in front of him, and attack a pile of ingredients with a small hatchet. He was always stripped to the waist, for he persisted in using the traditional charcoal burners in preference to the gas, and the heat was intense. He left for home several hours before we were ready to eat, so plates of food, beautifully arranged, were left in a slatted wooden cupboard lined with mosquito screening which was supposed to admit fresh air and nothing else. But absolutely no container was proof against the myriads of ants. Unlike their huge tightrope-walking cousins on the washing line these kitchen ants were tiny and would creep between the rims of plates put together in pairs to protect our meal. But we soon learnt the traditional method of standing the cupboard legs in water with a layer of oil on top; ants cannot swim. When we finally came to eat our supper the food was of course lukewarm at best. On the wonderful evenings when the microwave functioned, there was no problem. But saucepans of boiling water really did the job just as well.

Unbeknown to us at that time, there was one other microwave oven in Phnom Penh, hidden away in the kitchen of a remarkable gentleman called Ben. Ben was an Australian. He was one of those characters, larger than life in every possible way, that on rare occasions one is privileged to meet. Overweight and middle-aged, he had been wandering the world for many years and was a fount of erudite information. An ethnic musicologist by profession, his knowledge of Khmer art and music was immense, and his passion was the legends and mythology of Cambodia and their portrayal by the classical Apsara dancers. He worked with the Cambodian Ministry of Culture, and was like us a volunteer, but with OSB, the Australian equivalent of VSO. He had an immense heart and was generosity itself, opening his home to everyone. A constant clicking and whirring came from his back room where Khmer students from the College of Fine Arts in which he taught were welcome at any time to use his computer. He was not one to abide by petty rules, and woe betide anyone who tried to impose them. Everything about the way he lived was different. His back garden was a smallholding with pens of pigs and turkeys designated for practical use, a legacy from his Australian farming background; sloppy sentimentality certainly did not impede his hospitality. Under a trellis in front of the house hung row upon row of orchids in pots, collected during his many travels. The house itself of course bore the stamp of his personality. Its living-room was furnished comfortably, a joy to those of us in more straitened circumstances. There were woollen rugs from Vietnam on the floor, and blissfully welcoming long easy chairs. Books and busts of Khmer heroes sat on every surface. A full-length electric key-board stood against one wall. An elegant staircase led, on our earlier visits, nowhere; the flat roof above it was awaiting events which ultimately more than fulfilled expectations. Ben had at last created a huge room, but a room with only one solid wall. Front and sides were trellis work supporting a tangle of climbing plants and giving an airy freshness not often found in Phnom Penh. Presiding over all was a fleet of dogs, usually four or five in number. These were the lucky ones that Ben had rescued from the streets, bathed, combed, and fed until they were tamed into much-loved household pets.

There was good news for Tim on his triumphant return from Bangkok. We had been invited to Ben's for Christmas dinner. As in previous years, he was opening his house and garden to the entire English and Australian community in the city, and rumour had it that this was to be no mean feast, as we could well imagine. But there were still a few days to go, and a few days in Cambodia can encompass almost anything. Unrest had been grumbling in the city for the past week. As far as we could understand, the government was no longer able to pay its employees and so was sacking them. In addition, a large body of students was objecting to the corruption rife in high places. Demonstrations made legal for the first time by the Paris Peace Accords were erupting all over Phnom Penh. (It is interesting that there was total ignorance of the art of demonstrating. There were instructive articles in the Bangkok Times from neighbouring Thailand as to the niceties of method and approach.) On December 21st the medical students joined in, one of whom was shot and badly wounded. That evening, on the World Service all the way from London, we heard that he had since died. Even in our secluded part of the city we could hear bursts of gunfire continuing well into the night, but they sounded a long way away and our little music group had an evening assignation to rehearse at Ben's for a Christmas concert the following day. Life was going on as usual in the streets round about, and the cycle ride was a short one. The music, Pachelbel, Bach and Vivaldi, was very reassuring. Everyone turned up, and our efforts were amply rewarded with coffee and our host's homemade cakes. Pete, a recorder player fresh from his well-digging far from Phnom Penh and so ignorant until now of the riots, insisted on putting my bike in the back of his big white truck and driving me home, and as I wrote my diary that evening guns were still rumbling in the distance.

Next morning, James made a tour of the city to ensure that his flock was still alive and well. He suggested firmly that we all stay at home out of harm's way, and Tim and I were only too happy to oblige. Our more adventurous colleagues, however, determined to see all there was to see, went on a voyage of inspection and came back with dramatic reports. They found the centre of the city closed off, and our old friend the Asie Hotel inaccessible. Huge crowds of students thronged the streets, banners held aloft proclaiming 'This is a peaceful demonstration. Don't kill any more of us', for four in all had died the previous day. Bricks and stones, scattered all over the road surface, gave the army trucks crammed with riot police a bumpy ride. Occasional tanks and armoured cars lumbered past. We heard that visiting delegations from China and Vietnam who were to attend a conference had cancelled their visits. Khieu Samphan, the Khmer Rouge official who despite his murderous reception a few weeks earlier had been planning a second visit, discovered a more pressing engagement. The Bangkok Post was full of doom and gloom, reminding the public that the state of affairs preceding Pol Pot's takeover in 1975 had been much as now, and predicting a rapid return of the Khmer Rouge.

It so happened that a Dutch friend of ours, a paediatrician working in the provinces, was staying in a hotel near the city centre during a weekend visit to Phnom Penh. She spent much of the day under her bed, the riots raging beneath her upstairs window. As events quietened down, she pulled her table to the back of the room and sat down at her computer. Suddenly the glass in her window shattered and a bullet flew across the room, hitting the wall above her desk and ricocheting back so close to her head that she felt the breeze of its passing. Unscathed, I suspect she went quietly on with her work.

But despite all the alarm and despondency, peace gradually returned. A nine p.m. curfew was imposed, but that posed no problem to us as our Christmas concert was held earlier in the evening. We played in what until recently had been the Russian Cultural Centre, a stuffy building which smelt strongly of dead rat. When the time came to go home, we had reason to be very grateful to the young colleague who had insisted on borrowing a car to take and fetch us. Bicycles, he had said sternly, were not a good idea in the present climate. Emerging into the fresh air, we were faced immediately across the road by a riot policeman who instantly let off a few shots from his gun. (Many Khmers are trigger-happy. They shoot at anything, including thunder clouds which to the uninitiated can be quite alarming. Besides which, what goes up must come down.) We ducked behind our borrowed van, but he was not shooting at us. Without warning, the road had been closed to all but four-wheeled traffic, and it was an unsuspecting motorcyclist who was the object of the policeman's attention. At least he had the grace to fire over the poor man's head. Increasingly as time went by, motorcyclists were shot dead by fellow citizens who coveted their mounts. The Honda Dream was the model most popular with would-be thieves.

The next day, Monday 23rd December, all the schools were closed to prevent any further student protests. Apart from one or two bursts of gunfire after the evening curfew the town was unusually quiet. There was none of the frenetic pre-Christmas activity that does its best to spoil the festival at home. The crowded shops, festoons of streetlights and desperate last minute purchases seemed a million miles away; not in fact so very far from the truth. Any Christmas cards for home had been sent weeks before. None were for sale that first Christmas but instead we had discovered hidden away on several of the market stalls something much more interesting than a robin in the snow. Students from Ben's School of Fine Arts were selling miniature water-colours, paintings of palm trees and wooden huts, tiny boats and farmers working with their buffalo on the land. These cost almost nothing, and we bought quantities of them. Envelopes were sold separately. Made of poor paper, although cut in the right shape they were not assembled, so before posting our little pictures we had to set to work with the glue pot. True to tradition I had a moment of panic. I had not bought a present for Tim. One of the markets specialised in antiques, and there I found a heavy brass cowbell with a pleasing tone to rig up for visitors at our locked front gate. Although it never achieved its original purpose it did later come into its own as a burglar alarm. Attached to a nylon trip-line across the inside of our front door, it would have frightened us to death had any unsuspecting marauder sent it crashing from its perch on to the ground.

Christmas meant nothing to our Buddhist colleagues, and there was to be no public holiday. So December 24th was a full working day spent with Dr Vathiny in gynaecology outpatients, and it was not until the evening that our own festivities began. A sumptuous dinner, preceded by gin and tonic with slices of fresh limes picked from our own garden, of baked fish washed down with a bottle of wine and cheered by the arrival of our two young friends Caitlin and Bill from Battambang fired the Christmas spirit. Afterwards we listened to tapes that we had brought with us of a beloved Nativity play, faithfully produced year in year out at our local hospital at home, and of course of Christmas carols. And wonder of wonders we managed to catch live on our crackly short wave radio the Christmas Eve service of nine lessons and carols broadcast from Kings College Cambridge every year at three p.m. With a seven-hour time difference, it made for nostalgic bedtime listening.

Curiously, no Protestant service had been arranged for Christmas, and we had planned to attend midnight mass in the Roman Catholic church on the opposite side of Phnom Penh, meaning to ride the three or four miles on our bicycles. But the curfew was still in place, and though we toyed with the idea of ignoring it, we are not of the stuff of martyrs and went to bed instead. (This was a fortunate decision, for unbeknown to us the service had been cancelled.) So Christmas morning began with another service at that same church. Our visitors had come down from Battambang in their truck so we were able to do the little journey in style passing on the way underneath a well-known landmark known as the 'broken bridge'. This had once been a long bridge across the Tonle Sap, originally known as the Pont Sangkum, and built after independence from the French. It had been destroyed in the civil war in 1973, and now its two stumps protruded from either side of the river, yet another amputation testifying to the effect of war. Once in a fit of absent mindedness I nearly drove up and over the edge, for there was no barrier. At last, since we left, it has been rebuilt by the Japanese.

The service was very moving. It was held outside under an awning of plastic sheets laced together. It had been raining, and every now and again one of the sheets would deposit its contents down the necks of those sitting below. But the huge crowd, squatting or sitting cross-legged on yet more plastic took it all in good part, despite their Sunday best. Many of the little girls wore European style frilly nylon dresses, and everyone was of course barefoot. The three officiating priests were all white. This was only the second Christmas that Christianity had been allowed back into the country since the Pol Pot time, so no new Khmer priests had yet emerged from their training. The service was held in Khmer so we could not follow the spoken word in detail but it was clearly a very joyous celebration. The singing was strong and tuneful. We stood in line to receive Communion, Roman Catholic fashion, and the three priests got through us all with remarkable despatch. (I have since learnt that it is forbidden by the Roman Catholic Church for a Protestant to receive communion at one of their services. To whom should I apologise?)

Three other figures stood out from the crowd. Dressed in white habits and wimples with the well-known sky blue band across their foreheads, these were the Sisters of Charity, representatives of Mother Teresa's community in Phnom Penh. Their serene faces wreathed in smiles, they were giving the local traditional greeting to all of us on this beautiful warm sunny Christmas morning. I was not to know then of the interesting link I would forge with one of the trio.

Weeks earlier, a gigantic parcel had arrived for us at the office sternly labelled 'Not to be opened until Dec. 25th'. Now at last the time had come. Hurrying home in our borrowed truck we set to work. Its contents proved to be truly amazing, a joint effort by all four of our family and clearly assembled with considerable thought. There were books, glace fruits, a Christmas pudding, cosmetics, chocolate, toothbrushes, biscuits... the list could go on. Everything was wrapped and decorated, and by the time that we had raked around at the very bottom in the vain hope of finding yet more, there was overwhelming evidence that Christmas had well and truly arrived.

But the Feast was still to come. Armed with our small contributions, the four of us drove to Ben's house. Little tables and the inevitable pink plastic chairs had been set out in his colourful garden, roofed by a sky-blue plastic canopy. Clearly the menagerie had lost two of its senior members, for the serving table was laden with turkey, pork and ham, as well as vast quantities of salad and vegetables. Wine, beer, and soft drinks were there in profusion, and we all set to work with a will. As crackers were pulled, bright paper hats vied with brilliant tropical flowers for pride of place.

And so, after serious misgivings, our first Asian Christmas away from family and old friends was proving to be a very happy one. New acquaintances had by no means replaced the old, but how lucky we were to have fallen amongst such congenial and compatible company. But still of course family came first, and we had promised ourselves and our children the luxury of a phone call on Christmas Day. Alas, an afternoon spent at the only public telephone ended in disappointment. All lines were busy and as the curfew deadline approached our frustration grew. A few minutes before five, leaving ourselves just time to cycle the two miles home, we had to abandon the idea.

Chapter Thirteen

Christmas proved to be a landmark, for after it life settled into a pattern of sorts. Not that events became predictable, for every day continued to present surprises, but at least certain major themes emerged. Work and the weather dominated our lives.

At Christmas time, the sun shone and the breeze blew. The locals disappeared inside a variety of jackets and complained of the cold, while we Europeans rejoiced in the delights of a pleasant English summer. Occasionally we even had to pull up the green blanket that normally gathered dust at the foot of the bed. But already by the beginning of January things were beginning to change. During February and March the temperature rose imperceptibly but relentlessly. April loomed large before us, a prospect that brought dread to the stoutest heart. Ever since our arrival, everyone, locals and expatriates alike, had impressed upon us that the April heat would be almost unbearable. Sleep would be impossible without at least three cold showers a night. But long before April arrived, the high temperature and humidity were having their effect. By mid-morning, energy was draining away. The three mile cycle ride to and from the hospital twice a day was taking its toll. To climb the stairs up to our little house at lunchtime became a minor challenge in itself, and to remain upright whilst eating our bread and cheese and drinking pint after pint of water was a discomfort made pleasurable only by the prospect of becoming horizontal immediately afterwards. Despite the fact that even the inside of the wooden wall of our bedroom became too hot to touch we would instantly plunge into a slumber of bottomless depth. The town emptied well before midday. Only the cyclo-drivers remained, their sleeping frames sprawled over the passenger seats like rag dolls, hatted heads lolling, bare legs and flip-flopped feet lifelessly disposed at grotesque and hideously uncomfortable angles. Shady spots were at a premium. But April had not even arrived. We tried not to think about it, and my daily exercise to the hospital continued unabated.

It would be possible to base a fascinating textbook of medicine on that hospital alone, and over a period of just a few months. Apart from the medical problems themselves, the difficulties in handling them were legion. It was still early days. I still rode the rough muddy track leading from the main road to the ward in a daily state of apprehension, knowing that I was not yet fully accepted and uncertain of what impossible cases lay ahead. I was a woman, and must beware of stepping on sensitive male toes. Then the skills of my colleagues were so immensely variable. I quickly came to know which of them were good doctors and which were not. But even the good ones had sudden lapses, and I could take nothing for granted. Often it seemed that the teachers at the Faculty of Medicine in their efforts to ensure that medical education was up to date had failed to concentrate on the essentials. My colleagues had not been taught some of the simplest things and I quickly found that it would not do to correct them openly. I was not a consultant but an 'ordinary' doctor like themselves, and their pride was at stake. On the rare occasions when students attended the hospital, I felt free to be seen to teach. Then I would gradually become aware that the entire ward staff had quietly gathered round the bed, but to notice would have been fatal.

Anyone who has ever been examined by a doctor will remember the point where a hand, usually freezing cold, is gently laid upon your midriff. At least in Cambodia our hands were always warm, but gentleness was not in the vocabulary. With again notable exceptions, the victim's abdomen would be leant on suddenly and with enormous force. As this only happened at all when the patient had tummy ache, I could hardly bear to watch, though the average Khmer is remarkably stoical about pain. The only way that I could think of to correct this was by exaggerated care when it came to my turn but I do not think anyone noticed except doubtless the patient, who probably disdained such a pathetic approach as useless anyway. But I was equally guilty of cruelty in a certain medical condition. There seemed to be only one method of diagnosing amoebic abscess of the liver, a condition almost unknown in Britain and which I had never seen before. The shout of pain from even the bravest when the lower right ribcage was struck sharply with a closed fist left no room for doubt. There must be a better way, but when in Rome.....

Both students and doctors alike were impressive in their academic knowledge. The problems lay in its application, and, given the facts of each case, in working out the various possible diagnoses. Then there was the difficulty of realising that the wrong choice could have been made and that a change of course was needed. One such case was that of a young woman admitted panting for breath. When, after a careful and thorough examination of her chest, her lungs were pronounced clear and her heart sound, she was labelled as hysterical and no more interest taken. No one seemed to have looked further down and noticed that her abdomen was acutely tender, or to have discovered on questioning that she had missed a period. Far the most likely diagnosis was a ruptured ectopic pregnancy with massive internal bleeding. So little blood was left in the arteries and veins that the lungs were having to work overtime in order to circulate essential oxygen. This was a real emergency requiring immediate surgery. But it took a great deal of persuasion to alter course and call in the 'gynaecologist', a doctor who had simply worked in the gynaecological ward for a few months longer than the rest. The delay could well have proved fatal; fortunately for all of us it did not. A ligature tied tightly round the ruptured blood-vessels turned off the stop-cock just in time, and the tube in which the pregnancy had lodged was finally removed. Had the egg only managed to travel a few more millimetres and arrive safely in the womb, none of this would have happened.

This particular patient had been too ill to move, but in less dramatic circumstances, 'my' doctors would have been only too delighted to pass on the responsibility to Tim whose expertise in the operating theatre was already well recognised amongst the city's doctors. My own hospital director had tried to tempt him away to join us but officialdom forbad it. As time went on, an oddly familiar pattern established itself. Exactly as had happened at home, any outpatient cases that were beyond the capabilities of Vathiny or myself would be sent across to my specialist husband. We would scribble a referral note, issue geographical directions, and send the lady on her way. But paper was an expensive luxury, and supplies frequently ran out. Then all we could do was entrust the patient with a verbal message; surprisingly, the system worked very well.

Another example of unintentional neglect due to a hastily and wrongly made diagnosis was that of a young Vietnamese woman. In the absence of my medical counterpart Dr Chuoy the ward was being looked after by a locum. The unaccountable diagnosis that he attached to this unfortunate girl was malaria and treatment was given accordingly. Despite the lack of improvement, that seemed to be that. She was poor and she came from Vietnam, the age-old enemy of Cambodia; two unforgivable sins. The inescapable inference was, why bother? She had had nothing to eat for fifteen days before admission, and had obviously been half starved for much longer. Even so, it took a lot of pushing to activate the ward staff into finding her some nourishment from the paediatric ward which an NGO was supporting with a nutrition programme, and to look for tuberculosis which seemed a far more likely diagnosis. She was finally transferred to the Tuberculosis Institute down the road, but not before the poor girl had developed a deep vein thrombosis in her leg, and had added to her unpopularity by stealing from the woman in the next bed. As letters were never exchanged between hospitals, she was lost to sight. I doubt very much if she survived.

And so it went on. No criticism is intended. That there was any health service at all at this stage in the country's recovery was remarkable, and the level of skill and dedication in my own counterparts and many of the other doctors even more so. But inevitably, so soon after such total deprivation and degradation, there were huge gaps still in Cambodia's infrastructure, not least in the medical services. There was ignorance amongst insufficiently trained staff and also lack of motivation largely due to their low salaries and wretched living conditions. Admittedly there was laziness too, and the wards varied with the quality of the doctor in charge. Often a patient's admission procedure would be skimped. The notes would be derisory, the history-taking and examination virtually non-existent. For example, one day I came upon a man who had been admitted forty-eight hours previously. The fact that he was completely paralysed apart from some movement in his left arm had totally escaped the medical and nursing staff's notice. Another patient had come in in heart-failure. This time his condition was well documented and all the symptoms and signs neatly noted down. Or rather nearly all, for a vital one had been omitted. No one had thought to wonder why his heart was in such trouble, and so the measurement of his blood-pressure, the pressure in the arteries against which the heart has to pump, had been forgotten. It proved to be sky high.

Another more practical problem was the dire lack of facilities at the poor doctors' disposal. The situation of the destitute who faced death for lack of drugs was of course an ever-present misery. But it was not only drugs that were in short supply. Although the Khmers are very dextrous and so make excellent surgeons, the range of operations that they are trained to tackle is limited. A number of times Dr Long Ky and I on our ward-round in General Medicine would come to the bed of some young woman sitting bolt upright on her bed-mat, unsupported because there were no pillows or back rests, panting for breath. To lie down would be impossible, for then gravity would release its hold on the fluid that was already impeding her breathing, and her lungs would be swamped. Listening with a stethoscope we heard the harsh roar of a severely damaged heart valve, the typical long term aftermath of rheumatic fever. Usually the scarred valve had become too tight, impeding the flow of blood through the heart. In England right back in the 1950s surgeons had perfected a relatively simple operation to solve the problem. A finger, pushed through a small cut in the thin-walled upper chamber of the heart and then down through the tight ring of tissue would release the stricture and allow the blood to flow freely again. But no surgeon in the whole of Cambodia even in 1992 would dare to tackle this. There simply were not the operating theatre and anaesthetic facilities, and the danger of infection was too great. So these girls were destined for an early death. Pregnancy puts extra strain on a damaged heart and this is presumably the reason that we were only seeing this condition in the women's ward. Why we were not admitting new cases of rheumatic fever despite such strong evidence of its prevalence a few years previously was a more difficult question. Possibly it had been yet another product of the exigencies of the Pol Pot years or possibly, in Khmer eyes, the illness itself is not sufficiently severe to warrant medical attention. But more of that later.

Another big problem, too, is the vexed question of tests. In the West, investigations play an increasing part in diagnosis. The Cambodian doctors are well aware of this, and do their best to follow suit. But once again the facilities simply are not there. There are cupboards full of complex scientific instruments, mainly left by the Eastern bloc before its disintegration a few years previously, but most of them are broken and in any case there is no money to buy the necessary reagents. Nor is there anyone sufficiently skilled to repair them. But the staff in our little hospital laboratory were expert in the vital diagnosis and monitoring of malaria. For this, the only equipment needed is a needle, a microscope, a glass slide, and, extremely important, a practised eye. If I had malaria I would be far happier with a diagnosis made in Phnom Penh than in most English hospitals. But the doctors continually surprised and frustrated me by demanding more complex tests from the laboratory than its staff could perform, and then airily dismissing the results as wrong if they did not fit in with their expectations. More difficult investigations could be carried out at the national laboratory, the Pasteur Institute in Phnom Penh. But these were expensive, and there was no means of transport of samples from hospital to laboratory other than by the patient's relatives. I could not get used to the lack of bacteriology swabs, those long sterile cotton buds encased in test-tubes with which to collect infected samples. The patient himself had to be transported to the laboratory, usually in a cyclo, if this type of analysis was needed. When soon after we arrived my hand was infected by my spectacular dive into the town sewer, Bill and Caitlin gave us a cattle swab. It was at least eighteen inches long and correspondingly fat, but had the great advantage of making us all laugh. Later, Tim and I imported boxes of swabs for human use, but they will all have been used up long since.

These are just a few of the things that were lacking, a problem which, as I say, was not confined to health care. I did not often get depressed but the following quotation from my diary can only have been written when things seemed extra black.

'This is a desperate place. The aspirations are there, but the walls of the pit are too steep and slippery to climb without a ladder, and all but the bottom rungs are broken. There is no money to mend the ladder. Until and unless the ladder is mended, the people are utterly trapped and can only struggle helplessly at the bottom of the pit.'

But it was not just the doctors and their problems that caused unexpected difficulties. It was the patients, too, who presented even familiar illnesses in unfamiliar guises. This of course is not at all surprising when you think about it, but it was something that in my ignorance and lack of insight I had not anticipated. East or West, the human body is constructed in very much the same way, but other differences are enormous. The Khmers' attitude to illness is quite different from our own. They prefer to keep their troubles to themselves. In cases of sickness in their village communities, first the extended family and next the village elders are consulted, and only then is the local traditional healer called in. Great faith is still placed in remedies handed down the generations. When one of our patients with leukaemia found that with no access to chemotherapy we could do no more to help him, he drank a mixture of ground deer's horns in coconut milk. The remission that followed lasted several months. It is left to the desperate or to those whose outlook is becoming more westernised to make the journey to hospital. The concept of the family doctor does not exist. The nearest approach is the hospital doctor who has to supplement his meagre monthly salary of $15 by private practice at home.

So despite the high level of illness and early death in the country, the wards often remain half empty. There are other reasons too for this. Once again, money is a big factor. Our hospital, intended for the very poor, was supposed to be almost free. Each patient was asked to pay a few riels a night (a penny or two) but even this was not insisted upon. However, although I like to think and do believe that corruption there was minimal, money certainly did pass hands. Doctors and nurses and their families have to live. I was given a hefty tip by a patient on one occasion, who simply would not take no for an answer. So it was not surprising that many patients are afraid to go into hospital for fear of losing what little they have.

One of the worst examples of unintentional abuse, both clinical and financial, was poor Solon. He was admitted late one evening, and next morning when Long Ky and I went round the ward we found him lying flat on his back and apparently too frightened to move. His colour was good and there was nothing visibly wrong with him. He and his mother between them told us the story. A year previously when he was nineteen he had developed pain in his chest. He went to a doctor who told him he had a bad heart and that he must rest completely. He took a few of the tablets that he was prescribed and had bought in the market, but when he found they had no effect he put the remainder aside in a plastic bag. Impatient with the first doctor, he consulted a second one, who confirmed both the diagnosis and the strict instructions to rest, and sold him another collection of pills. Once again, when a few of each colour had been sampled and found wanting, into the bag went the half-empty packets, and a third doctor found. And so it went on. His mother, a Pol Pot widow and herself a farmer of reasonable means, had sold first her chickens, then her cow, and finally the roof over their heads to pay for her only son's treatment. She was at the end of her tether. Long Ky and I heard the story and listened to the boy's chest. My colleague's ears are exceptionally sharp, but try as we would neither of us could find any evidence whatever that he had anything but an entirely normal heart. More questioning elicited that immediately before his pain had started, he had had a bad fall, twisting his back. As the nerves from the spine travel horizontally round the body from the back to the front, it is perfectly possible for one of them, trapped in a minor back injury, to produce pain in the front of the chest. What we found made this seem likely. There was absolutely nothing to stop him getting up there and then and going back to work on his mother's farm, except that his wasted muscles would be of little use and that there was no longer any farm to go to. All their money had gone on doctors' bills and inappropriate treatment. The evidence, a large carrier bag full of useless pills, was there on the bed for all to see. And a fit young man had lost not just his strength but his entire fortune and a whole year of his life.

So it was not surprising that patients avoided doctors for fear of bankruptcy. Fear of many things was I think at the root of their hesitancy. When I pushed aside clothing to examine an abdomen I almost always found thin strings of tiny multicoloured beads wound loosely round the waist. These apparently were to placate evil spirits, something surely outside their Buddhist religion. There were other emotional pressures brought to bear, too. Time and again patients discharged themselves long before treatment had been given time to work, or had even begun, and often those who were, or thought they were, about to die were taken home. There were a number of different reasons behind this. Some of these were simple; lack of money, no family to care for them, impatience that a day or two in hospital had not wrought an instant cure. One reason was certainly sheer terror of the unknown, and particularly of the surgeon's knife. If an operation was unsuccessful, often the patient in waiting in the next bed would disappear overnight. But some reasons must have been much more complex, and I only wish there had been time and energy to find out more. In any event, it was all extremely frustrating. If a difficult case presented problems, I would often spend the evening at home with my books, such as they were, and draw up a plan of action, only to find an empty bed when I arrived next day. The patient had gone home.

I remember with especial sadness one such case. She was a young girl in her late teens, her stick-like arms and legs contrasting horribly with a belly so swollen it seemed she must give birth at any moment. But there was no baby inside, just pints of a clear yellowish fluid. Over the next few days, Long Ky and I did our best to sort out the cause. Of all the possibilities, the only one that might respond to treatment was tuberculosis. If this should be tuberculosis peritonitis, there was a faint chance that we could help her. Various simple tests supported this diagnosis. Dr Veng Thai, the medical director of the hospital, took a particular interest in her case, and by his authority we were given the rare privilege of use of the ambulance to take her to the Tuberculosis Institute. (There was an ambulance, which was probably of pre-Pol Pot vintage, but its driver often failed to materialise. He had to cycle many miles in from the country each day, and his wife was sick. The result of these difficulties was that he drank most of the little money he earned in rice wine and could not find his way to work. Who could blame him?)

However, we were in luck. Both ambulance and driver were available. There was even petrol; often, later on, if I needed the vehicle I had to buy a pint or two. Once I even had to buy a new tyre. Long Ky, the girl and her mother and I all climbed in, and off we went. She was so ill that she could not sit unaided, and her mother had to support her. The Khmer doctor in charge of the Institute had received special training from the French Red Cross who supported it, and clearly knew what he was about. He kept her there, and to my joy, confirmed our diagnosis. But it was not to be. Her mother refused treatment and took her home. On that same day, another girl, this time with tuberculous meningitis, discharged herself from our ward without treatment. Much time and effort had been spent on her diagnosis. Sometimes I wondered why we bothered.

Chapter Fourteen

The great advantage of not having a telephone was the certain knowledge that we would not be called at night for hospital problems. But the same did not apply to expatriates. The word soon got round that there was a good obstetrician in residence, and at any hour a big white truck would draw up at our gate and some heavily pregnant lady and her escort would appear to see Tim for advice or ante natal care. His usual procedure was to carry out the first examination in our house, and then to suggest that any further appointments should be held at the hospital. One morning in the rainy season, having arranged a meeting with a patient at January 7th, Tim negotiated the flood-water covering our own drive, splashed his bicycle through the mixture of rain heavily laced with sewage that lay foot-deep in the side roads, and finally arrived at his destination. The big low lying courtyard of the hospital was always one of the first areas to flood, and this day was no exception. The beds and their occupants had all been painstakingly moved to a higher level, and as he came through the open gate, it was a desolate scene that greeted him. The only living object in the vast sea before him was the pathetic figure of the patient he had come to meet. Marooned on some half-sunken island, she stood with skirts clutched about her plaintively announcing as she gazed round at the ever rising tide that her waters had gone. Pulling his imagination back from a wonderland of oceans of amniotic fluid, Tim managed to achieve both a dry room and some sort of medical examination. The news was not good. She was in premature labour, and there was no provision in this hospital nor any other for babies born too soon. A flight was due to leave for Bangkok in an hour's time; she would be well cared for there. Her doctor husband was told to get her on that plane by fair means or foul, but that he might even so have to deliver the baby en route. The story goes that his face went ashen grey; he was after all an administrative doctor and had not delivered a baby in years. They were on their way to the airport in minutes, only to find the flight completely full. Despite a desperate plea for help over the intercom not one European would give way. It was a Cambodian family who finally gave up their seats, enabling the poor lady to reach the haven of a modern maternity unit in Bangkok with minutes to spare and relieving her husband of further torments. The story has a happy ending, with mother and baby both doing well, and, back in Phnom Penh, a worried obstetrician breathing a very deep sigh of relief. It had been a difficult and delicate decision. On her return, she came to the house to show us her beautiful child.

We had plenty of other visitors too, some purely social and others who wanted to air their problems. The expatriate community was small and tight. People were pushed into one another's company, and gossip and feelings ran high. And it was hot. Tim and I did not socialise as much as our younger colleagues; we rarely went to the regular Saturday night parties that were given in turn by the various non government organisations (NGOs.) And so, because we were more distanced from the various relationships and intrigues that were happening round us, because we were older, and because we had a garden with shade to sit in, our friends would often turn up just for a chat. This gave us great pleasure and added enormously to our life. I think we all kept each other going. But what did not add to our peace of mind were the antics of Ret S'Mai, our one-legged guard. His tale is not a happy one, although eventually I think it had a satisfactory ending.

Ret S'Mai lived with his brother and sister-in-law. His brother, he said, was rich, but his brother's wife did not like Ret and would not allow her husband to give him anything but house-room. Within a day or two of his arrival with us, Ret complained that he had no money for cyclo fares and could not get to work. So we bought him a second hand bicycle, not as a gift, but as a loan for as long as he continued to work for us. He was absolutely delighted, and for a little while all went well. There were problems of course, but we pushed these aside as teething troubles. He was an uneducated lad from the country and would take time to learn our ways. After all we could not hope to set his poor ill-assorted feet on the upward path without some pitfalls. We pictured his future in a rosy glow, a future in which without doubt this heroic war cripple would make good. True, quite what good he would make remained at the moment a little obscure, and it did not take long to dawn upon us that far from clearing the murk was getting thicker. It is for instance difficult to retain faith in someone whose first positive act is to tip the household's accumulated garbage over the back wall into the next-door-neighbour's garden. We had already met this neighbour once. He was a gentle, shy old man, a retired engineer, who spoke an unusually elegant French. But as his angry face topped with white hair erupted over the garden wall, all sign of shyness had vanished. The gist of his outburst was would we please control our boy and fast, but it went on for some minutes and I can only hope he felt better for it. I did not. Faced with this reprimand, Ret simply shrugged. What else was he to do with the rubbish? We had no idea, but we made it our business to find out. Other neighbours pityingly explained that we should of course pile it in the road outside our house and set fire to it. Some of it burnt quite well.

A few days later, I noticed that Ret arrived for work on foot. Where was the bicycle? He had lent it to his younger brother, in town for a few days. A week went by, and still there was no sign of it. This time he told us that the loan had turned into a gift, as his brother's need was the greater. The lad lived in the country with their mother, and had no means of transport to get to school. Such generosity seemed praiseworthy, but the bicycle was not his to give away. Eventually we came to a mutual agreement; he would receive half wages until the debt was paid off. But within a few days I was peremptorily summoned to another kitchen conference and my heart sank. Ret could not manage on half wages, so what was I going to do about it? I did not like his tone, but perhaps the language problem was interfering with our mutual understanding and I took him to Kem the agency secretary who would act as interpreter. Finally we settled that he should work half time, and during the afternoons would earn money as a cyclo-driver. But from now on, contrary to his usual habits, he must turn up for work on time. The session ended with a ferocious argument as to when he had last been paid, and I felt his days were numbered. But the following morning, grin firmly in place, he was punctuality itself and worked hard in the garden. Once again he had won the day.

Next some dollars mysteriously disappeared from the house. Was he the thief? Almost certainly, but there was no proof. Then came the plea for a holiday. He had only been at work for a month, but his poor old mother out in the country was ailing and he must pay her a visit. If we gave him money, he would do us a great favour and bring back a special type of rice grown only in his mother's province, and some rare and delicious fish. The heat must have addled our brains, for we agreed. He was to be away one week. After an absence of two, he turned up. Sorry he was late, but there had been a terrible epidemic in his home village in which two of his brothers had died. He had felt obliged to stay longer to bury them. He did bring back a few pounds of rice which cooked up even more soggily than the market variety, but of course the fish had gone off on his way back and he had been forced to throw it away. How could we have been so gullible?

Meanwhile Tim, though much better since his return from Bangkok, was still unwell from time to time. One evening he had taken to his bed, feeling very sick. Ret had long since gone home. Suddenly I heard the dreaded nasal cry of 'Madame' from outside our locked gate. I went to investigate, and between the bars Ret poured out the following tale of woe. Another borrowed bicycle had developed a puncture and he had walked all the way from a roadside stall where he had taken it to be mended. (These stalls, dotted at intervals along the pavements, were equipped with primitive essentials for puncture-mending. A brisk trade resulted from the multitude of bicycles, for tyres were old and roads rough.) Ret had run out of cash and had no other means of getting home. So could I lend him money to pay for the repair? Even I realised that the figure mentioned was impossibly exorbitant, so there and then I decided to call his bluff. On the pretext of fetching money from the house I also collected the key for the front gate, and as soon as the grubby notes had changed hands through the bars, quietly turned the key in the lock. It was very dark, but I as I slipped through the opened gate I could just see the white flash of his T-shirt disappearing up the lane and then positioning itself above the rear light of a waiting motorbike. I watched the bike until it disappeared, turning away from the town centre. So this time surely I knew for certain that he was lying. But even now there was a niggle of doubt. Could he have gone round to the repair shop another way? Grabbing my own bicycle I pedalled dementedly off into the night, making a circuit of all the repairers in the vicinity. Of course there was no sign of the culprit. Back home, still clutching the bunch of keys in my hand and cursing myself for an unspeakable idiot, I went to bed. The next day, I asked my friend Alice to come and help me talk to him. She spoke Khmer fluently, and as a teacher was very experienced in dealing with young Cambodians. Acting as interpreter, she confronted Ret with all his unproved misdoings. Disarmingly, he admitted to every one of them. Of course we should have dismissed him then and there, but Alice like us succumbed to his charm. Moreover, Alice is a true Christian, and was only too happy to tell him that we would give him just one, but only one, more chance.

For a little while longer we jogged uncomfortably along. The saga of Ret's misdoings was becoming quite a talking point among our English colleagues, all of whom had got to know him as a regular cyclo-driver in the Asie days. One or two of them still argued forcibly in his favour. Most mocked us for our gullibility. But given time problems usually solve themselves, and this was no exception.

One day I arrived home from work, late for lunch. It had been a difficult morning, and I was tired and thirsty. As I opened the front gate, I simply could not believe my eyes. Running down the entire length of our concrete drive for perhaps twenty yards was a thick white line, glistening in the sunlight. It was neither central, straight, nor even. Starting at its widest, it wobbled its way back and to the left, narrowing as it went. Our garden was our particular delight. New plants had been put in among the old, and it was just beginning to make a showing. But far from the usual relief as one's eye rested on its gentle greens and pinks, now attention was riveted on this ugly urban monstrosity. The white line ruined the entire effect. There stood Ret, paint pot in hand, grinning all over his face. 'What have you done?' I asked. His face fell. He thought we would like it. He had seen pictures in books of Western roads. They all had white lines down the middle, and he thought it would make us feel at home.

Tim, returned just before me, had reacted in exactly the same way. Somehow this seemed the ultimate crime. Our precious haven was ruined. Get rid of it, we said. And anyway where did you get the paint? He had found a half empty pot left over from the window frames. And so the ultimate horror struck. This was no water-based paint that could be scrubbed off, but gloss, the best we had been able to buy. It was there for ever. Not so, said Ret. After fruitless scrubbing at it for a few minutes while we uncomfortably sat watching him while we ate our lunch, he disappeared to the back of the house. In a little while he returned and proceeded to paint over the line with a mixture of cement powder and water. It totally and instantly disappeared. We let him do it for it soothed all three of us. But in reality we all knew that as soon as the rains came the merciful camouflage would wash straight off, and the line would once more take pride of place.

Ret allowed us to digest our lunch and then asked to speak to us. It seemed that the white-lining had been intended as a softening up process which had gone badly wrong. He said he wanted to ask us a special favour. Would we buy him a cyclo? He was no longer able to earn extra money as the machine he had been using was borrowed and its owner needed it back. To our amazement he seemed surprised when we said no. We pointed out that we had lent him a bicycle and he had clearly sold it. We pointed out that this was not a spur to generosity on our part and that we had had enough. 'In that case' he said with great dignity 'I am very much afraid that I shall have to leave'. And leave he did. Believe it or not, we were rather sad. But the oddest thing of all was that this episode which seemed everlasting had in fact occupied just two months.

However the story of Ret S'Mai had still not quite ended. A few days later, a hatted figure on a shiny new bicycle appeared in our garden. It was Ret, come to tell us that he was going to marry a girl from his home village whom he had known for many years. We pitied her but congratulated him. The only problem was that he had to earn some money first; however, if he expected a reaction he was in for a disappointment. And after that he popped up from time to time, on each occasion looking a little more prosperous. He 'borrowed' his uncle's car and became a taxi driver for a while. Occasionally, as his English improved, he acted as an interpreter for the UN. But I do not think he ever did marry his childhood sweetheart, not while we were there at any rate. The last time I saw him he was waiting for me outside a shop, sitting as though by right on the bright red bonnet of our jeep.

The jeep. I could just say that we bought one to help out the bicycles and that would be the end of the story. But it was not like that. This was a very special jeep with a very special character, and it added a great many different flavours to our daily life. It was a purchase that had not been decided upon lightly. It was to be bought with our own money, and would have to be sold again when we finally left the country. A great deal of discussion as to its price, suitability, roadworthiness and all the rest had gone on between the two of us before the 'bargain' was clinched. (Bargain it was not; but let that ride.) In reality, I knew all too well from the first moment Tim clapped his eyes on it that this was to be our fate, the latest in a long line of eccentric vehicles that has passed through his hands over the years. Each and every one has been open-topped, exposing its very heart to all that the heavens have to offer. An outing in any of Tim's cars has always been the best way I know of distilling a whole skyful of fresh air into a brain-blowing battering bluster and sending my husband into transports of delight. I knew from the start that despite my boring better judgement I would agree, and sure enough as soon as I saw it in all its shining glory my heart was won and the deed was as good as done.

The jeep had just been painted a bright shiny pillarbox red which faded over the ensuing months to a matt pink. The workshop that had thus transformed it had been set up by two East Germans, who were members of an NGO with the suitable acronym of SODI. I do not remember what the letters stood for but I do know that one more on the end would often have voiced our feelings for our purchase perfectly. It certainly started as it meant to go on. The very day after we proudly brought it home Tim drove to work. Alas, by lunch time disaster had already struck. A noisy cloud of steam arrived at the front gate and chugged down our driveway, spurting boiling water as it came. As if by magic, the white line reappeared. Clearly the radiator had sprung an enormous leak, which proved to be just the first of a never ending series of breakdowns. It was a very old jeep, probably made at least a quarter of a century ago and originally brought in by the Americans. Its number plate proudly proclaimed PP 78, which presumably meant that it was among the first eighty cars ever to be registered in Phnom Penh. Not that we ever had any documents for it of any sort. As far as we could make out at the beginning, such things as log books, tax discs, and insurance and driving licences simply did not exist. Later we found that local drivers did carry papers of some sort and I think we were fortunate never to be asked to show any, especially on the two separate encounters I had with the police. On both occasions, I had failed to notice a No Right Turn sign and was stopped by a policeman in his strange two-tone uniform of air-force blue shirt and khaki trousers. I said I was very sorry, donned my most apologetic I'm-a-stranger-here smile and went to drive on. But that would not do. The first time, I was told that I must pay a spot fine of two dollars. I had no idea of the rules, and as this is only about £1.50, pulled out my purse with the thought that I had got away lightly. It was only when he tried to raise the stakes that I realised that in all probability there was no such law, and refused to part with the extra. Fortunately he simply laughed and sent me on my way. On the second occasion my captor was a middle-aged burly fellow who stood menacingly in front of the car, and said he would only move if I bought him beer. I was not beyond a minor act of corruption and said that yes, if he was thirsty I would buy him a can. He swelled visibly and indicated that he meant not a single tin but a tray of two dozen. At that I went on strike, for beer was not cheap and twenty-four cans would make a big hole in my allowance. Besides, this was not friendship but blackmail. No, I said, and there we sat, glaring at each other. We stayed there for a very long time, until at last a much younger man strolled over. He was clearly my policeman's superior, and after looking me up and down, he muttered something that I did not catch, and I was allowed to drive on. Had I known then what I heard later, I should not have been so self-righteously stubborn. One of the UN staff drove through a puddle, inadvertently splashing a policeman who happened to be standing nearby. The policeman shot him dead.

The jeep certainly took some getting used to. Of course it was left-hand drive with corresponding transposition of the controls. When I eventually mastered that difficulty, I found I had to double declutch, something that had fortunately been familiar many years ago when I first learnt to drive. But even so, rapidly gearbox trouble developed. Every now and again the engine would be stuck in neutral, the lever jammed solid. But far from being immobilized, the car continued on its way, quite fast, in some secret one-speed gear of its own. I rapidly learnt that if I gave it its head, suddenly there would be a clonk and all would function normally. But with little motor-bikes buzzing round me like a swarm of angry bees it could be distinctly unnerving.

Then the petrol gauge did not work. (Neither did the hand-brake, but that was merely an inconvenience). We had to measure with a dip-stick, and sometimes we forgot. Shopping had been difficult on bicycles, particularly for furniture. Rejoicing in proper transport at last, I had bought two heavy wooden desk chairs and several bags full of the week's food supply. Two miles from home, the engine spluttered and died. Alas the tank was empty. I took a cyclo to the nearest roadside stall where they sold petrol. At least I assumed it was petrol. There were a great many of these stalls, little tables laden with Fanta bottles containing a pink liquid. I had seen motor-bikes stop at them, and I did not think it was to refresh their drivers. Promising rapid return of the valuable empties, I took two of these back to the vehicle and tipped them into the tank. Back went the bottles and then came the moment of truth. Surely now the engine would start, but it remained stubbornly silent. Perhaps it really had been Fanta after all. A complex manoeuvre involving two cyclos and much gesticulating got me and my purchases home and Tim and myself back to the jeep again, still there for the simple reason that no one could move it. (Or could it possibly be that no one wanted it?) And neither could Tim who, after a consultation with the local garage, disappeared on a motorbike tightly sandwiched between two greasy bare chested mechanics. This was the reconnaissance party, gone to fetch the senior engineer who proclaimed that all was well and why had we been so stingy with the petrol?

And so it went on, and on, and on. If the wretched car gave no trouble for two consecutive days it was a miracle. Twice it dropped its propeller shaft on the road, once with an explosive flourish in the middle of the main highway, and the second time in a side street, gently and with sadness. On this occasion I had to ask two Khmer passers-by to help me push it to the side. It had been around for some time now, and its notoriety was spreading. They pushed, but not without one of them saying in impeccable English 'This is the most terrible car I have ever seen'.

But the equation was in perfect balance. Frequency of breakdown was exactly matched by ease of repair. The main jeep garage was almost

Dr Vathiny leaning against the jeep, with Mme Savun

next door to my hospital, and father and son who ran it gained great amusement from my never ending cries for help as yet again I arrived by emergency cyclo. The red jeep abandoned by some roadside became a common if moveable landmark. Friends would report sightings, and enquire tenderly after its health. The garage would collect and mend it, usually within a matter of hours. I do not think the bill was ever more than $4 (£2.50).

Our Khmer colleagues simply could not understand us buying such a vehicle. Why on earth did we not get a respectable white Toyota like everybody else? But our expatriate friends held quite a different view. Despite its age and afflictions it was a happy car and we got an enormous amount of fun from it. People loved to ride in the back for short trips round the town, though we quashed any suggestion of taking it further afield. With the best will in the world, we could not call it reliable and Cambodia is not a country in which to break down far from home. And in the ensuing months it certainly came into its own as a beast of burden, laden with people, supplies and large quantities of medical drugs. In fact I could not possibly have done my job without it.

But that was later. In the early days, it was just a heaven-sent alternative to the gruelling bicycle rides in the ever increasing heat. Poor Tim; I am afraid I came to use it much more than he did, for my hospital was a long way from home and he stoutly maintained that he enjoyed his daily walk or cycle ride to work. But Khmer women do not drive cars, or did not then. Add to this the nature of the beast and both its age and my own, and together we seemed to produce the eighth wonder of the world. For the first few months, everywhere I went heads would turn and mouths drop. Then would come the laughter and the universal cry of 'Yea bak lan!' 'Grandma driving a car!' I like to think that the laughter was friendly. But for joy-rides it was Tim who took the wheel and gloried in the car's eccentricities. On these occasions, unencumbered by doors or seat-belts, we would swap positions and I would happiy hand over the controls. It was not the easiest car to drive.

Chapter Fifteen

The very next night, we went to a concert. The College of Fine Arts was split into two separate sections, one next to the museum in the middle of the town where students studied art and sculpture, and the other on the outskirts. This was the centre for music and dance and it was here that two of our compatriots Alice and Catherine worked. They were good friends, with music as the bond between them, for they were both fine violinists. But there the likeness ended. With her slender figure and delicacy of features and complexion, there was a strangely fairy-like quality about nineteen-year-old Catherine. Her ramrod-straight back, with long blonde hair flowing out behind, made her too a familiar sight as she rode her bicycle round the town, her fair colouring in absolute contrast with those around her. Unlike the rest of us, she was not with any organisation but had come out entirely alone. Following a previous visit to the country and filled with a youthful zeal engendered by the obvious plight of the Cambodians, she had fought her impecunious way back against great odds and had found herself a place as a teacher in the music school. She did not much consort with Westerners. She came as near as she could to becoming a Khmer, lodging in an ordinary Cambodian household and living as one of the family in a wooden hut without water or sanitation and with rats in her bedroom. She had very little money and was often an anxiety to the expatriates with whom she was in closest contact. She was young, sometimes thoughtless, distinctly fey, and very attractive. She did not always wear 'suitable' clothes. But our impression was that despite her youth, isolation, and physical frailty she was well able to look after herself. Many people helped her too and, when I last had news of her, she was achieving remarkable results.

But that is jumping too far ahead. That night, she seemed very much a part of the ethereal beauty that cloaked the whole magical evening. Dressed in the classical Khmer sombot or skirt, she was to take part in a concert celebrating the opening of a new music and dance pavilion.

There were certain moments during our two years in Cambodia that demanded immediate special treatment, and this was one of them. In a little notebook, I tried to record their essence as best I could. This was as close as I could get.

'Tonight all our senses were satisfied. Imagine a full moon, shining through the open sides of a simple pavilion. The surroundings are open and green. As we arrive, our headlights throw up on a wall the magnified shadow of a bullock, huge and still, with its horns and strong neck. Inside, a harpsichord is playing. The music is modern and spiky. Against the wall stand wooden chairs, their backs carved in different patterns. Each pattern has its own double shadow standing behind it, clearly defined. A cello rests on its side and a violin leans upright in a corner, their rich curves and colours accentuating the starkness. For a whole hour the music flows, from strings and keys and vocal cords. All is serene, the performers intent and supremely content in their music-making.'

There was something both exciting and deeply moving about the College of Fine Arts. That so much emphasis should be placed on matters of soul rather than of body in a country decimated by the recent horrors is of course as it should be but not as it always is. But then music and particularly dancing are central to the Cambodian culture. After every major event, good or bad, the people will get together and dance, or will even dance alone. As I fruitlessly sheltered under a tree one day, I watched a child respond to the first rains with a spontaneous ballet of the utmost elegance. Stripped almost naked, she unselfconsciously let herself go, leaping and turning with a supreme and unhurried grace, her slender body and limbs curving into a series of perfect arcs. Soon other children joined in and the moment was gone, but it had been her own expression of relief from the heat and I envied her.

So the College was vital to the country's recovery, and it was here that children came to learn the traditional Apsara dancing, a technique that can only be perfected if pupils begin early. The beautiful boneless movements of arms and hands for which this dancing is so famous has to start with the elastic ligaments of childhood. The School of Dance had reopened eleven years previously under the guidance of the ten per cent of performers who had survived the Pol Pot era. Of these, Madame Chea Sami was the most revered and took the lead in training the new generation, many of whom are children of those who died. I never found the time to go and watch a teaching session, but I once saw the children put on a performance in that same dance pavilion.

There are a number of traditional dances, many of them based on old Hindu legends. It is an extremely intricate art, in which all humans, both male and female, are played by girls. Men take the specialist roles, such as the mythical giant and monkey. To understand it fully requires detailed knowledge, for each step represents some thing or some emotion, such as love, anger or embarrassment. We understood almost nothing as we watched the children enact their roles, but even in our ignorance we could appreciate their budding skills and of course their fabulous costumes. Later we watched other children's dance troupes too, youngsters that showed every bit as much enthusiasm if not quite the same skill, and always my favourite character was Hanuman, the white monkey, proudly played on each occasion by a lithe and athletic boy.

Hanuman is one of the most important characters in the legend of the Ramayana, for without him all would be lost. Less than three weeks after our arrival in Phnom Penh we had had the unique privilege of watching the first full shadow puppet presentation of this story since 1974, before Pol Pot's invasion. Just four sets of these puppets are left in the whole country, of which the only complete collection is the one we saw that night. Immediately before the Khmer Rouge takeover, the puppets, life-

Children performing a traditional dance

sized stencils cut from stiff buffalo-hide, were packed in boxes and left in the house next to the theatre. The boxes were opened by the Khmer Rouge who evidently failed to recognise their contents and left them untouched. Had their importance been realised, these cleverly crafted silhouettes would, no doubt, like so much else, have been wantonly destroyed.

The Ramayana legend is a Hindu epic, known throughout South and South-East Asia. It is two thousand years old, and tells the story of the incarnation of the Hindu god, Vishnu, who comes down to earth as a handsome Prince, bringing with him his goddess wife. The purpose of his visit is to destroy a ten-headed monster who rules over an army of demons on the island of Sri Lanka. Helped by Hanuman, the white monkey, he eventually succeeds in his task, and they all live happily ever after. This legend and the stories of many other battles that stem from it are frequent subjects of Khmer art as well as dance. There are excerpts from it portrayed in the bas-reliefs at Angkor Wat, and it is depicted in paintings on the walls and ceilings of the throne-room of the Royal Palace in Phnom Penh, though these of course are much more recent. In the olden days a thousand years ago, to dance the Ramayana was to perform a religious ceremony. This picturesque portrayal of the triumph of good over evil was thought to bring peace and to smooth away all disharmony between the gods and their human subjects.

One of the most important functions of the College was to keep alive this ancient Khmer mythology, passed down by music, dance, and word of mouth from generation to generation. But the world does not stand still. Some of the greatest exponents of Western music are appearing in Japan, Korea, China and other Far Eastern countries and in the years before the evils of 1975 Cambodia had been part of this movement. Its flourishing symphony orchestra had been the pride and joy of the musical elite until that too had fallen prey to the devastatingly destructive powers of the Khmer Rouge. When Alice suddenly appeared in their midst, violin slung on her shoulder by a stout strap, how musical hearts must have lifted and musical hands itched to get back to work. Alice was there to help them, and if Western music was what they wanted then that was what they should have, despite her own private leanings toward the traditional.

Amongst other tasks, Alice trained the school orchestra. This had only just come into existence before our arrival, and when we first heard it perform early in our stay it sounded much like any average orchestra in any average English school. Even then, though, there was one notable difference. The fluid action of the children's bowing arms, all moving in a remarkable union, was quite unlike the stiff-wristed pull-push of most European learners. The gift of natural grace was as clearly manifest in the violinists as in their dancing counterparts. By the time we left two years on the improvement was extraordinary. Fully recognizable now was the huge potential of this young orchestra, the only one of its kind irrespective of age in the whole country.

The next intake of volunteers to appear a few months after our own arrival reflected perfectly the country's needs. Their skills were respectively medicine, hydrology, and flute-playing, and we found it impressive that our agency in far away London should recognise the equal importance of all three. It is easy to imagine the raising of inelastic eyebrows at the notion that a fancy flute-player could compete in value with specialists in malaria and the management of water. But the choice was absolutely right, and so Mary joined Catherine and Alice at the school and became a vital member of the team. But in those early days it was Alice who was fundamental to the success of Western music, a success that was very nearly doomed to failure by an unexpected and alarming turn of events.

Alice is a missionary who after working in South East Asia for over thirty years had recently come to Cambodia. At the time of her arrival the government had only just allowed Christianity back into the country and it was unwise to say the least for her openly to continue her missionary work. The Overseas Missionary Foundation to which she belongs had sent her in as a music teacher, but such is her dedication that despite the danger she continued to work in promoting the Christian faith amongst the Khmers while at the same time helping them with their music. Towards the end of 1991, she applied for a routine renewal of her six month visa, but to her surprise and distress her application was refused. The reason was a political one. Concealed in the cupboard under the stairs of her house was a cache of religious books. The news had spread amongst the local Christians that this was a distribution point for much-needed literature, its content still heavily frowned upon by some Cambodian officials. Somehow the secret got out and the information was passed to one particular member of the communist government who, already suspicious, determined to get rid of her.

Her present visa had only a few days to run when the blow fell, and everything and everyone associated with her was thrown into turmoil. The Director of the Music School threatened its closure, saying he could not run it without her support. Ben, the Australian working with the College of Fine Arts, was beside himself and moved heaven and earth to obtain a reprieve, but without success. The Protestant church was saddened beyond measure, and produced wonderful and eloquent prayers for her safety and happiness. It was a great personal blow to me too. I had come to rely on her friendship, her serenity, and her provision of the weekly escapism of music-making, all of which were important in this otherwise alien world.

Ten days later, her time was up. She had given me the cases of music that we chose from each week. She could be very stern, and I had received strict instructions that I was to keep our chamber group going at all costs. I had neither her musicianship nor her authority, and knew that this torch passed on to me was in grave danger of a spluttering extinction. The moment of her forced departure happened to fall on a Friday, the very day on which we always met. Our assembly that evening felt rather like a memorial service. We must attend out of respect for the dear departed, but the pivotal point was no more.

How wrong we were. As we sadly unpacked our instruments, there she was! The Head of the British Mission had appealed on her behalf, and she had been given a reprieve, admittedly for one week only, but surely the rest would follow. It was Catherine, her fellow fiddler, who had persuaded the British Ambassador-to-be to plead her cause. He succeeded where all else had failed, and Alice will go down in the Mission's annals as his first consular case.

But this after all was Cambodia. One week on, and events had taken another about turn. The visa was not after all to be renewed and Alice's suitcases had to be repacked. This time it was the Earl of Caithness, visiting the country on behalf of the British Government, who came to the rescue. Citing the clause on human rights laid down in the Paris Peace Accords, he finally and irrevocably overturned the Cambodian minister's decision. Alice was awarded a full six month's visa and everyone's worries were over. This was a truly happy ending. The Protestant church rejoiced, and the occasion was marked by a celebration chocolate cake, appearing and disappearing at our next Friday bonanza. Alice was no mere missionary/musician, not she. Her chocolate cakes are the stuff that dreams are made on.

It was her twin hats of music and religion as well as our own inclination that first took Tim and me to the international church. Its congregation was drawn largely from members of NGOs (non-government organisations), many of them Americans of strongly evangelical persuasion. There was no priest, and worshippers took it in turn to lead the service. Sometimes at these church meetings we had an outside speaker, usually a visitor to the country who was interested in taking part in our home-made service. The most memorable of these was a Khmer pastor, head of the Cambodian church in America. He gave us a fascinating outline of the history of the Protestant church in this his home country. Although Roman Catholicism had been introduced by the French in the late nineteenth century, the first non-Catholic missionary had been a pastor by the name of Hammond, who arrived in 1923. It was he who translated the Bible into Khmer, the edition that they still use to this day. But progress in the spread of Christianity was very slow, and was in any case seriously disrupted by the Second World War, during which all missionaries were imprisoned by the Japanese. After 1945, the numbers of Christians gradually built up again, accelerating as time went on until once again everything was brought to an abrupt halt, this time by the arrival of Pol Pot with his vicious veto on all religion. Some missionaries escaped; others, as well as a number of the new Cambodian Christians, came to a horrible end. At least one was crucified, nailed up to his own front door. At last Pol Pot's troops were finally driven out and refugees began to trickle through to the camps on the border with Thailand. To the great joy of many of the workers in the camps, it emerged that the Christians had not after all been wiped out but had continued to meet in secret throughout the Pol Pot years. As they filtered through to relative safety and security, they brought with them not just stories of horrendous hardship and incredible survival, but accounts of persistence in their faith against all odds. One man described how he had buried his Bible in the ground early every morning and then dug it up again after dark so that he could read and be refreshed. But right up until 1990, just the year before we arrived, Christian gatherings were forbidden. From that day to this, Christian groups have been springing up throughout the country in ever increasing numbers, although the government still makes their life far from easy.

So on most Sunday evenings, just before five o'clock, I would balance my violin in my bicycle basket and set off for the church, where Alice led a little group of musicians in the accompaniment of the hymns. I have to admit that my behaviour was not always impeccable. As I have said, members of the congregation took it in turns to lead the service, and while many of them were excellent, there was one particular gentleman whose approach was very different from anything that I was used to. He had a strong singing voice and would lead the congregation in a rendering of songs from the evangelical hymn book that I found unbearably slow and sentimental. In Alice's absence one day, I could endure it no longer, and as we set off on the next verse, somehow or other my errant fiddle broke into a fast and furious gallop. The body of the church responded to a man, and the next few seconds were a glorious romp. But the revolt was doomed to failure. The rest of the hymn, announced our leader, will be sung unaccompanied. The reprimand was absolute, but I had no regrets. It had been worth every scampering semiquaver.

It is sad that in the Protestant church there are so many different opinions, and that even in the small gathering of expatriates in Phnom Penh these differences should manifest themselves. But I confess that I was greatly relieved when the Church of England authorities received royal permission from King Sihanouk to set up the first Anglican church ever. Our first pastor moved in at great sacrifice to himself, his wife, and their three daughters, for their plans had been in a very different direction. Don Cormack performed wonders in the short time that we knew him, and we were enormously privileged to listen to some of the very best sermons that I have ever heard. He had previously spent many years working with Cambodians both inside the country and in the refugee camps on the Thai border and has recently witten a fascinating account of the history of the Cambodian Christian Church entitled *Killing fields, Living fields*, already in its second edition. He was therefore an ideal choice for this post, and in a unique position to introduce Cambodians to the Christian faith. There was no building in which to hold services, so he converted the ground floor of an existing house into a simple but beautiful little whitewashed church. But all was not quite sweetness and light, for in the unavoidable absence of his organist wife, it fell to my lot to struggle through the accompaniment to the service on a battery-run keyboard, the nearest we could get to an organ. I am no pianist, and I truly think my pulse rate reached more dangerous heights on Sunday mornings than at any other time during those two variegated years.

Chapter Sixteen

As time went on, the backcloth of this unfamiliar life grew gradually broader and its colours richer. Tightly woven, every square inch of it was filled with incident, threads thick and thin twisting together into the tangle that made the experience one of such peculiar fascination. The big events shone out in blocks of colour, but only by contrast to the duller ones of every day. It follows that these were equally important, and if the telling of them seems disjointed, so was the way we lived. Confusion can only add authenticity.

It was the little things that made us feel we really belonged. A few months after our arrival, we were invited to another party. The infant mortality rate in Cambodia is one of the highest in the world; survival for the first month after birth is an achievement, and traditionally is marked by a celebration. Cha's new baby had successfully reached this milestone, and we were invited to join in the family festivities. The event took place at their home, a wooden house very much like our own and set in an open patch of ground in a quiet side street. But unlike ours, this one was filled to capacity. The central figure was Cha's mother-in-law, a youthful grandmother who made biscuits for a living. Then came her four children, their spouses and her grandchildren. At the top of the pile was Great Grandmama, a silent infinitely wrinkled crone who sat quietly in a corner as all good grandmothers should. There were no rooms in the house, or rather just one big one open to the rafters, and here the whole family lived. Samut proudly showed us her bedroom, curtained off in a corner. It contained the bare necessities. There was just room for her bed hidden under a white mosquito net and for a chest with a looking-glass on it; coloured pictures from magazines were pinned on the walls. Other flimsy partitions disappeared back into the gloomy depths, for all the windows, unglazed as was usual, were at the front of the house. So it was here by the windows that we sat for the party, on straw mats on the smooth wooden floor, beautifully polished by the soles of generations of bare feet. No one wears shoes inside. The very first lesson in etiquette is that they must be left on the doorstep. Slip-on footwear is essential for obvious reasons, so functional buckles and bows are out. Khmer women dress very elegantly, but the many cheap stylish sandals for sale in the market were all too small for my large English feet. We did not take our shoes off in the hospital, and so I could at least go to work decently shod. Incidentally, to point the sole of your foot at anyone is the height of discourtesy, so beware how you sit on the floor.

In the centre of the circle a cloth had been laid, and what a feast we had. There were Chinese noodles, soup, stew, salad and for pudding little jelly cubes from a packet. We each had a green coconut in front of us, the top of its husk neatly sliced off with a chopper leaving the white rind. A modern straw penetrated the depths of this ancient drink, and I know of nothing more thirst-quenching, or for that matter more hygienic, on a hot day. But no Cambodian party is complete without cans of fizzy drinks which were available in ever increasing variety as time went by. I was given Coca Cola, and the men all drank beer.

We ate and drank and conversed as best we could. Then came the photographs, which I am sure were a wonderful record of the proud parents' wedding, elegantly mounted in an album. I only hope I held it the right way up, for I had forgotten my spectacles. This was a pity, as Tira the bride is very beautiful and must have looked dazzling in her ornate wedding dresses. Khmer weddings are convoluted affairs which involve several changes of clothing by both partners, and the photographs would have been very enlightening. We never attended a full ceremony which was for close friends and relations only, but I do know that it involves sitting entirely still on the floor for hours on end, a considerable test of endurance. We did go to a number of wedding feasts, invited out of politeness by our young Khmer colleagues. Each guest was led to one of a number of tables usually arranged on the pavement under an awning. Fresh arrivals filled up each table in turn, and as soon as its number was complete, but not before, the meal was served. This was puzzling at first. Why was food and drink flowing free next door while we sat hungrily waiting? But once started there was no stopping, and course followed course. Familiar companions at table explained that the disgusting slimy black lumps which looked like giant leaches were a delicious species of mushroom, or that the knobs of meat-covered bone came not from cats but ducks. Once at a particularly gynaecological dinner I was faced with an obnoxious looking dishful of chopped cow's womb, which tasted as foul as it looked. Occasionally I would find myself seated with strangers and had to fend entirely for myself. Bare-footed urchins ran between the tables, grabbing half finished cans of coke and beer and discarded scraps of food as chairs emptied, for no sooner had the last person finished at a table than everyone got to their feet and left. There were no ceremonies and no speeches. It was all very matter-of-fact, particularly as regards payment. When either arriving or leaving, each guest passed the receipt of custom, a white shirted man sitting at a small table with lists and piles of envelopes. There was no set charge, and at my very first wedding I had been advised to wait until the end to assess the size of the contribution. This free market economy seemed to me sound practice, and I stuck to it.

The last wedding feast I attended celebrated the marriage of a woman doctor from my hospital. She had always seemed a rather sad lady with a difficult home life for her mother had cancer and needed ever-increasing care. Sokhon was an adequate doctor but with little enthusiasm for the gynaecological work she was doing, and it seemed that life was passing her by. I was surprised when I was told of the forthcoming marriage, for I had heard nothing about a boyfriend. In fact there had been no courtship. This was a marriage arranged by the dying mother, presumably so that her daughter would not be left alone, and Sokhon had met the boy only once before the wedding. I could hardly recognise her at the ceremony in the traditional glittering gown and head-dress and wearing heavy highly coloured makeup. She looked radiant and insisted on a photograph of the three of us. By the time I left the country she was pregnant, and I wish them every happiness. Arranged marriages are still common in Cambodia.

One day we got home from work to find our driveway entirely full of rank upon rank of neatly parked motorbikes. The house looked like ours, and the number on the open gate, always kept locked, was correct. So there was no mistake; it was our driveway. Now what? At once we were accosted very charmingly by the student son of our neighbour opposite (not the white haired French speaking engineer of garbage fame). His father was 'celebrating' the first anniversary of his wife's death, another Khmer custom, and would be delighted if we would join him. I was extremely tired and wanted nothing more than to flop. But it was a kind and courteous thought, though I imagine largely prompted by his need for parking space in our garden, and it would have been uncivil to refuse.

Once again the event followed exactly the same format. Circular hire-tables and pink plastic chairs filled the garden that we looked at every day from our balcony, and we passed a pleasant evening chatting in French to the six Khmer gentlemen seated with us, all dressed in the statutory grey trousers and open necked white shirts. Wives and daughters are nearly always left at home.

The sight of a funeral procession in the town was quite a common one. The coffin, simple or extraordinarily ornate according to means, was the centrepiece of a trailer usually pulled by a motorbike. Round it would be seated the white-clad 'religious', elderly ladies with hair clipped short who were living out the last few years of their life in a pagoda, or shaven headed monks in orange robes. But the preamble to such a procession threw me badly one day. There were two streets in town where carpentry shops were centred. I always enjoyed wandering round them with their great piles of rough timber, watching the processes by which planks were turned into furniture, some pieces beautifully crafted, others cheap and clumsy. I loved the smell of sawdust and the creative activity going on all around. By now the proud possessor of the jeep, I set out one afternoon to collect a desk that I had ordered just a few days before. But the joiner's shop had vanished, replaced by an exotic funeral parlour. The pavement outside was entirely taken up by an ornate work of art, a coffin carved in a wonderfully intricate design. On the top stood a framed photograph of a middle-aged man in spectacles, presumably its occupant. As I stopped in admiration I happened to glance past it and there was the interior of my shop, its normal frontage cleared to make room for this new display. I collected my desk from the young man inside who showed no visible sign of bereavement, and I never did discover whether it was the owner lying there or whether they were simply advertising their wares.

The young carpenter may well have been hiding his grief behind a smiling face, for the deepest sadness was often disguised by laughter. Take So Peap for example, the young man who followed Ret S'Mai as our guard. His father had been 'executed' by the Khmer Rouge, or rather had been hit on the back of the head with a hoe until at last he died. Peap, then a little boy of five, had watched the whole procedure from behind a bush and had finally run off terrified into the forest. His description of this unspeakable event was so interrupted by giggles that we could scarcely follow it. There can have been no other way to share such horror.

But laughter conveyed humour too. The Khmers have a great sense of humour, and the heroic villain of this next story was still laughing several days afterwards. One Friday evening I drove out as usual to play in our chamber music group. Tim undressed and went into the bathroom for a shower, leaving the door ajar. To his alarm, as he stood under the dribbling shower-head there was a rapid padding of bare feet across the adjoining wooden floor, the door banged shut and the bolt was shot home on the other side. He was well and truly locked in. He shouted and thumped with such persistence that after some time the bolt was cautiously drawn back, and as the door slowly opened a terrified pair of brown eyes peered in at him through the crack. Cha the cook, thinking we had both gone out together, had heard footsteps upstairs. Bravely he had crept in on his bare feet and cornering the burglar in the bathroom had surely taken a notable captive. It must have been a rich moment when the truth dawned that far from being a bandit the figure revealed in all its sodden naked glory was his boss. He and his friends certainly enjoyed it to the full.

Odd things happened in the expatriate community too. On the whole, members of NGOs were an earnest group. There were a few misfits who had come for the 'wrong' reason, but most of the white population were do-gooders in the best sense, people who were motivated by pity and a wish to help. So it was not exactly a glamorous society. Clothes were directed at comfort and not at fashion, and the universal daytime young female wear consisted of T-shirts and bright cotton trousers. I always wore a skirt, but only because I found it cooler. Imagine a day, New Year's Day in fact, spent in the dirt and squalor and deprivation of the hospital. Then imagine a wonderful swim in the sparkling blue cleanliness of the Hotel Cambodiana pool, surrounded round its edge by our Western fellows, their noses deep in erudite papers on the problems of rehousing refugees and the rights of women. Afterwards, refreshed and with dripping hair, we walked to the car park. And there, standing all alone, was an apparition from another world. Beautifully coiffured fair hair framed her lovely oval face, made up to perfection. Tall and slender, she was clad entirely in black, with form-fitting silky trousers and an elegant top that could only have come from an exclusive fashion house. She sparkled with gold, necklaces, bracelets and earrings all glinting in the brilliant flashes of sunlight that fought their way between enormous blue-black thunderclouds.

Momentarily rooted to the spot, we pulled ourselves together and asked if we could be of help, for she looked a little forlorn. Her request for a pair of scissors, particularly from a couple of swimmers carrying almost nothing but their towels, did seem a little unlikely until we noticed the roll of elastoplast held in a manicured hand. Proudly I remembered a Swiss knife that I had been given before leaving home for use in a Cambodian Emergency. It was in my handbag, and clearly its great moment had come. Explaining that she had fallen off her motorbike, she hacked off a length of Elastoplast. Tim stepped forward, ready and more than willing to stick any length of plaster on any proffered part of her anatomy. But once again, things were not quite as they seemed. Turning away from us, she proceeded to repair a slit in her petrol tank, cracked by the fall. There, standing in a car park in the seedy capital of the saddest country in Asia, a hot eerie wind of hurricane strength suddenly whirling about our ears and the sky black with thunder, she solemnly handed us her card. Her looks did not belie her, for its elegant script proclaimed her to be the owner of an art gallery in a major European city. At that moment, it just did not seem possible that the two worlds could co-exist.

But that was not quite the end of the story. It seemed that she was staying with her mother, and please would we keep an eye on her after her own return home? Her mother, a professional photographer, was living with a young Cambodian artist just round the corner. She turned out to be a lady in ankle socks and flowing skirts who took photographs of the old-fashioned posed variety, white-gloved hand on breast against a background of Gothic columns. Her boyfriend, who must have been less than half her age, painted pictures of such obscure design and so fraught with meaning that our efforts at interpreting them were a total failure. I am afraid we did not try very hard, and the friendship did not flourish.

Even odder than the appearance of this apparition from another world were the continued antics of that baffling resident of our own, Iain the lying Scotsman. His Walter Mitty life of dreams was very firmly entrenched in the flesh-pots of reality, and he wrought increasing havoc among the young ladies of the town. Strengthened by a goodly measure of brandy for breakfast, he would set out to charm the city, men and women alike. Long after he had gone every cyclo driver who took us for a ride, however bad his English, would manage to enquire fondly as to Iain's health. He did have great charm despite the horrible black singlet he wore instead of a shirt, but those of our group closest to him began to find him more and more of a responsibility. He put in fewer and fewer appearances at the engineering school where he was supposed to work. He took a young Vietnamese girl into his flat to live with him. She could speak no English, and he ruled her with a rod of iron, trading on her devotion. Events began to come to a head when word got round that she was pregnant. And by a remarkable coincidence at this precise moment a letter arrived from home. It was a long chatty letter from his mother, and right at the end it mentioned, seemingly almost in passing, that his father was very ill and was going into hospital the very next day for a coronary artery bypass operation. Please would Iain come home?

The next thing we knew was that he had gone, on compassionate leave and bearing with him by a strange irony fifty dollars lent to him weeks previously by Christopher, the only one of us to have seen through his sad tale of stolen money when we had first arrived in Bangkok. None of us have ever heard from him again. Happily, the young Vietnamese was not pregnant after all and was able to go home to her parents, something that would have been culturally impossible had the rumour been true.

We learnt so many things. As power cuts grew worse we learnt to buy ice by the metre from a street vendor, a little girl with a large axe who chopped slices off a block wrapped in wet sacks to keep it cool. We learnt to boil our drinking water for twenty minutes and then filter it, and that the filter clogged up with a disgusting brown sludge if it was not cleaned every few days. This came as no surprise, for we had been told that water and sewer pipes, both of them rusting and rotting, ran side by side, their contents mixing freely. We learnt to rinse all eating utensils in drinking water, and to clean round the bathroom basin with a saucepan cleaner rather than a cloth. We coped with the leaking roof when the monsoon arrived; on one occasion the water flowed under the front door from a flash flood on our balcony in such a tidal wave that the settee on which Tim was at the moment examining a patient became an instant island. I kept a special shoe for the sport of cockroach-bopping, though rumour had it that the myriads of eggs released in the squishy mess only increased the problem a hundredfold. At least the wretched animals did not spend the next few hours with all six legs waving in the air, slowly and helplessly dying on their backs, as happened with the spray cans of Instant Death bought in the markets.

The list could go on for ever, but I hope that is enough to give a taste of everyday life. Of course things got on top of us at times, and homesickness lurked continuously. But to us it was a huge adventure, a time of living to overflowing capacity and surrounded by a warmth of comradeship and humour that beggared anything we had known before. We were lucky to be there.

Chapter Seventeen

The hospital work continued with its daily crises, its mixture of success and failure, triumph and frustration. As I felt increasingly at home I came to enjoy it more and more, greatly helped by the warm-hearted support of my Khmer colleagues. But in all honesty I did not really feel I was achieving a great deal. Dr Choy in particular was better at coping with the limitations imposed by poverty, and my contribution was small. So I made no objection when Dr To Ream, director of the Maternal and Child Care section of the Municipality Health Department, suggested that I come with him on a tour of inspection of the city health services. There were seven districts in Phnom Penh, each with its own dispensary or cottage hospital with outpatient facilities and short-stay beds. Patients with more serious illnesses would thence be referred on to one of the major city hospitals such as our own. So I spent several afternoons being chauffeured round in the ambulance, which made a very pleasant change. Our journeying took us well outside the city limits, for the outlying districts, though still within the civic boundaries, were in effect right out in the country and it was a relief to see cattle and paddy fields and to breathe fresh air. Every dispensary that we visited was clean and in good shape and had clearly been recently restored. In each we were politely greeted by the Khmer doctor or medical assistant in charge. It did seem that the patients were conspicuous by their absence, but this was explained by the timing of our visits. All routine medical work was carried out in the mornings by reason of the climate. I was told that the pristine condition of these buildings, so unlike that of the poor old decrepit municipal hospital, was entirely due to charity. Each had been restored by a different NGO and it gradually dawned on me that there was perhaps more to this tour than sightseeing, though I was far from guessing the magnitude of the task in store.

The seventh and last dispensary that we went to was as different as could be from all the others. It was a very large square brick and concrete building of 1960s era with a flat roof. The windows were boarded up, their shutters hanging crooked by a single hinge, and the ground in which it stood was a jungle of scrawny scrubby undergrowth harbouring old drink cans and bits of plastic surrounded by the remnants of a broken-down fence. The only redeeming features in this scene of desolation were some beautiful mature fruit-trees and the relatively open country round it. From the next door house came a continuous roar of machinery and an uninterrupted flow of the thickest blackest smoke imaginable gushing out into the road. This establishment turned out to be an ice-making factory, probably the origin of the yards of ice that we bought from our friendly street-seller at home.

We arrived in late afternoon and our driver hooted at the big double wooden gates, firmly closed and spanned by a faded blue sign. This, with its red cross painted at either end and white curly Khmer script between, proclaimed it to be a medical institution of some kind, but its decrepitude gave heart-sinking warning of what was to come. A boy ran to let us in, and after covering the few yards of concrete driveway we were greeted at the front door by a tiny lady in a white overall with short straight grey hair and a huge bunch of keys dangling at her belt. I shall never forget my first sight of the vast entrance hall. It was like an enormous underwater cavern, its ceiling way up under the roof and its walls, originally pale blue, so uniformly grubby that a macabre cave-like gloom encompassed the intruder. At one corner of the tiled floor was what once must have been an ornamental fishpond, its sunken base broken and dirty. Beyond, a boxed-in wooden staircase, doubtless ultra modern in its day, went up to a sort of minstrel's gallery off which led a maze of rooms and passages. Our little lady with her gaoler's keys became our guide and led us hither and thither, up hill and down dale, always preceding us and unlocking door after creaking door. There was almost no light for the windows were either boarded over or shuttered, but the few rays that struggled in were sufficient to show us the layers of dust and dirt that covered every surface. Some of the rooms had once been wards and contained the old iron bedsteads that I had come to know so well. One door was not locked, and I could scarcely believe my eyes when I saw that on a bed just inside lay a young woman, not merely alive but bright eyed and smiling and clutching a new baby to her breast. The impression that to reach her I had to struggle through a tangle of age-old cobwebs must be false, but for a moment I had truly felt that I was trapped in a time warp. Jerked back into the present, we went to the labour ward where this miracle birth had taken place. The antique birthing couch was bloodstained, and there can have been scarcely room for the midwife to stand between it and an enormous rough-surfaced stone sink. The whole of the upper half of one wall was open to the sky, for the glass had long since broken and the prevailing wind must have blown monsoon rains straight in on both the mother and her attendant midwife. Against another wall stood the instrument cupboard. It was impossible to see through the grime on its glass doors, but the turning of yet another key allowed me to look inside. All it contained was a single dirty speculum and two or three candle ends, guttered wax down their sides. These gave the lie to any idea of electricity, for though occasional bare bulbs hung from ancient lengths of flex, almost continuous power cuts in this part of town made them virtually useless. Candlelight can have been the only illumination for the birth of babies during the twelve hours of darkness. There must have been a pair of scissors somewhere; perhaps Mme Savun, our medical assistant guide, kept them in her pocket, safe from pilfering hands.

Downstairs again, we wandered through yet more rooms until finally at the moment that darkness fell we sat down on the stairs and held an impromptu conference. Optimistic pressing of the light switch delivered nothing, and we could scarcely see each other as we sat there, but out of the gloaming came the request that I had been half expecting. 'We would like you to start a women's clinic here'. At that moment, it seemed an impossibility. How could I even begin to contemplate such a thing? The building was Hitchcockian. I had no money, no staff, almost no language, and certainly no experience in setting up any such project. The whole episode must surely be a nightmare. On the other hand, the work that I was already doing was not up to much. It was more of interest to me than of use to anyone else. If this was what was really needed, then at least the idea should not be dismissed out of hand. I promised to think about it, and went home to wash off the accumulated dirt of thirty years. If there was any water.

Weariness begets worry, but the opposite is also true and as the next day dawned so did the beginnings of a cautious optimism. It was our habit to get up early and enjoy the cool of the morning, eating home-made muesli on the balcony and watching a pair of tailorbirds, tails erect, flitting from twig to twig of the old mango tree. Sometimes bulbuls would be there too and often a plaintive cuckoo would serenade us, his mournful descending scale very different from the cheerful call of his Western cousin. But that day my mind was elsewhere. There would be no harm in making a few enquiries, and where better to start than with our Field Director and with my gynaecological colleague. James in the office was intrigued. It was an appealing project, both because the request came from the local authority and not from outside, and because it would be something from nothing. The cupboard was bare and but for us was set to remain so. There could be no harm in taking it one step further.

So next I talked to Dr Vathiny, my young, cheerful, attractive gynaecological counterpart, she whose charms turned the knees of certain of my English male colleagues to water, their prosaic thoughts to flights of poetry. But I needed to talk not poetry but gynaecology, so for once my female gender was a help rather than a hindrance. Vathiny took the clinic proposition entirely in her stride. Why not? What was the problem? When I raised the minor matter of funding, she looked at me scornfully and brushed it aside. She shared the view of most of her countrymen that Western streets were paved with gold. The concept that our agency supplies people not cash remained throughout my time quite beyond the collective Khmer comprehension.

A meeting was called at the rundown offices of the Municipal Health Department by its director, Dr Abdul Koyaume, a member of the Muslim Khmers who come from Kompong Cham, a province north of Phnom Penh. Whatever faults he may have had, Dr Abdul Koyaume was blessed with an infectious enthusiasm and a rare ability to see beyond present problems to a brighter future. He had it all planned in his head. I could choose whatever staff I needed to run the clinic, both from those already working in the dispensary and from elsewhere, subject to his approval. They would cost me nothing, for they would still be employed by the municipality. I would of course have to find the money for everything else, he said, but that would pose no problem to a rich Westerner. He went on to outline plans for a sample survey, in which I would visit a certain number of local households chosen at random, to discover the health needs of their women. These needs would then be supplied free, by me.

The whole idea was beginning to take shape, to seem marginally less impossible. Enthused by Dr Abdul Koyaume, I considered my next step. It seemed logical to seek advice from other NGOs experienced in setting up similar projects. So I went to see Brenda, an Irish midwife who worked for the group Concern. Everyone knew, respected, and liked her, a diminutive David tackling Goliaths galore with the catapult of her own resilient personality. Brenda was not encouraging. She poured out a list of all the things I must do before I could even think about it. I must talk to yet more NGOs, to the neighbourhood Khmer Women's Association, to local government officials, to the present staff at the dispensary. Who would be my counterpart? How would I find one? And what about funding, for without that I could achieve nothing. I had a bad cold, and it all seemed just too difficult.

But I was not dead yet. Next day I went back to Vathiny in her dirty claustrophobic hospital room, labouring away day in day out at the same old job. The new clinic would only function for two mornings a week. Could she be tempted away just for these few hours? Would she help me set it up? Would she act as my counterpart there as well as here? The lead part in any survey would be far better played by her for quite apart from the language problem she would be more understanding of her fellow countrywomen's problems than would a foreigner. So would she come visiting with me? Her unequivocal answer to all these requests was a delighted yes please. But both of us knew that her release from the hospital hung on the decision of the Director of Health and personally I felt pessimistic. She was doing far too good a job already.

So now everything possible had been done to secure not just any counterpart but the best there was, and all we could do was await the decree from above. Next on Brenda's daunting list was more advice from other NGOs. So I called on the local director of World Vision, an American organisation based on an evangelical Christian ethic, large in size and substance and high in ideals, but low that day in understanding and compassion. An exceedingly patronising young man spent the next hour telling me that firstly the idea itself was not a viable one, and secondly that even if it had been it was clearly completely beyond my capabilities to develop it. I managed to thank him politely, but could not refrain from pointing out that the purpose of my visit was to ask for advice on its fulfilment, not for reasons why it was impossible. But despite my show of bravado, I felt like a pricked balloon. As a complete novice, I could not really set myself up against the advice of such a large rich and powerful organisation. But then again maybe I could.

There followed yet another meeting with even bigger and better

Cambodian bigwigs. As we seated ourselves round the long boardroom table, glasses of weak tea in front of us, Dr Abdul Koyaume turned to me and informed me that the proceedings, normally in French, would be in English out of courtesy to my director James who was no linguist, and I was to translate. My French is not bad, but I knew that the skills of interpreting were far beyond me. I also knew that I was in no position to argue, and that there was no way out. James opened the meeting with the sort of flowery flow expected of him, gushing expressions of appreciation for imaginary honours tumbling over one another with never a pause between. After what seemed minutes he stopped at last and everyone looked expectantly at me. I could neither remember exactly what he had said nor was capable of putting it into French. There was a tense pause and then I took the only possible escape route and said 'Il dit merci' (he says thank you). Everybody laughed and the ice was broken. We got through the rest of the meeting somehow; in fact, their English was every bit as good as my French. Out of it came two vital decisions; I could have Vathiny, and it was possible that VSO might produce some funding. Up to £10,000 is occasionally made available. My nursing colleague Tom and I were to apply for the biggest grant, to be split between hospital and clinic.

So it was with a light heart and considerable excitement that I took James to look at the building straight after the meeting. In full daylight it did not seem quite so gruesome. We were told that it had been built by an eminent Cambodian physician as a combined residence for his own use and a private nursing home. But his occupancy had been brief, cut short by the arrival of the Khmer Rouge. The house had been laid waste with doors and windows ripped off their hinges, and the doctor had been murdered. In the room that was later to become our consulting room the wall was peppered with bullet-holes, and I often wondered about his end. After our brief look at the building we went on a tour of the surrounding countryside to see what sort of life our potential patients led. It was very rural. We drove along a rough earth road built on top of a dyke with tiny shacks perched along its edge. Below and beyond lay farm land, now the brilliant emerald green of paddy-fields but which in the rainy season would be transformed into a huge uninterrupted lake. As the enthusiasm of my field director grew so did my hopes for my half of the £10,000 grant for it was his influence on the accountants in London that would be the deciding factor.

There may be sewage in the drinking water and cockroaches in the cupboard, but nothing can stop the relentless march of science. A fax machine standing idle in a candle-lit office may seem an anachronism, but, given the opportunity, it works as well in Phnom Penh as anywhere in the world. And it was by fax a while later that Tom and I heard we had got our grant. To us at that moment £10,000 seemed an immense sum. Kind, gentle Tom; his first thought was that now we could buy mattresses to give comfort to bedridden patients, their skin worn through in sores the size of dinner plates from continuous lying on rough straw mats. Mine sprang to the clinic. What was to stop us now?

Chapter Eighteen

It is one thing dreaming dreams, but quite another turning them into reality. We were faced with a hundred and one decisions. Repair of the building and purchase of equipment were urgent priorities. Nowhere in Cambodia could Tom and I buy the instruments and other resources that we needed, so it was essential to look elsewhere. Goods advertised in glossy Western brochures were far too expensive. Travel to Bangkok would use up precious dollars on air fares, and in any case prices there were high. Ho Chi Minh City or Saigon, capital of South Vietnam, seemed our only hope and here we were in luck. A friendly Australian lady with the unlikely job of teaching English to Cambodian army generals had a contact there. He was a Vietnamese representative of a large international drug company, with many friends among the local pharmacists and medical suppliers. He was prepared to arrange for bulk purchasing of small instruments at remarkably low cost, and he also knew of several secondhand equipment shops in Ho Chi Minh City where we could look for larger items. If we sent him lists of our requirements, he would do all he could to help us. And so we set to work. Vathiny was invaluable, there were no major disagreements, and the job was soon done. Now we must await a summons from Saigon.

Meanwhile, work at the hospital continued and everything else had to be fitted in round it. The most urgent task was to carry out renovations to the dispensary, for it was no use possessing businesslike new equipment if there was nowhere to put it. Vathiny and I decided to choose just two rooms to use as surgery and waiting-room. The staff, who had for years provided some sort of skeleton medical service despite the dreadful working conditions, seemed as excited as we were and put themselves out to help us. The large room that was pockmarked with bullets was an obvious first choice and its present medical assistant occupant insisted on taking himself off elsewhere and giving it to us. But with its pitted, cracked, and filthy walls, boarded windows, and ceiling stripped bare of its original ornamental timbering, even here we were faced with a sorry sight. Leading out of it was an unexpected discovery, a 1960 state-of-the-art bathroom, tiled in turquoise and complete with a matching suite of bathroom fittings. Nothing but spiders came out of the taps, and the lavatory, set in a patch of ominously damp cement, was black with an unthinkable encrustation. But it was a bathroom and water could surely be brought in from the tap in the garden; cleaned up, we could use the basin for washing our hands, and even the lavatory had possibilities.

I went to look at the small brass tap lying outside in a patch of mud. I turned it on and out came a tiny dribble. I raised it a few inches from the ground and the dribble stopped. The water came from the city mains and by the time it reached this outlying area the pressure was too low to provide more than a token supply. But even this was worth having and could be carried to our bathroom in buckets. Why not use a hose? Because there was no money to buy one. So on to the equipment list went hose and bathroom water-pot.

Our chosen waiting room was another vast chamber forming an open L with the entrance hall. From it, big double wooden doors led to the garden, and a second small door to the surgery. Its ceiling was wooden and its walls painted the usual duck-egg blue. Add thirty years of neglect, and you have the picture. There would be room enough in here for the entire local population to sit and wait.

Builders' estimates came next. Our Khmer colleagues in the clinic had friends in the trade, but so had I. Peter, who had helped us to buy mattresses, was by now well established at the head of a big building project. He brought his Khmer foreman to the dispensary, and together they walked slowly round, pen and clipboard in hand. By the time they had finished, I could begin to visualize premises not just practical but pretty too, for appearance was important to attract clients, suspicious of any change. Peter's costing came to £500, far higher than the estimate given by the clinic's odd-job man and a big chunk out of my share of the grant, but it was worth it. It would be work well done.

Slowly things were taking shape, but still we had no drugs nor money to buy them, for this was an expendable item excluded by the grant. Vital to the success of the project, I could put off the problem no longer. So I went to talk to Dr Pene Key. A century ago before we left England it was she that Tim and I had visited in her London ODA office, and who had clearly thought that the pair of us in coming to Cambodia were biting off far more than we could chew. Meantime she herself had accepted the invitation of the Cambodian government to come out and assist in the setting up of a new health service. She was a highly influential and highly respected figure, and I knew that if she approved of the project she would help if she possibly could. But it was again with a certain amount of trepidation that I approached her office, this time in the cool premises of WHO, for I knew that she did not suffer fools gladly.

She was kindness itself and listened carefully to my story. I was anxious to put before her not just the immediate problem of my little clinic but the much wider issue of the lack of provision for drugs in the hospitals generally. As illustration, I told her of the plight of an eight month pregnant girl who had been admitted in an acute attack of asthma. An injection of adrenaline, an emergency drug carried by most Western doctors as a matter of course, could be life saving. The hospital adrenaline was ten years out of date. Of two ampoules purchased by her husband in the market, one was unlabelled and the other simply stated 'Made in Paris'. Both were battered and scratched and our 1980 bottle seemed preferable. But it did not work. The patient survived, but only just.

Dr Key seemed interested in the clinic, though this did not prevent her from asking a great many shrewd questions. She could not suggest any definite source of free drugs nor of funding for them, but why not try the Vicar of Bangkok? She went on to explain that he ran a charity for deserving causes, and perhaps I could be put in that category. The fact that our area included a large number of brothels might well be an added draw, she said. Whether or not it was the prostitutes that appealed to the parson will never be revealed, but my begging letter elicited a promise of $1,000 worth of drugs. I was not to know at that stage how long they would be in coming, but when I heard that my agent, the Rev M.M. was not merely the vicar of Bangkok but of the whole of Thailand, Laos, Vietnam and Cambodia too, the weight of responsibility seemed to lift from my shoulders. With all that earthly and heavenly power behind me, who knows what we might achieve.

Suddenly Tom and I were summoned to the office. The message had come through from Ho Chi Minh City that all was ready, and we were to leave on our shopping spree in two days time. Certain pieces of equipment had been ordered from Echo in England, an organisation set up by retired missionaries where old medical equipment is made new and despatched overseas at minimal cost. Some we would buy locally. But it would be up to Tom and me to use up the rest of our grant in just one day, and the final forty-eight hours were spent in a frenzy of last-minute discussions and decisions.

At five thirty on the morning of Friday 20th March we were off at last. As a great favour we had been lent the VSO truck. Our excellent driver, Mr Ra Chea, took the wheel and the Australian teacher Carol, Tom and myself settled back to enjoy the seven hour drive ahead of us. A long stretch of road through wooded countryside took us to the ferry crossing over a river. We arrived just in time to see the boat pull away, but some refreshment at a riverside café while we waited for its return was in any case a welcome diversion. When asked whether I would prefer my coffee black or white, I proudly answered with the Cambodian phrase which literally means 'coffee with liquid from the breast of a cow'. What comes is always the same; a glass filled to the brim with pitch black coffee solidly supported on an inch of sweetened condensed milk that is neither liquid nor has seen the inside of a breast for a very long time. It is, however, delicious.

Across the river and back on the road we quickly reached the Vietnam border. There was the usual long wait at the customs shed where we were pestered by pedlars selling every variety of food and drink. However, our driver had prepared all the right paperwork, and eventually we were off again. The border marked a noticeable change in our surroundings. Now we were driving between huge tidy fields in one of which stood three enormous bamboo fans, deeply curved in the shape of the back of a basket chair. Made for winnowing rice in season, today they stood lonely and desolate against the grey sky, giant sentinels guarding the growing crops. Along the side of the road we would pass groups of shabby shacks with among them little stone houses thatched with bamboo leaves, reminiscent of Irish crofts at home. Most prominent of all were several larger church-like buildings, also made of stone but standing by themselves and all painted a shade of pastel pink. I was told later that these were meeting houses for members of the Caodaist faith, a combination of the Buddhist, Confucian and Christian religions, in which there are some very strange goings on. It was invented by a civil servant in Cochin China, and involves a Pope with female cardinals, prophecy by planchette, and a sainted version of Victor Hugo pictured in the uniform of the French Academy with a halo round his tricorn hat.

Or so Graham Greene tells us in his book *The Quiet American*.

At last, in early afternoon, we arrived in the outskirts of Saigon. The immediate impression was of a brighter, cleaner and more cared-for city than the one we had just left. There were still the familiar fleets of cyclos and motorbikes and nothing felt particularly strange but there were notable differences. This could have been Phnom Penh Mark Two, or even Mark Ten, for perhaps in a decade 'our' poor tired city would look like this. School must have just come out for everywhere were girls on bicycles, all attired entirely in white, the hip-length tunic with its high neck and long sleeves overlapping white trousers. More seemly clothing could not be imagined apart from twin triangles of brown skin appearing through slits in every tunic's side seams, greatly appreciated by my male colleagues. This unusual school uniform was no longer made of silk but of nylon, and how unbearably hot it must have been. I am sure the girls were glad of their geometrical ventilation. The women too wore very similar garments though many were sleeveless, their arms covered instead with the long white gloves that our great-grandmothers wore 'for best'. This I was told was to protect them from the sun, as pale skin is considered a sign of high breeding. These ladies would have looked extremely elegant but for the fact that most of them were astride motor-bikes, a travesty from which our modest side-saddled Cambodian girls would have turned with demure disdain.

We drove straight to Carol's hotel, booked in advance and looking temptingly comfortable. But with our humble volunteer status we had to turn elsewhere, for our top financial limit was roughly half the cost of a night at the Majestic. Alas, we did not know that this was a public holiday in Vietnam, and every hotel was full. Our long and fruitless search through crowded streets led us eventually to the door of a once magnificent French building dating from colonial times. Unlike several hotels we had seen it was shabby rather than sleazy and we rang the bell. Tom put our usual question of 'have you any rooms?' to the Vietnamese gentleman who answered. He looked us up and down, first me and then Tom, all six foot four inches and twenty seven years of him, and finally said 'yes, you can have the honeymoon suite'. I expected my young companion to demur, but not a bit of it. 'Fine', he replied, 'and can our driver come too?'

Just inside, an old fashioned lift peered out through its ornamental wrought iron gates, the ancient wheels and pulleys dispirited and lifeless.

So we trudged up three flights of an elegant curved staircase, depositing Chea in room number twenty-seven on the way. Up and up we went, Tom and I the strangest pair of newly-weds you could hope to meet. But Tom's sanguine acceptance of the situation was rewarded when the ceremonial throwing open of door number thirty-nine revealed not one but two huge bedrooms boasting two beds apiece. The Vietnamese must have curious honeymoons, a subject perhaps for further research but on another day. We each had an en suite bathroom. Everything in my own worked after a fashion, but Tom's was a failure, so girt with a towel he used mine. On one of my two beds was a clean bottom sheet, with grubby head cushions and blanket and a bright blue mosquito net. I was not alone, for Tom was nearby and I had for closer company a large bat, a corpulent cockroach, and an unseen but loudly squeaking presence behind the wardrobe. And to think I had let my fancy dwell on a comfortable room and a hot bath. But if life had been like that this book would not have been written; in any case, under the sky blue canopy of my bed net with its skirts firmly tucked in against all comers I slept the sleep of the dead.

Next morning faced with a hectic day we got up early and sat down to breakfast at a café across the road. Our food had just been put in front of us when suddenly and explosively Tom shot to his feet, yards of him convulsively straightening like a human Jack in the Box. The round table turned turtle and cascaded its contents all over him, noodles from his bowl of soup festooning his knees and a sodden stain spreading across his trousers. The unsuspecting cockroach that had crept up his trouser leg must have been as astonished as the rest of us. Judging by our appreciative audience, it was the funniest piece of street theatre that the passers-by had witnessed in years. But no lasting harm was done, the table was righted in a moment and fresh supplies brought by a joyful waiter. Tom, unperturbed, brushed off the noodles and shrugged his shoulders. He had not brought a change of clothes, but no matter.

The next eleven hours were spent in intense activity. Under the initial guidance of our medical contact we rushed hither and thither, from a curious courtyard occupied entirely by pharmacists already hard at work collecting up our instrument order, to a large equipment supplier, and back again. Naturally there were problems, for various articles had failed to materialize, and we had to make do with second best. Many of the metal instruments were imprinted with the mark of a well known charity, but we took care not to enquire into their history. Left to ourselves, one supplier proved elusive and it took us ages literally running through the streets in the hottest part of the day to track him down. A coffee seller with her Vietnamese-English dictionary was our salvation, directing us to a treasure trove of excellent secondhand equipment. A few minutes of panic followed. Our precious truck had vanished from its parking place in a notorious part of town and we feared it had been stolen. But all was well. Chea had simply taken himself off for a little joyride.

Late in the afternoon we went back to the chemists' courtyard to find the huge packing-cases waiting, their contents ready to be checked item by item. Working against the clock, we just finished as darkness fell, and we were done. The truck was loaded with an examination couch, autoclave, steriliser, oxygen manometer, instrument trays and crates and boxes of specula, scissors, syringes, forceps and all the other items listed on the reams of cheap paper that we had covered in the last few weeks. We drove it to a lock-up where it would be safe, and made our weary way back to Carol's Majestic Hotel. We must have been a sorry sight, sweaty, dirty, and dishevelled, and Tom still with the sinuous pattern of spaghetti adorning his trousers. Late as we were, for we had a dinner-date with our pharmacist host and his wife, I was sent up to Carol's bathroom to clean up. How I resisted the temptation of a soak in her bath I shall never know, but a hot shower, the first for six months, was a taste of heaven and a luxury hardly even dented by the necessity of climbing back into the same set of clothes. Further restored by dinner in a clean and comfortable restaurant, a trio playing in the background, we were driven back to our shabby French palace. The bat had left me through a hole in the window's mosquito screen, but my other companions were still there and together we passed a second peaceful night. Before first light next morning, an insomniac Vietnamese fly-on-the-wall would have witnessed Carol, Tom, Chea and myself enthroned in cyclos and careering four abreast through the empty Saigon streets, an international chariot race with its goal the lock-up garage. Mercifully our loaded truck was still there with nothing obviously missing and we were soon off on our long drive home.

The sun came up as we travelled through the cool and peaceful countryside, dozing in our comfortable seats. For a while the scenery became more rugged, and far below us we could see a river running between steep wooded banks. But the sudden appearance as we rounded a bend of two wheels of an overturned bus sticking out over the roadside brought us wide awake and screeching to a halt. The body of the bus lay upside down below road level held there by trees, and gruesome images flashed through all our minds of who or what it might contain. With a nurse, a doctor, a surgical couch and box upon box of instruments on board, we could hardly pass by on the other side. So it was with some relief that, peering over the edge, we saw that the carcass was rusty and that there was no sign of humanity, alive or dead. We discovered later that the crash had happened weeks before, and there had been no survivors. We simply had not noticed the protruding wheels on our outward journey, so steep was the truck's final resting place.

Apprehension ran high as to our reception at customs on the border. Would our hard-won booty be confiscated? or at the least would we have to undo hours of packing to prove we were not importing Kalashnikovs or crack? But Carol had taken the trouble to obtain a letter of intent from the Vietnamese Ministry of Health and armed with this we sailed through in double quick time. We had just one more interruption to our homeward journey. As we were nearing Phnom Penh who should Carol spy at a roadside café but a group of 'her' generals, sitting over glasses of amber liquid. Judging by her unusual loquacity when eventually she rejoined us, this was not tea, and we were all in the best of spirits when we arrived home in the early afternoon. It had been an excellent trip.

Next on my list was a meeting with a representative of the local Women's Association. I had no clear idea of what we would discuss but as the clinic was to be for its members, clearly support from the Association would be useful. I expected that Vathiny and I would go together to meet their delegate for an informal chat, and was a little surprised when I found that two high officials from the health department, both of them men, were coming too. However, surprise was something that I was teaching myself to suppress for given its head it would have been almost permanent. Any emotion saps energy and I had none to spare. It was a hard lesson to learn, and I still had a long way to go; as I walked into the dispensary that morning, I realised just how far I was from achieving it. The entire vast entrance hall was full of benches on which sat rank upon rank of ladies, all dressed in their best. In front of them was a white-clothed table with four chairs to which I was escorted with the utmost deference. At once the expectant chatter hushed to a sudden silence as all rose to their feet. Dozens of pairs of brown eyes fixed on me as I took up my expected position, dozens of pairs of brown hands were raised palm to palm in the traditional greeting of respect. It was crystal clear that a speech was expected of me and I had simply no idea what to say. My worst nightmare had come true and once again there was no escape.

Fortunately the clumsy process of speaking through an interpreter gives time for thought between sentences, and as Vathiny smoothed out my stuttered rubbish into a convincing flow of Khmer, I managed to cudgel my brain into some sort of order. All began to go well, and I suppose I must have become over confident. An Idiot's Guide to Aid Work that I had recently read suggested that members of local communities should be encouraged to raise at least a nominal sum of money to pay for services. But at the mention of the word money it was as though a curtain of ice had come down. The hitherto increasingly friendly atmosphere palpably froze, and all was lost. The extent or indeed the nature of my crime was never really made clear, but I certainly received a sound rebuke from the Assistant Director of Health, a man I did not greatly care for, and was left wondering whether the damage evidently done could ever be repaired. It was yet another example of the absolute dependence of the Cambodian people on outside help. For well over a century they had been cared for and told what to do first by the French and then by the paternalistic Sihanouk. They had been bewildered and all but destroyed by the events of the Pol Pot era, when most of the men and women who would have become their natural leaders had been killed. The people were still searching for their identity, and only now just beginning to take responsibility for their own destiny. This was to change very soon, but at that time was still only too evident on every side.

Chapter Nineteen

It had been decreed that every penny of our grant must be spent by that curious date April 5th, the end of the financial year, and the next days were spent scurrying round Phnom Penh markets in a concentrated effort to fill gaps that were left. 'Yea' with her puce face and dripping hair became a familiar figure in the market, and one of some concern to the lady stall-holders sitting comfortably in the shade, fanning me as I steamed past clutching bowls and bins and brooms and bulging plastic bags. Vathiny once again was a tower of strength, always looking cool, unruffled and immaculate. I wonder how she did it. Baking tins were bought from kitchen stalls to act as instrument trays. A smart white television trolley, the only one of its kind, was added to the collection and became the envy of the whole hospital in its elevated position of instrument trolley in the general medical ward. We never managed to find another, even a year later when funds were not so tight.

The next item on the agenda was something I had really been looking forward to: we were to begin the pilot study of the health needs of our future clients. Health and habits are inextricably mixed and only by talking to the women in their own homes were we going to get any real idea of what we could do to help them. We had already designed a questionnaire which had been translated and then typed in the Khmer script by the hospital secretary, a gentle lady who always treated me with the utmost respect and politeness without detracting one jot from her natural and very self-contained dignity.

So it was with considerable excitement that, on the morning of April 6th, I drove along my usual route to the hospital. Certain groups of houses had been selected on a geographical basis and we planned to visit as many of these as possible over a given number of days. That morning we drove through an area where the contrast between rich and poor was all too evident. Large villas set in gardens were interspersed with tumbledown shacks, and my heart sank as we seemed to be heading straight for a rich man's castle. But I was quite wrong, for we stopped a few yards short of its front gate, bolted and barred in a manner more suited to a fortress than a private house, and got out instead in front of a tiny cabin almost completely overshadowed by its monstrous neighbour. It was erected on legs in the traditional fashion, and the only means of reaching its open door was by climbing a short rickety wooden ladder, having first of course kicked off our shoes and left them on the ground below. (It is interesting to compare departing guests in the West and the East. At home, most leave with scarcely a backward glance, whereas everyone in Cambodia turns right round again to face the house. This, though simply to enable them to push their feet back into the shoes that are pointing the way they came, adds a nice formality to the proceedings. I have never known anyone park their footwear in reverse to allow them a rapid getaway.)

Sitting on the wooden floor, I had plenty of time to look around me while Vathiny talked to our first client. Built originally of bamboo the house, like its owner, had evidently fallen on hard times. Two of its walls were made of corrugated paper and flattened cardboard cartons advertising Coca Cola in large upside down letters. Flapping brightly coloured rags filled in the gaps and a third wall had been replaced by a worn sleeping mat badly frayed at the edges. The fourth was largely open to the elements. I had plenty of time, too, to worry about the fate of this poor family in the approaching rainy season, for the few banana leaves that were left in the roof would do little to keep out the torrential rain that was to come. The only furniture was a hammock made of a coarse dark-coloured cloth and slung diagonally from corner to corner of the hut. The tiny swelling in the depths of its folds proved to be a new-born baby, rocked from time to time by one of the three undersized children that were huddled together for protection against the intruders. All three were coughing, and the smallest one had pus running down his cheek from a half closed reddened eye. There were still more occupants crowding the confined space, for a visiting neighbour with a small girl at her knee had come to keep the children's young mother company. Otherwise there was nothing, nothing at all. There was no furniture, not even a sleeping mat, the only one having presumably been requisitioned to replace the worn out wall. There were not even any cooking pots.

The owner of this pathetic establishment seemed only too happy to chat with Vathiny and to answer her questions. She confirmed what was obvious to us already, that there was hardly any money coming in. Her husband was a cyclo driver and spent nearly all the little he earned on the local rice wine. I wondered what kept them alive. While she was talking she extricated the baby from the suffocating folds of its hammock and put it to the breast where it suckled contentedly, evidence that at least she was sufficiently well nourished to produce some milk. I could not follow all that she was saying but I was fascinated by her reaction to questions on family planning. There was no need to be a linguist to interpret on her face the look of delighted astonishment when she learnt that there were ways other than total abstinence of preventing the arrival of baby after baby. It seemed that she knew absolutely nothing about even the natural rhythm method of contraception, and she could scarcely contain herself with delight as the possibilities were explained to her. As we went on with our survey and also talked to others who had carried out similar projects elsewhere we found that this ignorance was almost universal. The women had all realised the basic fact that it takes two to make a baby but beyond that was a yawning chasm of mystery. A commonly held belief was that conception resulted from a mixing of the couple's blood. Fortunately most of the mothers breast fed their babies for at least two years, and this, though by no means a foolproof method of contraception, does at least reduce fertility at the time.

It was time to move on to the next house. This was a hut of similar size and design but here there was obviously more money coming in. Its interior was much darker merely because there were not so many holes to let in the light. It was neat and tidy, with saucepans complete with lids ranged against the wall in one corner and signs of cooking outside at the back. We were welcomed by two smiling young women, each with a baby in her arms, the owner and a cousin visiting from the country. Once again they seemed quite happy to answer quite searching and personal questions, and once again reacted with incredulous delight to suggestions about family planning.

On we went, this time to a large rooming house at the end of a muddy cul de sac. It was a concrete building, dilapidated but solid enough, housing an entire family in each of its ten rooms. We had time to visit only one of these, a palace compared with what we had just seen. The tiled floor was reasonably clean, and the walls and high ceiling, though grubby, were in sound repair. There was plenty of room for two of the big low wooden beds in common use, each decorated on its bed-ends with small looking-glass panels and each spread with a sleeping mat. The owner of this desirable residence had five children, and as we interviewed more of her neighbours sitting outside in the shade of the building it became increasingly obvious that the number of children in each family was directly proportional to the age of their mother. The last woman that we talked to, a little older than the rest, seemed rather better off. At any rate, she was the only one who was able to answer 'yes' to item eleven on our questionnaire which read 'do you have enough money to feed your children well?'

And so we came to the end of our first morning's visiting. We had not achieved numerically as much as we had hoped, for in Vathiny's hands the interviews took a very long time. Surprisingly she seemed as shocked as I was by the extreme poverty we had seen, and had felt bound to discuss and advise on many subjects well outside our official brief. But I am sure it was time well spent.

Chapter Twenty

Time in the East, however it is spent, does not have the same significance as in the West. It might seem that there was little else to do before the clinic could be opened; we had merely to visit a few more houses, decide exactly what drugs we needed and ask our priestly patron in Bangkok to put them in the post. Just how far this fell short of the truth once more only time would tell.

For one thing, the festival of the Cambodian New Year was almost upon us, in secular terms the equivalent of Christmas in the West. Phnom Penh shuts down for several days, giving everyone a chance to escape as far as possible from the intense heat and humidity that holds the country in its grip at this time of year. For some this simply means staying indoors. For the few lucky ones like ourselves it makes it possible to leave the noisy dusty confines of the city and go to the seaside.

A group of our fellow volunteers had invited us to join them in their truck. Much as we loved our jeep it was far from trustworthy, and the road down to the coastal resort of Kompong Som is not to be taken lightly. It passes through Khmer Rouge territory in wild and mountainous countryside and demands considerable respect. We were strongly advised to travel in convoy, each truck flying its official organisation flag, and to make our journey during daylight hours. This presented no problem as the whole journey would take less than four hours. But a permit from the Ministry of Foreign Affairs was still required for a journey of more than fifteen kilometres outside the capital. Somebody had to put in the necessary request and in my innocence I volunteered for the job.

At least it gave me the opportunity to visit the impressive French colonial building in which the ministry was housed. As I walked through the front door I was stunned by the magnificence of the huge entrance hall and of the sweeping broad and carpeted staircase that soared upwards into unseen realms above. Lush potted plants, their exotic blooms mirrored in floor tiles that had been polished to an incandescent brilliance, stood between tasteful furnishings. A porter in uniform sat at an elaborate desk, a telephone at his elbow, and I began to think that I had magically strayed into another country altogether. Not one of the hospitals possessed a telephone. The Ministry of Health, the only other government building that I had seen, was as dilapidated as the rest of the city. Why such startling contrast? I had plenty of time three days later to ponder this conundrum, and the answer must surely be that this was the face of Cambodia turned toward visiting foreign dignitaries. It was a praiseworthy effort but a pathetic one, for their disillusionment would be both rapid and total.

That day I simply put in my request for a travel permit and went away, with precise instructions that I was to return at nine in the morning three days later when the document would be ready for collection. I went back exactly as requested. I should have known better. For two hours I sat on an elegant chaise longue upholstered in red velvet, only to be asked with the utmost deference to come back at two. The afternoon's performance was an exact repetition of the morning. Finally I was told to leave with the assurance that the document would be delivered to my home the next day. Even I did not believe that one, and in the end we went anyway, without it. But nobody could say I had not tried.

An hour after dawn a few days later our convoy set off; there were only two trucks in it, but we hoped this qualified. (The dictionary does not define the minimum number.) This was our first holiday outing from the city apart from our one day trip to Angkor soon after we had first arrived, and we were all more than ready for the break. Even the journey was enormous fun. After navigating the traffic on the outskirts of Phnom Penh we drove along roads that grew gradually more deserted until we were passing through empty pancake-flat countryside. Then, far away on the horizon, there appeared the misty outline of a hill, small and insignificant at first but growing encouragingly bigger as we approached. As fields and farms were replaced by wilder land, a sorry sight met our eyes. It looked as though the whole wooded face of the countryside had been carelessly shaved with a giant razor, leaving behind a bristling stubble of severed stumps. On either side of the road this prospect stretched for miles until, in the distance where the plain rose into the mountains, we could see the dense unbroken coating of the forest as it must once have been everywhere. All round us there was evidence of tree-cutting. Neat piles of logs stood at intervals along the roadside between tiny hamlets of ten or so tumbledown straw huts. We stopped momentarily at one of these villages and got out to stretch our legs. To my astonishment, an unusually tall Khmer man came straight up to me and gave me the traditional greeting. 'I was a patient at the municipality hospital', he said 'and surely you are the doctor who drives that red jeep.' Thus spreads notoriety.

We drove past several huge trucks grinding along beneath their burden of mighty tree trunks. More picturesque but sending the same message were teams of buffalo, each pair yoked to a single immense tree dragged painstakingly along on a two-wheeled axle. On a later trip to this same coast we were able to visit the port in the company of a reporter as intrepid in her quest for information as the rest of her kind. An imperious wave of her UN card allowed us through the gates and along a pier to the dockside. We talked to the official in charge of one of the logging ships who smilingly agreed that the quantity of timber being exported to such places as Singapore and Hong Kong was well over the permitted limit. The illegal export of hewn trees over the Thai border from the north west where the Khmer Rouge have their biggest stronghold is one of their best sources of funding.

That day, though, we were in holiday mood and not too bothered by the problem of deforestation or anything else. Or so we thought. But as the mountains closed in on our two lonely little vehicles and with nothing but wilderness in sight, I think each of us felt an inward shudder. There was menace in the air and it was a relief when Tom broke the silence. 'Perhaps', he said, pointing to a heavy column of smoke rising from the jungle, 'perhaps that's the Khmer Rouge frying bacon and eggs for their breakfast.' If they were occupied with matters of such grave importance they would have no time for us. In any case, it was not long before we had left the mountains behind us and were sitting in a pavement cafe on the outskirts of Kompong Som eating our own breakfast. It was still only half past nine, but we were hungry.

Buckets and spades and rubber rings were the very last things we expected, but there they were for sale in this pretty little town built on hills next the sea. It was here that, in the past, Prince Sihanouk used to come for a holiday. In those days the town was called Sihanoukville, and since his return from exile it has gone back to that name. But for us it will always be the one and only Kompong Som. There were plenty of signs that this had once been a thriving seaside resort. Just inland from the sea stretched a long esplanade ornamented with pleasing sculptures of animals, and it did not take much imagination to picture wealthy Cambodians in a previous era strolling along in the cool of the evening to get up an appetite for dinner in one of the sophisticated French restaurants. But now weeds were growing up through the concrete and the only legs being stretched were our own.

We had not come all this way to study history. We were here for a holiday, and reverting to childhood we just could not wait to fall into the sea. Scrambling down from the man-made paraphernalia, we found ourselves looking out over a sweeping bay bounded on one side by a rising cliff-top and on the other by a rocky arm reaching far out into the water. Contained between these two was a sea of the deepest turquoise blue, its colour gradually fading to a glassy clarity in the ripples that lapped the sand. Never before had I seen sand so white and clean and of such depth that it actually squeaked as we trod on it. Man Friday's footprint would have come as no surprise. And to complete the picture, in the middle of the foreground was a simple wooden fishing boat, the weathered green of its hull blending perfectly with the water that rocked it gently to and fro. It was the contrast between this idyll and the city we had left that morning that was so overwhelming. Into the half a year since we had left home our little group had crammed half a lifetime of new experiences and we were tired, needing time and space as we had never needed them before. Here, spread out before us, was the perfect remedy. Miraculously for the moment all of it was ours to enjoy, and we had simply to bask in it, to absorb it to the full like sunning seals.

Stripped of our clothes and clad in swimming costumes and layers of sunburn cream, we set out to explore. Although there was none of the detritus of human habitation, no rusty cans nor even a single plastic bottle, we were surrounded by evidence of other forms of life. Shells, bleached white like the sand, were everywhere, but to find perfection was rare enough to make the search exciting. Every now and again we would come upon one so intricately sculpted and of such exotic design that it was impossible to leave it behind, and my own treasure trove was one of the first things I packed when we finally came home to England. There were small shellfish in the rock pools and giant jellyfish in the sea, but my favourites were the wind-crabs, tiny creatures scuttering along the beach, as insubstantial as the sea spray from which they seemed to have come. And above all was the breeze, gloriously dancing over the rocks and up and away through the palm trees' rustling fronds, a blissful coolness that came off the sea and blew away city cobwebs and the intense April heat.

There was just one minor problem. One of the legacies left by Prince Sihanouk in the 'sixties was a number of concrete holiday bungalows hidden amongst palm trees only a few yards from the beach. These had lain empty for years and we had assumed we would have no difficulty in renting one for a few dollars a night. But here we came unstuck. We were not the only people to have rediscovered Kompong Som. The advance party of the United Nations whose presence had been agreed upon in the Paris Peace Accords had got there first and every bungalow was taken. But somehow it did not seem to matter in the least. We had brought sleeping mats to sit on, so why not put them to their proper use as well? It was the dry season so there would be no risk of rain. What could be better than sleeping out under the stars? So we set up camp in a little wood adjoining the beach, sent a few willing volunteers to find a market and buy provisions, and embarked on one of the most glorious days that I can ever remember. There was no sign of the UN, for it emerged that they were not actually in residence but simply keeping everyone else out with a permanent booking. We had the whole beach and seemingly the entire South China Sea to ourselves. It was such a comfortable sea, too, with none of the usual difficulties of temperature and turbulence. Rocked by waves of perfect size and shape it would have been the easiest thing in the world to fall asleep and float off into the sunset. But we all kept an eye on each other, and after a day of contented idleness, sunset found us instead in our wood lighting up the three charcoal burners that one of our number had had the foresight to bring with us. Peter was our self-appointed quartermaster and chef, ably assisted by Tom. Potatoes, rice and cabbage were all bubbling nicely and tantalising whiffs of grilled fish fresh from the sea were just beginning to set the juices flowing when we discovered that after all we were not alone. Perhaps it was the smell that drew them to our hideaway but suddenly we found ourselves surrounded by a group of Khmer gentlemen who were clearly not best pleased at our presence. It emerged that they were from the little hexagonal cafe that served the bungalows, and their all too clear message was that it was against all rules and regulations for us to be camping here. Amazed that there were such things we put up a strong fight, but they were adamant. At last we persuaded them to allow us to stay provided we moved closer to the restaurant where they could keep an eye on us. They made out that they were concerned for our safety but from whom or what they did not say. They were certainly worried about their own pockets, for they refused to allow us to do any more cooking. From tonight, we were to eat in their cafe or not at all.

As we cleaned our teeth in the sea and spread our mats on the shore in preparation for the night ahead, it did not occur to us that we might be cold for this was something that simply never happened. However the breeze that thankfully kept the mosquitoes at bay was enough to make me forage in my bag for a sarong bought in Phnom Penh market, which doubled as skirt and changing wrap. Now it had turned blanket and I spread it out over me before settling back again to look up at the stars and the half moon that was glinting on the sea and dimming the fireflies' light. It was nearly idyllic but not quite. The sand looked soft but was actually quite extraordinarily hard, attacking bony prominences with painful persistence. There was a great deal of tossing and turning up and down the beach, but eventually, lulled by the sound of the waves just a few yards away, we slept the sleep of VSO children of all ages out on a remarkably good spree.

Next morning we managed to escape detection as we boiled our pan of water on a fire of driftwood for breakfast coffee. Then, before the sun got too hot, some of us set out to explore the forested headland that

Fishing village at Kompong Som

stretched out into the sea. We were in for more surprises, for as we walked the well-worn path that led from the beach into the trees, within ten minutes we came upon a busy village that had been completely hidden from us. Nobody seemed to mind as we wandered past the open sides of the little huts that crowded in on either side of the track. Dogs barked and children stared, their parents responding politely to our greetings as scraggy chickens squawked and scuttled from under our feet.

Soon the huddle of huts was left behind and we walked on between giant trees with the unfamiliar liquid calls of jungle birds sounding from the heights of their topmost branches. After a few minutes we saw the glint of water through the forest ahead and realised that we had crossed the base of a peninsula and were approaching a second bay. Just as we reached it a twist in the path revealed signs of more human activity, for here in a clearing, surrounded by rough planks cut from the trees, was a pair of Noah's Arks. Rising from each of the sturdy wooden hulls was a little half-completed house. Though these must have been for fishermen rather than the animals that went in two by two, it really did seem that at any moment Ham or Japheth would appear with a hammer and a mouthful of nails. But there was no sign of anyone at all, although nearby were a couple of small huts like those in the village we had just left. (On a later trip we found the arks a little nearer completion but no sign of the huts. Afraid that this meant that the project had been abandoned, we enquired about it in the village. Surprised, our informant told us that this was normal for the time of year. In the wet season boat-building was temporarily halted and the huts were moved back to the company and protection of neighbours.)

The next two days passed in a happy haze. We dozed and read in the shade of palm trees, sustained by a constant supply of drinks from huge cool-boxes that we had brought with us. We swam in the sea with obsessional frequency, washing away the sweat and stresses of the past months in an almost ritual cleansing. Once I went off exploring on my own, scrambling on the rocks at the tip of the peninsula between 'our' two bays. Suddenly two little brown boys erupted from nowhere, leaping from rock to rock ahead of me and clearly teasing me into an attempt to follow them. I soon gave up, but found that they had led me to the far side of the point where a macabre sight met my eye. Apparently floating on the surface of the sea were twenty or so straw-hatted human heads. To my relief, every now and again one of them would move in a purposeful way and it gradually dawned on me that this was not some sacrificial rite but a group of women at work. Under the shallow water was a labyrinth of rock pools, and attached to the heads were invisible bodies squatting on the sea-bed, catching crabs.

It may well have been these very crabs that were served up to us that evening at the shabby little restaurant standing on the edge of the sand in the second bay. We had been told about it by a previous visitor who insisted that we must get there before sunset. We arrived when the huge red sun was still well above the horizon, but even so we were only just in time. Imagine that you are standing there with us, your feet bare on the firm squeaky sand. The sea sounds in your ears and smells salty in your nostrils. Just be there, and watch with us that gigantic fireball slide down the smooth slope of the sky so fast that it is only moments before it disappears, snuffed out by the sea. In seconds, islands, dull blobs on the far edge of the ocean, turn black as pitch against a sky where each glowing tint slips so fast into the next that soon there is no colour left and the whole world goes grey.

So now we could only just make out the other feature which had given fame to this isolated hut. The side which presented itself to the visitor was made entirely of soft drink and beer cans. These had been painstakingly strung together in long lines which, hanging closely side by side, made a gigantic bead curtain. Penetrating this clanking partition we found ourselves in a fair sized room, two long tables with chairs arranged round them filling most of the space. The only food on the menu was fish, but in mouthwatering variety. It was a little trying to sit through a lengthy first course with everyone but me burrowing away at the shells of a huge pile of crabs, but to join them would have been more than my life was worth, for they make me as sick as anyone has ever been and lived to tell the tale. However the rest of the meal was well worth waiting for, and we finished our feast feeling comfortably replete and with enough empty beer cans stacked on the table to add at least one more string to the curtain wall. Apart from the beer the bill was negligible, and this proved to be just the first of several happy evenings that we spent in this restaurant during the several trips we made to the coast. On one occasion we were devastated to find it gone. But we need not have worried, for it had simply been moved lock stock and barrel further down the shore like the boat builders' huts. Another time, one of us left an expensive video camera behind, worth a fortune to any of the locals, and we were deeply touched when the wizened proprietor took the trouble to walk two miles to return it to us.

We had three whole days in paradise and then it was time to go back. Sad though we were we felt mightily refreshed, and we knew that at some point soon we could return. What we did not know was that never again would it be quite the same. More and more aid workers were pouring into the country, and very soon not just the advance party of the UN but their full force of twenty thousand would be arriving. We paid several more visits to Kompong Som and it was always wonderful, but somehow that first visit remains unique. Never again did we repeat our impersonation of beach-bums, and as increasing numbers of people arrived so amenities to serve them began to creep in. It was not many months before we got there to find a Khmer entrepreneur with a fleet of windsurfers for hire. It is difficult to imagine a better location for them and they gave great enjoyment to many people, but gone possibly for ever was our seaside Garden of Eden.

Our departure from that first visit was played by the book and, setting off in good time, we got safely back to Phnom Penh well before dusk. Others were not so fortunate. It was not unusual for Khmer families travelling in private cars or taxis to be the victims of attack, robbery at gunpoint which sometimes ended in tragedy. But for expatriates such events were almost unheard of although extreme caution was advised at all times. It would be wrong at this point not to pay tribute to three brave people, two of them English and one Australian, who lost their lives on this same stretch of road almost exactly two years after our first trip. Dominic and his girlfriend Kellie ran the Cafe Rendezvous at Kompong Som, a restaurant so popular that we never managed to eat there. But few people knew that it also served as a refuge for the town's street children whom Kellie took under her wing. The couple's good deeds to sick youngsters were many, often paying for their treatment out of their own pockets. On April 11th 1994 Dominic, Kellie and Tina, a young visitor from England who had only been in the country for three weeks, were snatched from their taxi by guerillas during a regular run to stock up on supplies from Phnom Penh, and were later killed. Dr Peter Carey, Oxford historian and chairman of the Cambodia Trust which supplies and fits artificial limbs to Cambodian mine victims, attended their memorial service in Phnom Penh. On an earlier and happier visit, he said, he had found Cafe Rendezvous a 'revelation in a demoralised society, and a haven from the realities of Cambodia', and that Dominic and Kellie 'offered care in a superlative place, in a place of few superlatives'.[2] We know that they were happy and fulfilled there, in a country that held all of us in the grip of its extraordinary mixture of beauty and ugliness, good and evil. There will be many who miss them sorely, not least the homeless children whom Kellie loved so much.

Chapter Twenty-One

Confined once more in the heat and noise of Phnom Penh the world gradually dragged itself back to work, though it appeared that to prolong the holiday any excuse would do. The anniversary of the entry of Pol Pot into the capital seemed to us a strange date to celebrate, but nevertheless the timely arrival of 17th April at the end of the festival of the New Year meant yet one more day when nothing functioned normally. Tim's job was the first to settle back into its usual pattern, or so it seemed. But once again events were to take an extraordinary turn. There was nothing to suggest as he set off for work on his first morning back that today was to be any different from every other day. Little could be further from the truth.

There was a certain Swiss paediatrician working in Phnom Penh. Not content with his skills as a doctor, this remarkable man was also a first-class cellist, or 'entertainer', as he liked to call himself. Back in his home country, he would organise concerts in which he not only performed the classical cello repertoire with exceptional talent, but also sang, to his own cello accompaniment, songs that he had written himself about the war-stricken children of Cambodia. These concerts must have been very popular (he gave one in Phnom Penh to a spellbound audience) for he made a great deal of money which he spent on building, staffing, and eventually running, a children's hospital in the capital.

It so happened that on this particular morning the new hospital was to have its ceremonial opening and unbeknown to Tim all the Cambodian doctors at January 7th had been invited. When he arrived at work as usual, he found the hospital courtyard full of armed soldiers. Surprised though not unduly alarmed, he began to make his way to the wards. But this was not to be. All of a sudden a khaki-clad figure, gesticulating and brandishing a gun with alarming energy, seized him by the arm and forced him in the opposite direction. Objecting strongly to this manhandling he managed to shake himself free, but with armed men on every side he felt he had little option but to go where he was told. As he was hustled towards a back exit from the hospital, he speculated on the meeting that he was at last to have with the notorious Pol Pot. To him, this was simply the fulfilment of a half-formulated fear, an expectation almost, that had been with him from the beginning. But instead of being bundled out of the hospital and into a truck as he had anticipated, he found himself pushed through a side door into Intensive Care. His captors unceremoniously shoved him towards a bed on which lay a soldier in blood-soaked khaki, shot through the chest and brought by his anxious colleagues to the nearest hospital. Never mind that it was a hospital for women, nor that all the Cambodian doctors had mysteriously vanished. Here was a skilled white surgeon, who would surely save their friend. But as Tim approached the bed, mightily relieved on his own behalf as the reason for his kidnap dawned upon him, the poor fellow breathed his last. I would have died of fright; Tim simply seemed rather disappointed to have missed meeting Pol Pot after all. (Or so he says. This is surely sheer bravado; he must have been scared to death.)

One way and another it was nearly the end of the month before we continued with our pilot study, and I began to wonder whether we would ever complete the preparation for our clinic. However, at last we were off again at the start of a day which, though again it seemed normal enough at the time, will always be to me linked with tragedy. This time we took with us from the dispensary a nurse whom I had not met before and who carried with her a smart little metal attache case. It seemed that today's formula was to be different for when we arrived at our destination, instead of going straight to the first in the neat row of palm huts and continuing with our questioning we waited outside in the street. We must have been standing full in the sun, for I remember its almost blinding rays as they glanced off the lid of the nurse's case and the medical assistant's shiny bald pate. In a moment, we were surrounded by a buzzing horde of flies and pot-bellied children, a miserable malnourished bunch covered with boils and skin rashes. Opening her gleaming case, the nurse, looking enviably cool and efficient in her spotlessly white overall, began to give out pills and potions in response to the medical assistant's requests. His examinations were perfunctory to say the least. A quick poke under the ribs in the general direction of the liver was the most anyone was given, but in any case the ensuing issue of worm pills from the drug bag was clearly what was needed. An impossibly wrinkled old crone, her ancient skin encrusted with the dirt of ages and hanging in folds off a pair of scarecrow's arms, pushed her way through for her share of the booty. Not so an old, old man, so piteously doubled up with pain that he seemed rooted to the spot and was in danger of missing his turn. I was nearly tripped up by a chicken running amok in the scrummage, its few remaining feathers sprouting from a skin that had been scratched red raw. Someone dusted off an upright wooden chair for me to sit on, and thus enthroned I asked what we were waiting for. It turned out that we were serving a double purpose, for not only was this ad hoc clinic a gesture of medical outreach to the community, but we were also an official delegation seeking the village chief's permission to set up our medical centre. He was nowhere to be found, so we continued instead with our survey.

We had already discovered that the women's crying need was for contraception and on this second day of our tour the evidence increased with every family we visited. The first woman we talked to was in her early thirties, thin and careworn and with one eye blinded by severe corneal scarring. She told us that of her ten pregnancies no less than five had been aborted, and as time went on I found that this was a common story. Desperate to keep their husbands and knowing full well that the men would turn to prostitutes if not kept happy at home, the girls could deny them nothing. Some I came across had had as many as ten abortions, and these were certainly not performed as the nice sterile packages obtainable in the West. There were horrendous rumours going around of 'midwives' to whom these girls turned in despair, unscrupulous women who would pummel their victim's abdomens for hours or if necessary days on end in an attempt to kill the foetus. Other 'operations' were carried out by slightly less barbaric methods, but none of these penniless girls could pay for proper medical attention.

Our morning finished at last, and emotionally drained by so many stories of poverty and deprivation, Dr Vathiny and I joined the rest of the team to wait for the hospital transport to pick us up and take us home. As we sat in the shade, a funny little incident took place that sticks in my mind. The nurse whose professionalism and calm cool presence in the midst of the clamouring crowd that morning had so impressed me took out of her pocket a pair of clippers and began to cut her toe-nails. It was an act that seemed quite out of keeping with her previous businesslike efficiency, and the memory of it somehow increased the sadness of her final pitiful misfortune.

A few weeks later I was working in the intensive care ward of the municipal hospital when a cyclo arrived at the open door, a lifeless figure lolling beneath its canopy. The unconscious girl was lifted bodily by the driver and one of the male nurses and dumped unceremoniously on an empty bed. She was pale and sweating with a blood pressure that scarcely registered on the sphygmomanometer, and after my colleague Dr Chuoy had given her a careful examination he pronounced her in the last stages of septic shock. Always worried by severely ill patients, on this occasion he seemed even more than usually troubled and I asked him why. He looked at me curiously. 'Don't you recognise her?' he said. I looked again at her ashen face and realised at last that this was none other than the nurse with the shiny silver case. Further examination showed that the overwhelming infection was coming from her womb, but try as we might, with the few antibiotics available to us we were unable to help her and she died. Later we learned that she like so many had conceived because there was no practical alternative, and had tried to end the pregnancy with this disastrous result. Here if ever it were needed was proof of the urgency of providing help for these girls who surely had already been through enough suffering to last them several lifetimes. Ridiculously, as I glanced at her feet now lying there so still it was the fact that her toenails would never again need cutting that brought home to me the pathos of such an unnecessary death.

Chapter Twenty-Two

'Chust call me Klaas', said the big man dressed in khaki shirt and shorts. I was cycling home to lunch one day when I passed him standing at his garden gate. Suspecting that he was one of the newly arrived members of the UN that we had heard so much about, I stopped to greet him as every good neighbour should. His name was Brigadier General Klaas Roos, and he turned out to be the director, no less, of the UN civilian police, which was to become known as Civpol. Like everything else nowadays the UN brought with them their own jargon. Their correct title, the United Nations Transitional Authority in Cambodia, was rapidly shortened to UNTAC, a label that quickly became attached to almost any foreigner.

There could be no doubt of their arrival. Insidious at first, as in their absentee occupancy of the seaside bungalows, by the time three more months had passed the place was crawling with them. Twenty-one thousand men and women from a hundred different nations had converged on this little country, and could not be ignored. Their presence coincided almost exactly with the rest of our stay, for the peacekeepers left at the same time as we did.

There were pale blue berets everywhere. The worn out roads in Phnom Penh became even more hazardous, with greater and greater numbers of huge white trucks scattering local traffic quite unaccustomed to such speed. A Cambodian bus was knocked off the road by a careless UN driver resulting in seventy-six casualties, some of them fatal, and this was by no means an isolated incident. The fact that the rainy season and the peacekeepers arrived simultaneously did not help. Roads that are a foot or two deep in water are not the easiest to negotiate.

Then there was the effect on food prices. The soldiers were paid in dollars; a lot of dollars, far more than they were used to. (The average cost per UN head for their eighteen-month stay was roughly $262,000, or £175,000 pounds.) I noticed that Dr Chuoy stopped going to the hospital cafe for his ten o'clock breakfast. Taxed with this, he said he could no longer afford to. The value of the riel had plummeted, and now he breakfasted at home on yesterday's leftover rice, eaten cold. But I have to admit that, as regards food, UNTAC did us expatriates a favour. The first supermarket opened almost at once, and 'Le Shop' became a regular Saturday morning port of call on my way home from work. The taste of the first Danish frozen chicken that we bought there and cooked in our biscuit-tin oven was memorable. More and more Western-style shops were to follow, as entrepreneurs of several nationalities cashed in on the bonanza. The markets were flooded with perfect replicas of UN flags, the famous berets and even pairs of pale blue shorts.

It was the end of our peaceful occupation of the one and only swimming pool, at the Cambodiana Hotel. UNTAC moved in and took it over. Most of the time they just stood in it, yelling at the top of their voices to their buddies. They all seemed to be enormous men, and they gradually got even bigger, running to fat from enforced inactivity. There simply was no longer any room to swim. Keeping them busy and fit was obviously a problem, and I was impressed by the efforts of their officers to deal with it. On my way to work I used to pass the Indonesian contingent's makeshift barracks. Sometimes I would meet a platoon of them jogging along the street, the sweat glistening on their black backs, their arms thrusting in unison like rows of synchronised pistons. At other times they would be hard at work clearing the muddy pond outside their barracks' gate, working in formation with little hoes to give space to the pink lotuses that had been choked with weeds.

The peacekeepers did themselves no favours with the rest of the expatriate community, particularly in their treatment of Khmer women. It seemed that they had been given remarkably little teaching on hygiene and the spread of disease, and there can be no doubt that they are partly responsible for the huge rise in the number of Cambodians infected with HIV. My favourite prostitute at our clinic had become pregnant by one of them, well before our arrival on the scene. She certainly knew nothing of condoms until we taught her. The inexcusable philosophy of those at the top seemed to be that boys will be boys, causing a storm of protest amongst aid workers, particularly those amongst us pleading the cause of women's rights.

All these are facets of the UN presence that we saw or experienced ourselves. What we did not see, confined to Phnom Penh and with no inside knowledge, were the great efforts that were being made to do a good job and to succeed in the enormous task that had been set them at the Paris Peace Accords.

Their ultimate aim was to set up and run elections, so that the Cambodian people could decide for themselves on their own future. But before they could do this, four other matters had to be tackled. First, all civil war must stop. There must be an end to the fighting that had been going on for years between the four political parties, and each must disarm its soldiers. Three of them began to hand in their guns, but not the fourth. No, said the Khmer Rouge. Secondly, the UN must set up a ruling body, the Supreme National Council, to manage the country until a government was finally chosen. This was to include its own representatives, and delegates from each of the four Khmer parties. Three of them played their proper part, but not the fourth. No, said the Khmer Rouge, not until you play fair and abide by other rulings made in Paris.

The Khmer Rouge were evidently doing their best to make trouble. But there was little they could do at the moment to interfere with the UN's third task, to repatriate almost 400,000 refugees from the civil war who had fled to refugee camps set up for them on the Thai border. (It was in one such that our Khmer teacher Darra had lived with his family for many years). The camps had saved countless lives, but now it was time for everyone to come home. Hopefully, the civil war was over and the people could start to rebuild normal lives. But the immediate motive for their repatriation was that only those living on Khmer soil would be allowed the all-important vote. It was a huge task, tackled head on by the UN High Commission for Refugees. However things did not go smoothly here either. Landmines, floods and malaria made land that on paper had been promised to every family totally uninhabitable. The people were used to being looked after, with schools and health services on the spot. Now they were out on their own, miles from anywhere and without work, food and medicines. Starvation and disease once more began to take their toll, and there were many tragedies. One day, another limp figure was delivered by cyclo to Intensive Care where I happened to be lingering on after Dr Chuoy had gone home. The message that came with him informed us that he was a returnee who had attempted suicide with a drug overdose. He was already dead, a fact that altogether failed to register with the medical assistant on duty who wandered slowly off to search for an elusive stomach tube. The possibility that this could be an acute emergency had evidently passed him by. Here was a young man who had left the camps full of hope and enthusiasm, and had found nothing but despair. He was by no means alone in his troubles. But the project went ahead. Villages were built, the newcomers began to find their feet, and all in all the UNHCR was reasonably happy with its progress.

The UN's fourth and final duty before the elections was to teach the people the principles of democracy, to explain to them how they could have a say in their country's future. To carry out this difficult task, over four hundred UN volunteers were drafted into the country and it so happened that amongst their number was one of our friends. This intrepid band of people from many different countries and walks of life had received no previous training. Straight from a high profile advertising job in London, Felicity was paired up with a Norwegian boy, a total stranger, and sent to live with him in a tiny wooden hut in Ratinikiri, a province in the remote north-eastern corner of the country. Their only water was in a nearby river. Their food supplies were purchased weekly from a distant market, and the bread they ate was mouldy for five days out of seven. Their task was to teach the local villagers around them the basics of democracy and how to vote. These were primitive uneducated

Tribeswoman from Ratinikiri province

people from indigenous tribes whose language was not even related to Khmer. The men hunted in the nearby jungle, occasionally coming home to their bare-breasted women-folk with the ultimate prize, a tiger. They had never seen a camera, and when asked to pose for a registration photograph, would kneel in front of it with their hands held up in the traditional attitude of respect. Small wonder that some of them came round a second time, making the final registration count one hundred and twenty per cent. Felicity had the time of her life.

But while all these projects were going ahead, the main political happenings were in sad disarray. One of the four parties had collapsed, leaving only three in the fray. Of these, the Khmer Rouge went its own way, making trouble and directing troop movements that could only suggest a return to outright warfare. While the guerrillas sat on the fence, their AK47s at the ready and playing for time in which to think up their next move, the remaining two parties were increasingly at each others' throats. The Cambodian People's Party, or CPP, which had been in government until the arrival of the UN and was still under the leadership of the communist Hun Sen, was the more aggressive. Their attacks on the Royalists, whose clumsy acronym was Funcinpec and who were headed by Sihanouk's son Ranariddh, became increasingly physical rather than political. The UN was in dire trouble, itself sustaining attack and under criticism from all sides.

And then what everyone had feared actually took place. The Khmer Rouge pulled out of the rapidly approaching election. It certainly seemed at the time that now most of the point had been lost. The whole idea had been to let bygones be bygones and to include the guerrillas in a political settlement in order to stop the endless fighting. The country was desperate for peace, and now it seemed that it would once more elude them. Certainly the Khmer Rouge set out on a campaign of terror, doing their utmost to upset the elections. CPP were not so far behind, attacking Funcinpec headquarters, blaming the UN for bias against them and threatening the peacemakers if they dared to interfere with their activities. Things were coming to a head, and no one knew what would happen. The Khmer Rouge made all sorts of dire threats. They would attack the polling booths. They would burn down houses while their owners were out voting. They would position cameras inside the ballot boxes so that voting would no longer be anonymous. The UN authorities in New York started to panic and ordered all UN families out of the country. Sandbags sprang up overnight round the central UN building, which also housed the Supreme National Council. All expatriates were asked to lay in emergency supplies, and I remember wondering quite what good the dozen bottles of dubious drinking water that I dutifully bought would do if Pol Pot came to town.

In the midst of all this turmoil something else was happening, an act of great courage and commitment that should have come as no surprise in this country of contrasts. Following the teachings of Buddha, four hundred monks and nuns were walking all the way from Angkor in the north to Phnom Penh in the south in a traditional March for Peace. Early in the morning of their departure, they were gathered in a pagoda for meditation when a grenade was thrown in through the open door. Although it failed to explode, one of the weaker brethren, frightened by the incident, suggested that they might cancel their trip. But he was met with a stern reply. 'Buddha has saved us,' said Maha Ghosanda, head of the Inter-Religious Mission for Peace and leader of the march. 'Indeed, that is why we must walk.'[3]

It took them eighteen days. They marched through gun battles and torrential rain, sustained by crowds who had left jobs and families to line their route and give them rice and water. Soldiers came and prayed, not just that they themselves would remain unharmed, but that their own shooting would miss its mark. By the time they reached Phnom Penh on the very day before the election, numbers had swelled to three thousand. Impromptu prayer meetings halted the traffic in the capital over the next two days, and Prince Sihanouk himself greeted them with a heartfelt plea for peace. And where was I while all this was going on? Tethered to the house by yet another stomach upset. Friends who took part told me that it was a unique and wonderful experience, and with that I must rest content.

One more night, a night of nervous anticipation and excitement, and then at last the great day of the election dawned, 23rd May 1993. It was teeming with rain. The polling booths were guarded by armed soldiers. Many thousands of Cambodian officials, including Dr Chuoy, moonlighting to earn some extra dollars, were at their posts in various supporting roles. And what happened? Absolutely nothing, or rather nothing untoward. There were no explosions, no blazing houses, almost no violence at all. Instead there were long, long lines of people, soaked to the skin, clutching their registration cards and patiently waiting their turn to vote. The turnout was perhaps not so extraordinary when you consider what was at stake. Civil war had racked their country for as long as the younger people could remember. Peace was what they wanted above all else, and so they came out in their thousands and stood in the pouring rain. They knew the risks but they did not care. Here was a chance for a different life, and nothing would stop them from taking it.

The elections went on for five days, and by the end ninety per cent of the people had voted. It was an emotional week in which the whole population, ourselves included, seemed to rise higher and higher on a rose-coloured cloud of euphoria as the threats of violence subsided. But excitement too was rising as the results came in. The two major parties were running neck and neck and the tension was palpable. At last came the final outcome; Funcinpec had won by a small margin with fifty-eight seats as against CPP's fifty-one.

Several effects were immediate. CPP were furious and behaved, as one would expect, like spoilt and unsporting schoolboys. (So much for the reply given on polling day by Hun Sen, CPP's president, when he went to register his vote. When asked by a journalist if the CPP would turn over power if they lost, he replied 'I am one of the great sportsmen of the democratic game.'4) The whole thing, they said, was grossly unfair. But unlike most schoolboys, any retaliation would be with guns, not fists, and many terrified Funcinpec workers took to their heels and fled in terror for their lives.

Prince Sihanouk, alarmed by the small majority and the evident instability that it would bring, tried to take over on his own but was dissuaded. In the name of democracy, the world said, it simply would not do.

The Khmer Rouge had been dealt the biggest blow since they were driven out by Vietnam fourteen years previously. One theory of their apparent collapse is that they had miscalculated, thinking that in the face of CPP's pre-election violence the other parties would pull out and once again become their allies, hopefully headed by Prince Sihanouk himself. It did not work, and now they were left stranded. For the moment.

Funcinpec of course was happy, but faced with a coalition with their bitter opponents their pleasure must have been sorely tempered with pain.

So what happened next? There were, of course, endless repercussions which continue up to the present time, but our own story is in danger of getting lost and these must wait. The extent of CPP's rage, its aggressive manoeuvres and the right royal row that resulted from them, the return of the princely prodigal son, the further machinations of the Khmer Rouge, and above all the efforts to form a coalition between two such disparate political parties, all this must wait until the end, where the reader will find it in a political postscript.

Chapter Twenty-Three

Ten months before the elections we went back to England for our mid-term break. Our son was to be married and nothing would keep us away. The happy event and a month of hot baths, good food and general resuscitation did wonders for mind and body, and though it has to be said that we were dreading our return, it would have taken a major event to prevent it. The first year, spent largely in preparation for what we hoped to achieve, had not been a particularly comfortable time, and we had absolutely no intention of wasting it. So when the moment came, off we went, sad to leave but in good spirits and with high hopes. We need not have worried. It was remarkable how much at home we felt as soon as we got off the plane at Pochentong airport and travelled once more down the straight tree-lined road into the city. This time we were going to our own little house and to jobs that had taken shape and were familiar, a very different state of affairs from our first arrival ten months before. To my own surprise, I felt really pleased to be back.

It did not take long to get into the Cambodian swing of things again, the leaking drain from the bathroom basin, the broken water pump, the food cupboard seething with ants. Without a pump, the tank on the roof soon ran dry and we had to tip buckets of water over each other's heads like everybody else. Our drinking water filter broke too, and we were reduced to drinking bottled water that sometimes was sterile and often was not. The electricity supply certainly had not improved in our absence, so that candlelight in the evenings became the rule rather than the exception, and the little girl round the corner was kept busy with her chopper and her yards of ice. Although our Cambodian colleagues seemed reassuringly pleased to see us back again, it was disappointing to find that nothing had advanced in my absence. Months on, the charitable church in Bangkok still had not sent the promised drugs, Dr Vathiny still had not started the course on family planning that she had been promised at the gynaecology hospital, and alterations to the water supply at the clinic still had failed to happen. It was the same old story.

It seemed that nothing in Cambodia got done unless a great deal of breathing was done down a great many necks.

But all these annoyances were suddenly overshadowed by a frightening event which came close to a disaster. When I arrived one morning at the hospital, Dr Vathiny failed to appear, a most unusual situation. Rumour had it that there had been an accident, but it was only later that the details emerged. She had gone to visit her sister's stall at the New Market. A would-be burglar, planning a raid on a jewellery counter, threw in a grenade to clear a path for himself, killing or wounding twelve people. It just so happened that Catherine the violinist, our young friend who taught at the music school, was passing by and saw two blood-stained women staggering out of the market, arms round each other for support. She stopped to help, and realising who they were took them to the military hospital where Vathiny's husband worked. The surgeons were able to remove most of the fragments of shrapnel, but when I went to see the sisters at home a few days later it was obvious that they had been lucky to escape worse damage. Vathiny had a hole right through her ear lobe. I had been determined to open the new clinic quickly come what may. But a colleague peppered with shrapnel was something that I had not reckoned with, and a second event that came hard on the heels of her convalescence all but brought the whole project crashing about our ears. We were within an ace of being sent home for good.

Almost immediately after our return from England, one of our daughters came out for a visit. Although Tim and I had both gone back to work her stay seemed like an extension of our holiday, and so it was with a double sadness in our hearts that we finally saw her off at Pochentong airport. But now it was time to look forward, to face the future and accept the challenge and excitement of the next few months. We had a year left in the country. We knew now what we wanted to do and more or less how to do it. We felt refreshed and energetic after our break, and both of us realised that to make the most of the time left it was vital to keep as fit as possible. But this was easier said than done. It was too hot to take much in the way of exercise and Tim, an Olympic athlete in his day, had been reduced for some time to running round and round the emptiest room in our house. On the very day of Penny's departure he launched into such a determined attack on the climate with a series of muscular antics of such ferocity that the wooden sitting-room floor was pooled with sweat and the moans and groans that were squeezed out of him reached an alarming intensity. Afterwards in preparation for a supper guest he took a much needed shower, but when after a very long time he eventually emerged it was obvious there was something seriously wrong. It seemed that he had no idea that we were about to have a visitor, and when I reminded him who it was he denied all knowledge of her although she was an acquaintance of some months' standing. Gradually, the awful truth dawned that he had lost his memory. He could remember nothing of our daughter's visit; he did not even know that our son had just got married, and when I reminded him that we had been to England for the wedding, his disconcerting reply was 'England? That seems a bit excessive.'

I tucked him up in bed and took his blood pressure, which was perfectly normal. Clearly something had happened to his poor brain, and I could only think it to be the result of extreme physical stress in extreme heat. But what was I to do? There was no comforting GP to ring up for advice, even if there had been a telephone. There was no Cambodian hospital in the whole country that I would let him be seen dead in, let alone alive. At this moment came a knock on the front door and our dinner guest arrived. She was not a close friend, and I found the whole situation a little difficult to handle. What does one say in this situation? 'Do sit down, and what would you like to drink. By the way, my husband has just lost his memory'? For all I knew he would appear at any minute, stark naked and wandering in his mind, and although I am sure Pru can cope with anything it could have been disconcerting for all three of us. But I had to share this nightmare with somebody and together she and I decided on seeking the help of James, the Field Director with the pink socks. Pru pedalled off into the night to fetch him, while I stayed with my patient who every few minutes asked me what was happening, and when I explained about his excessive exercise, repeated with maddening persistence 'have I had a shower? I feel clean'.

James arrived very quickly, and poor Pru disappeared off home, unfed. After another council of war, James too disappeared for a while. With the advent of large numbers of UN troops, a field hospital had been set up outside the city in the old university building on the road to the airport. This was staffed entirely by a contingent from Germany and was a godsend to the whole community. Although its primary function was of course to treat UN personnel, its very able doctors were happy to help both the local Khmer inhabitants and any of the expatriate community.

We had already met one of the young physicians, and James had gone to ask for his help. After an hour or so the two of them returned together, and Dr Alex carried out his examination. When he had finished, he voiced the fear that we all felt but none of us had dared confront. Tim, in this godforsaken country, had probably had a stroke, and what did I want him to do about it? There is not much to be done about it in any country, but Alex was anxious to admit him, and as I had asked for his advice I had at least to listen. Wonderful though the UN hospital might be, it was a place of last resort. The beds in the long rooms that served as wards were almost touching, most of them occupied by victims of the motor-cycle accidents that were so common, young men groaning in agony from appalling injuries to their unprotected heads. Even if Tim should get worse, there was little or nothing that they would be able to do for him there, and rest and quiet would be impossible. Fortunately Alex was too junior to admit patients without seeking permission from his superior, so we had a short reprieve whilst once again he and James set out in the agency truck to seek advice. And gradually while they were gone what I had hoped for but hardly dared expect took take place. Tim's memory reconnected itself, and light began to dawn. By the time they had returned with the news that in any case the hospital was full, he was almost back to normal and the immediate crisis had passed.

The medical crisis, that is. But we had a long way to go yet. The following day, Tim was evacuated as an emergency to his old haunt, the Bangkok Nursing Home, this time with me in tow. I had been badly frightened, and suspecting that Tim might well be sent straight back to England, packed up as many of his belongings as possible to take with us. As an added complication, we had just received a shipment of an ill-assorted collection of medical equipment and drugs from home, a donation to Tim's hospital. With the strong possibility that he would not be coming back all this had to be sorted into the appropriate piles for distribution, so with the victim sitting in the middle directing operations, feeling perfectly well by now and unable to see what all the fuss was about as he could not remember any of it, I scurried hither and thither like a demented hen. I did not have time to wash off even the surface dirt and sweat before it was time to climb into the agency truck for the ride to the airport. Amy, the four-year-old daughter of our Field Directors who came with us on the drive, summed things up with disconcerting accuracy when she said, looking up at me quizzically with her bright blue eyes, 'What's the matter with your face, Liz? It's gone all crumpled'.

It was not until we were well past the wheel chair with its two white-coated attendants waiting at the foot of the Bangkok gangway, Tim striding out in front as usual, that the truth dawned. We had been casting our mind back to the journey, wondering which of our fellow passengers had been bravely coping with illness severe enough to merit such treatment. But standing in the main arrival hall, apparently unmet despite carefully made arrangements, we realised the chariot must be for him. Should he run back and fetch it, he wondered?

The next few days were spent in a whirl of medical activity. Tim could not have been given better or more thorough treatment anywhere in the world. For the patient, the highlight came with the arrival at his bedside of a consultant neurologist from Bangkok's leading teaching hospital. It was not so much her expertise that took his fancy, although that turned out to be considerable, but her other qualities. He still talks of her with a dreamy look in his eye. A string of investigations including a brain scan showed nothing wrong, and the conclusion reached was that he had not had a stroke, that there was nothing whatever the matter with him now, but that he had briefly suffered from an episode of something called Total Global Amnesia, or TGA for short. This is a transient condition brought on by extreme exercise in extreme climatic conditions, and is very unlikely to repeat itself. The relief was of course enormous, and when could we go back? 'Oh, whenever you like,' but we were not averse to the suggestion of a few days rest. It was my first experience of this wonderful haven with its air conditioning, hot showers, and garden glorious with bougainvillea, and where from my camp bed alongside Tim's high hospital one I could look out across our balcony at the birds congregating above the lake in which turtles made their home.

We had, however, reckoned without our agency's conscientious London doctor. Despite the gamut of tests, all of them negative, and despite the firm opinion of the local neurologist who had trained at our own leading neurological hospital in London, Dr J was adamant. Tim was on no account ever to set foot in Cambodia again, and was to come straight home as soon as he was fit to travel. Perhaps she will listen to the opinion of an English neurologist, we thought, and in any case we would value a second opinion. We wanted very much to go back and get on with our jobs, but certainly not at the cost of Tim's health. We chose a friend and colleague back in England who was noted for both clinical acumen and common sense, and the faxes started to fly. Within a few hours, the reply to Tim's summary of history and hospital tests had arrived, written in the specialist's own hand to save time. When he agreed precisely with the Thai doctor's diagnosis and prognosis, our last lingering doubts disappeared and, as yet another fax disappeared down the telephone line to the agency office in London, we felt confident that all would be well. But once again our hopes were dashed. Dr J remained adamant. Did I want to lose my husband, she asked, when I finally managed to speak directly to her on the telephone? It was useless to point out that Tim was no more likely to expire than any of the rest of us and probably less so. She was responsible for volunteer health, she did not want a death on her hands, and we were to come home.

The argument went on for days. Our own Field Director gave us great support, and it was not until a meeting of the senior agency officials in London had been called to discuss the impasse that Dr J was finally overruled and we were given a three-month stay of execution in which to round off our projects and our truncated Cambodian lives. It was far from perfect, but a great deal better than nothing. Who could tell what the next few weeks would bring?

I did not entirely waste my time in Bangkok, for I was able to visit the church office of the charity that had promised drugs for the clinic. The Rev MM was away, but I noticed a small box of assorted medicines sitting on a shelf, and asked if it was for me. It was. So when, battered but unbowed and with the box under my arm, we finally arrived 'home' to a heart-warming welcome, and when I found that Vathiny had not only fully recovered from her ordeal but had actually completed her family planning course as well, it really did seem that the clinic might finally get under way.

Chapter Twenty-Four

On Friday, 18th September 1992, almost a year after our arrival in Cambodia, our new clinic was declared officially open at last. This was a red-letter day, and careful plans had been laid to mark it with due ceremony. Properly typed invitations were sent out to the director of the Municipal Health Department and his officials, not such an easy task when typewriters in the Khmer script are few and far between and photocopiers starved of electricity. Enough equipment had to be put on show to make a reasonable impression. An inspection the day before had shown us that the clinic staff had tried really hard to make the whole building look presentable, and of course our two 'new' rooms were spotless and shining, but the bathroom with its unlikely turquoise matching suite had clearly been forgotten. It was filthy, with the lavatory bowl's disgusting encrustation still all too firmly in place. I made a fuss and produced money to buy a bottle of pink liquid indecipherably labelled in Vietnamese which I was assured would do the trick. I did not hold out much hope, but the staff must have worked like Trojans for by the next morning it looked as good as new.

Life begins early in hot countries, and the Grand Opening Ceremony was billed to start at eight a.m. When I arrived half an hour earlier, everything had already been prepared. A long table had been set up in the big entrance hall, and rows of the ubiquitous puce plastic chairs were waiting to receive the illustrious backsides of visiting dignitaries. The dispensary chief Monsieur So Phon had evidently gone to great trouble to make and hang on one of the walls a huge blue notice. He had pinned on to a sheet a series of large white cut-out characters in the Khmer script which no doubt made a grand proclamation suited to the occasion but might equally well have said 'Grandma Go Home' for all I knew, for I never had learnt to read.

Exactly at the appointed hour, the Khmer officials drew up in their white Toyotas and it was time to begin. Speech followed interminable speech as one after another the visitors rose to their feet for it seemed that everyone had to have a turn, but at last it was over and we all made for the feast laid out next door. The table was set with a white cloth decorated with vases of drooping long-legged flowers, and we dined off unripe bananas and broken biscuits. But any failings were due to lack of cash rather than enthusiasm, and we all knew that the few funds available would be better spent on the clinic than on this funny little formal ceremony.

The first session, held four days later, was not an outstanding success. There were no patients at all for the first hour, the new microscope was uncooperative and the slides that my colleague attempted to stain spread their purple dye on to everything in sight except the germs we were looking for. And anyway with the sudden demise of the electricity all pretence to a scientific approach came to an end. These were just teething troubles, but something much more serious was to happen that I feared would get the project off to the saddest possible start. Gradually the women did begin to appear in ones and twos, curious to see what the white doctor whose presence was advertised at the gate was doing. The very first to arrive was a girl who was nearly at full term with her second baby, and when with our brand new equipment we checked her blood pressure we found it to be sky high. This lady was in imminent danger of eclampsia, a condition in which fits suffered by the mother can result in her own as well as her baby's death. It was imperative to admit her straight away, and I tried hard to insist that she climb into the hospital car that was waiting for us and that would drive her back to our maternity unit in the centre of Phnom Penh. But no; she had a toddler at home that she could not possibly leave. Much against my better judgement we agreed that she should go home, make the necessary arrangements with a neighbour, and come straight back. Of course she failed to return, and when I asked for her address, I was given a look of such blank astonishment that it was clear that no such thing had ever been recorded for anyone. What a lot I had still to learn.

So it was with a heavy heart that I drove home, for I felt certain that neither she nor the baby would survive. It was a sorry start to a venture embarked upon with such high hopes. But of course we had to go on, and the following week I drove the jeep to the hospital where once again we were to load staff and equipment into the hospital truck for our onward journey to the clinic. But the truck failed to materialise, a situation which was to repeat itself with frustrating regularity, and finally running out of both time and patience we transferred back into the jeep and set off. The dispensary was five miles from the city in the rural suburb of Tuol Kork, the last section of the journey along a muddy track subject to deep flooding in the rainy season. That morning the rain was coming down in torrents and the rough road had vanished, its place taken by a lake some hundred yards long. I had never driven the jeep through deep floodwater and had no idea how it would handle. Setting my course towards the distant point where the track finally re-emerged we plunged in deeper and deeper and I began to fear for our safe arrival. But I need not have worried; we sailed through without a problem in the world. The water that came up through the floor soon drained out again and we reached our destination relatively dry shod.

Once again custom was slow. The morning dragged on and we were looking hopefully at our watches when suddenly the consulting room door burst open and Som An, the medical assistant on duty, erupted into the room. Please would I come straight away to the delivery room where there was a patient in labour with an extremely high blood pressure? Together we ran up the stairs and into the labour ward, and there on the couch with her feet up in stirrups, as large as life and very far from dead, was my patient of last week. She was in strong labour and I checked her blood pressure. As the needle shot up the scale so did my own level of adrenaline, and this time I was taking no chances. Before anyone had time to object, I had pushed the midwife into the jeep, followed by the labouring patient and her husband complete with sleeping mats and we were off. It was far too dangerous for her to be delivered in the dispensary, for we had none of the right drugs for her condition nor the facilities for a sick newborn baby (not that there were any of those in the hospital either). The jeep set off purposefully down the road and into the flood. I had no worries on that score this time, for had it not it just skimmed through without a murmur?

It was not the engine that gave out but the gearbox, which did have a habit of jamming. And jammed it was, completely solid. Deep in water, it was impossible to carry out the manoeuvres that sometimes put it right. There I was, stuck in the middle of a muddy pond with one of the worst obstetric emergencies there is and without so much as an aspirin. We were completely marooned, with no one in sight except for a couple of fat pigs contentedly rooting for scraps on the shore. Never in my life before had I prayed so hard and never in the jeep's life before had the gearbox come unstuck of its own accord. But within seconds we were off again, within minutes arrived at the hospital, and within two hours a beautiful healthy boy was born.

So far so good. But still very few patients were turning up, and I began to wonder if we had made a dreadful mistake. Perhaps I had completely misinterpreted the women's wants and the whole project would be a dismal failure. This new worry drove out the old, the lack of continuing supplies of contraceptives and medicines. We could count the number of patients we saw at each of our two weekly sessions on the fingers of one hand, and it seemed that our one big pot of red and yellow ampicillin capsules, given out for want of anything better for all sorts of infections, would last for ever. The Bangkok church charity seemed to have abandoned us, but anxiety on that score had faded from my mind. One day came a rude shock. Our 'pharmacist', an untrained but willing Cambodian who had taken on the job of guarding our meagre stores against marauders, showed me the antibiotic jar. It had a single layer of capsules left, just covering the bottom. We had no money left. What was I to do?

I have no doubt that, in Cambodia at least, miracles do still happen. That very night there came a knock on the door and there stood Dr Pene Key, busy reorganising the health service for the entire nation but still finding time to come round to our house with a cardboard carton of unwanted drugs in her arms. And so it went on, unexpected donations of large quantities of medicines arriving from drug companies in England as our wants became known, and finally a gift of the unimaginable sum of eight thousand pounds from the 'Small Project Fund' of the British Embassy, to be spent as we thought fit. On each occasion, previous supplies had dwindled to almost nothing, and we had been in grave danger of committing the cardinal sin of starting something without the means to continue it, which is so much worse than never starting it at all.

The contraceptive story was a similar one. Realising as a result of our survey the great need for coils, condoms and 'pills', I had taken the opportunity while we were at home on our mid-term break to visit the International Planned Parenthood Federation (IPPF) in London. It was our last day, I remember, and, running late as usual, I raced through Regents Park where their central office is located and arrived exhausted and panting just as they were about to lock up for the night. Taking pity on me, someone gave me a brief interview and some pretty posters to stick on the clinic wall; at least I had shown my scarlet face and made my presence felt. The effort proved worthwhile, for after a number of begging letters written on my return I received enough supplies from IPPF for every one of my potential five thousand patients for a year. No one else that I wrote to gave any response.

Happily, as the supplies appeared so did the patients. Word had got round at last that this was indeed a free clinic, without snags or strings attached. Now when we arrived in the mornings there would be crowds of girls standing outside or waiting in the big hall, all dressed in their brightly coloured blouses and long skirts, and all nodding and smiling as we bustled in with our microscope and shining stainless steel drums of instruments and swabs. We still found it easier to transport everything backwards and forwards from the hospital, where storage was safer and sterilisation marginally more possible. Several of the staff became proficient in inserting coils, and many of the patients took surprisingly well to the daily discipline of the pill.

But despite all our efforts, our store of condoms remained almost untouched. The husbands simply would not use them. This was the start of a major tragedy, for had they done so it might just have been possible to prevent the spread of the illness that will soon bring yet another wave of death. There had been no known cases of AIDS in the country when we arrived, and less than one in a thousand of blood donors was testing positive in the newly introduced HIV screening programme. By 1993, two years later, the number had gone up by twenty times, and now, in 1996, has more than doubled again for the general population (women attending reproductive health clinics). But amongst the prostitutes the rate is eight times greater than the average, no less than four hundred cases per thousand, or forty per cent.*

Less than half a mile from the dispensary is a major source of this infection, the biggest Red Light district in the city. If you were to drive north through Phnom Penh, up to the broken bridge (now at last repaired) and then turn left past the College of Fine Art, you would

* Rates of HIV in May-June 1996: female sex-workers 41%; military and policemen 12%; women attending reproductive health clinics 4.5%. *HIV and Sexually Transmitted Diseases in Cambodia*, Caroline Ryan and Pamina Gorbach, University of Washington.

find yourself on a narrow bumpy unsurfaced road built on the top of a long straight dyke. On either side, your senses would be soothed by the sight of a large lake, its surface covered with the lush growth of the big pink flowers and luxuriant leaves of lotus plants. On both sides of the road, you would pass a row of picturesque wooden houses on legs, their fronts joined to the road by wooden planks, their backs almost overlying the water. And then you would be struck by the extraordinary number of young ladies. You would see girls everywhere, a row of them on a bench lounging outside a house, some leaning on doorposts, or a group of them standing in the road gossiping until scattered by your car. And something else would strike you too: the unnatural chalk-white of their faces. These are the prostitutes, frightened children hiding behind their clowns' masks of powder and paint, only their eyes betraying their misery.

Misery and tragedy are the substance of their lives, from the reasons for their presence here, through their ill-treatment by 'owners' and clients alike, to the eventual inevitability of an early death from AIDS for many of them. But none of us knew much about them at that stage. What we did know was that the husbands of the 'respectable' ladies who sought help at the dispensary were frequent visitors here and that the can of worms that they opened by their refusal to don protection would inevitably spread its contents far and wide. It was essential to persuade these girls to attend our new clinic, both for their own good and for everyone else's.

But this was easier said than done. First we simply made sure they knew about it and that they were invited. Nothing happened. Next, we went visiting. The senior members of our dispensary team set out one morning on a brothel crawl. We knocked on the door of each little wooden house in turn and one or other of my Khmer colleagues spoke to the owner, man or woman or sometimes both. It rapidly became clear to me that I was simply a figurehead. I was not asked to take any part in the conversation, but I knew enough of the language to understand the speaker's reasoning. If Yea had come all the way from England to help them, surely their girls could bestir themselves sufficiently to walk the few hundred yards to the clinic.

Although this effort too proved ineffectual, it gave all of us a chance to see what went on behind the rows of doors, usually closed but often that day left open while the householders listened to what my colleagues had to say. It was a shock, to say the least. Just inside one house was a second open door leading into a tiny cubicle. The bed inside it, covered with a multicoloured cloth, was crumpled and filthy. On the wall at one end and a few inches above the bed was a large patch of black grease, about the size of a dinner plate. I never could decide whether it was their combined heads or feet that were responsible. Most front doors revealed a series of cubicles resembling nothing so much as cattle stalls. In one house, these looked new and clean; in all the rest, they were sordid and shabby. Although as we neared the end of our round it was well into the middle of the morning, while we talked a young girl looking bleary and rumpled emerged from her stall, followed minutes later by a youth casually zipping up his fly. It was all extraordinarily insalubrious, a total contrast to the seeming normality of the smiling well-dressed people with whom we were chatting at their front doors.

We had suggested on our rounds that the girls should come to a special clinic just for them on Saturday mornings. We thought that the prostitutes might feel less shy, and that it might be easier too for our usual clients. We came away from our tour horrified and nauseated by what we had seen, but encouraged by our reception and more than ever determined to succeed. For three consecutive Saturday mornings we went through the motions of collecting all our equipment and getting ourselves to the dispensary, sitting in solitary state for a couple of hours, and then going home again. Clearly this was not going to work either.

So what should we do now? I went to the office to pick our Field Director's brains. He looked at me pityingly; you take the clinic to them, of course. Why had I not thought of that? I consulted with my Khmer colleagues who continued to astonish me with their interest and co-operation. At this stage they were getting no increase in salary for their activities, and not only were they having to work much harder but were doing so in an area which both geographically and emotionally was considered totally unrespectable. They seemed to accept this new idea with their usual enthusiasm, and in no time at all we had arranged with the owner of a 'hotel' on the dyke (in effect a glorified brothel) that we should rent a room on his premises every Saturday morning for a couple of hours. Now the girls would have no excuse not to attend. The clinic would literally be on their doorstep, and their owners could even keep an eye on them, to make sure they did not stray.

Chapter Twenty-Five

A few days after our tour of the brothels and just a month before our second Christmas, a new phenomenon burst upon our lives. Until now, all our entertainment had been of our own making. There were parties and visits to street-side bars. We played music to each other, and joined in silly games. Some expatriates proudly owned television sets, but the films they showed, always of course in Khmer, were restricted to just two themes. The identical heroines, screeching their lines in ear-splitting monotony, were endlessly victims of either undying love or ferocious violence, usually both. The same went for the cinemas. Several people owned video players but there was a scarcity of films to show on them. Short-wave radios crackled too much to be good for anything except World Service news, a major lifeline. A portable CD player, a present from home that very next Christmas, became a treasured addition to the range. Tim and I brought back from our holiday in England several Shakespeare plays which we read to each other by candlelight, each of us playing half a dozen characters. I wonder what the neighbours thought.

But on November 13th, 14th and 15th 1992, history was made. For the first time ever recorded, an English play was performed in Cambodia. The Phnom Penh Players proudly presented Tom Stoppard's 'The Real Inspector Hound' in Crackers Restaurant, the best eating place in town. A stage was erected, and after dinner had been served at the many little tables among the potted plants the curtain rose. It was a superb performance, the brain child of Ben, the big Australian musicologist who did so much to make all our lives easier, and to an uncritical audience reached the height of professionalism. There were minor difficulties but they only added to the fun. Christopher had volunteered to play the corpse, on stage throughout but an undemanding role for someone without acting experience. Or so he thought. He had reckoned without Peter tripping over him and a feather wafting its way into his ear. His self-control was admirable. But the star of the event was the charlady, whose over-enthusiastic shaking of a feather duster had led to Christopher's plight.

In real life Carrie was an English teacher who had come out to Cambodia six months after our own arrival. She gave language classes to the teachers at an agricultural college set on the banks of the Mekong, about fifteen kilometres out of Phnom Penh. A little wooden hut had been built and blessed by monks just for her on the edge of the great river, the bedroom window designed by special request to give her a view of the moon rising over the water as she lay in bed. It was a beautiful place and she held several wonderful parties there, sending the college boat to fetch and carry us. But despite its romance it was an isolated and lonely life, and at weekends Carrie liked to ride her moped into town, often sleeping in our spare room. We got to know her well, but even so it was hard to recognise her as the middle-aged portly cleaner in head-scarf and overall who in my opinion stole the show. But they were all extraordinarily good, and their successors have continued to entertain Phnom Penh's foreign community to the pleasure of all.

Despite such distractions, a constant nagging at the back of our minds reminded us that we had very little time left. The three months' notice that we had been given due to Tim's temporary lapse of memory was nearly up. All through these uneasy weeks, we had been comforted by the support of the people round us. Tim was an important member of the community, and no one wanted to see him go. His counterpart at the hospital, Dr Chhun Long, was a frequent visitor at our house, turning up on his motor-bike to sit on our balcony and discuss problem cases with a much-respected teacher. There were constant comings and goings up and down our drive. Younger friends came to visit and to be entertained by stories of his past athletic adventures. Other expatriates brought their aches and pains and unborn babies. But even so, when he was finally summoned to the office and told that he could stay after all, we were surprised and touched by the reception given to the news of his acquittal. Of course we ourselves did not want to leave. To be forced to cut short our medical activities just as they were beginning to bear fruit would have been a great disappointment, and the reprieve came as a great relief.

So it was with light hearts that we took a few days off to attend the first ever VSO conference in Cambodia. Although it meant putting off the start of our new and exciting Saturday morning prostitute project for another week, I cannot honestly say that I was disappointed, for the meeting was to be held at our beloved Kampong Som, that haven of warm seas, white sands, and lethal (for me) crab for supper. None of us had any idea of what we were in for, imagining that this was really an excuse for a break. However in this we were sorely mistaken, for a complex and comprehensive programme of lectures, discussions and demonstrations had been arranged which kept us all busy from morning till night. But the hours between sunrise and the first lecture were blessedly free, time which our vet friend Caitlin and I were determined to fill with bird-watching. Caitlin was an ornithological convert. She had never shown any interest in birds before we met, but rapidly became a serious addict. In fact, I soon came to fear that I was to be instrumental in threatening the hitherto unshakable vet partnership, for her Welsh boy-friend, Bill, could see no attraction in it whatsoever. It bored him to death. (No doubt it still does, but fortunately for me, they are now safely married.)

Kampong Som was a wonderful place to look at birds. Just to be outside at dawn in such surroundings was treat enough, but to see our first hoopoe ever made it doubly memorable. There were brilliantly green blossom-headed parakeets screaming their way across the sky. There were drongoes, those marvellous little soot-black birds with tails so long that it looks as if a stick must have got caught up on the end. And best of all, drinking at the edge of a pond that we suddenly came upon in the forest, was a coucal. Caitlin condescendingly put me right on this one, for she had seen one before. The size of a crow, its glossy black plumage showed off to perfection a pair of brilliant chestnut wings, their rich colour glowing like ripe chestnuts in the early morning sunshine. They were all so beautiful.

We finished our conference with a carol concert round a fire of driftwood on the beach, to remind us that 25th December was only a few days away. A few of the group sang a song or two, and someone gave us a rendering of a poem. Mary, the flute teacher at the music college, piped a few tunes, and with me on the fiddle accompanied the carols. We played some Irish jigs. But it was a fairly muted affair for I think we were all tired, and early bed before an early start in the morning was the order of the day. A few lucky ones stayed on to celebrate Christmas on the beach, but for the rest of us it was time to get back to the dust and noise of the city. Our own Christmas was made very special by the presence with us of another daughter, who was able to taste for herself the delights of a festival spent once again eating turkey and plum pudding amongst the bougainvillea in Ben's garden.

And then it was back to work once more. Although none of our team really had much hope of success, we had laid careful plans for the first clinic on the dyke. If anyone should turn up, it was vital to give the right impression. In any case, I wanted very much to make it as efficient and comprehensive as possible. We had already been carrying out a simple examination for gonorrhoea using the microscope, but screening for syphilis is more complicated and involves a blood test. The Khmer head of the Pasteur Institute in Phnom Penh was one Madame Lye. She was an excellent pathologist, speaking good French and taking orders from no one but very co-operative if she felt like it. Perfectly happy to carry out the tests that I was asking for, she even lent me a dozen stoppered glass tubes, almost her entire supply, in which to put my blood samples. It was well over a year since anyone had investigated the prevalence of HIV among the prostitutes, clearly at very high risk, and neither Madame Ley nor I could see any reason why we should not include a simple spot test for this while we were about it. It was cheap, and she had the necessary reagents in kit form. Anonymity was of course of the utmost importance, particularly as there were rumours going round that girls who had previously tested positive to a 'disease', nature unspecified, had mysteriously disappeared, possibly for ever. In any case it was impossible to pull those carrying the virus out of circulation for they had no other means of survival. This initially came as a great shock to me as I am sure it does to others, but it was exactly this life and death dilemma that made the founding of the clinic and others like it of such extreme importance. The need for education was paramount.

I was very impressed with our Khmer team on that first Saturday morning on the dyke. They unloaded the usual equipment from the hospital car and settled themselves into the dark little bedroom that we had rented as if they had done so every day of their lives. I took no part in the arrangements. They persuaded the landlord to produce a table for the hall, and appointed the senior male medical assistant to take blood samples from any girls who might appear. The staff's knowledge of AIDS and HIV was minimal, but I insisted that they wore gloves. I had little fear that they would prick themselves, for they were very adept at injecting veins, but this was an obvious precaution. To my astonishment, a steady stream of girls began to arrive. Each proffered her arm for a blood test with nothing more than the usual teenage grimaces and giggles, and then came into the consulting-room clutching her blood sample in its unnamed numbered tube. There, she was given a full examination of her poor little tail-end, often inflamed and sore and frequently covered with venereal warts. This is no place to give in detail what we found, but how some of them could physically bear the agony that their occupation must have caused I shall never understand. The choice between that and a beating from their owners must have been very difficult to make. Some were only fourteen and had not even reached full puberty. These children liked to crowd in in twos and threes, filling the tiny room with its single bed to capacity, and making the heat almost unbearable. They chattered and giggled and looked up each others fannies through the speculum as if it was the most natural thing in the world, fooling about in a bizarre and heart-rending variant on a schoolgirl escapade.

All of us were finding this unfamiliar and deeply sad situation difficult to cope with, not least the soft-hearted Dr Vathiny. She talked for a particularly long time to one girl, tall and strong and older than the rest. It seemed that her mother was ill, and that she needed $50 (about £30) to pay the doctor's fee; she had come up from the country to earn the money just two days before and hated what she was having to do. Vathiny was clearly upset by her story, and on the spur of the moment we asked her if she would like to leave. Yes, she said, and with no more thought the decision was made to take her with us when we finished. At the end of the clinic she set to with a will, helping the staff to load the car. She clambered in with the rest of us, and when we had completed our morning's work came with me in the jeep. I had been told that Mother Teresa had set up one of her Houses on Achar Mean, the main street, and that the nuns who lived there took in waifs and strays. I was not at all sure of its exact locality nor indeed of anything else, and it was only then, as we drove along side by side, that I began seriously to wonder just what would happen if my information was wrong. What would Tim think if I turned up at home with an ex-prostitute in tow?

But my anxiety was needless, for the house was easy to find. It was a pleasant airy place, the smiling faces of its occupants proof of their welcome there. The Sister of Charity in her blue and white habit did not turn a hair at my request, and said that of course they would take her in. The only proviso was that she should be found a job as soon as possible.

But at least the immediate problem was solved, and I rode home in my fiery steed feeling gloriously self-righteous from my noble deed. It was not until bedtime came that the utter stupidity of my impetuous act struck home. No doubt this young woman had registered with one of the Madams, perhaps had even been given money by her in advance, and I had actually kidnapped her. What sort of start was this for a doctor hoping to build up the confidence of the people with whom she was supposed to be making some sort of rapport? There was little sleep for me that night, but once again my worries proved to be unnecessary. Calling on the nuns the next day, I was told that my protege had already run away, in their opinion probably back to the dyke to earn the money that she needed for her mother. This story seemed to get round with the speed of light, even to expatriates working a long way out of town, and people teased me about my kidnap for weeks to come. But hopefully no harm was done and yet another lesson learned.

So now my thoughts could turn back to the real purpose of the enterprise: to teach these young girls the dangers of their trade and how they could protect themselves and others. Though assessment of the present situation would be useful, HIV testing is a sensitive matter and I had not taken on the proposed programme lightly. It had been discussed with many people and given a great deal of thought. This was one of the biggest concentrations of prostitutes (two thousand of them were said to live along the dyke, where the whole community was dedicated to their existence) and it did seem that little was being achieved in AIDS control. At that time, this was a disorganised country with few official surveys and trials, and here was a unique opportunity to find out facts. Letters of intent to the minister of health and my immediate employer, the director of health of the municipality of Phnom Penh, produced no replies, and so Madame Ley and I went ahead.

My word. The whole place exploded in a storm of protest. Visiting delegates from UN health departments came to see me and tore me to shreds. I am sure they thought I was doing my own testing under the bed, with one of those home chemistry sets. At a regular monthly expatriate health services meeting somebody rose to her feet and announced in deeply shocked tones that Someone was actually testing for HIV. But the result of my instant 'confession' was surprisingly reassuring; Oh, as long as it's only you, they said. Looking back, it was the Americans who made all the fuss, and continued to take me to task for some time to come. Possibly they were jealous, and wished it had been their idea. It is presumptuous of me even to hope that my activities went a little way towards giving everyone a much-needed shake-up in the AIDS field. Certainly more thought is being given to it now, and official testing has been going on in a number of areas.

Although I still could not see that there was anything wrong with what we were doing, I am not at all sure that I would have been brave enough to carry on in the face of this storm of protest. But something else stopped our ill-fated programme dead in its tracks after just three weeks. For three consecutive Saturdays, a steady flow of girls had turned up at our makeshift clinic, happily accepting what had become our routine procedure of blood-testing followed by an examination and advice on AIDS and condoms. And then, the fourth Saturday, nothing. No one. What had happened? What had we done? Eventually we sent out our spy, a young and attractive male assistant nurse whom all the girls enjoyed and who unbeknown to me had been drumming up custom for the last few weeks.

When he came back, he had an interesting tale to tell. At the previous session, we had taken a sample from one of the girls for microscopic examination at the hospital. It had proved to be positive for gonorrhoea, and that morning I had sent for her to give her some antibiotics. This was enough to send them all bolting down their rabbit-holes, for evidently the rumour of enforced 'disappearance' following a positive diagnosis of anything was far from dead. We had learned our lesson the hard way, and clearly there could be no more testing that did not produce immediate results on the spot. The premises did not lend themselves to anything but the essentials, and blood tests had to stop. It was weeks before we had regained their confidence.

We had been attracted to this particular hotel by the big sign outside, painted with a blue cross. As this announced to the world that its owner possessed a medical qualification of some sort, we had hoped for his cooperation and had not been disappointed. The hallway in which we took our blood samples served several different purposes. Usually we would arrive in the morning to find the owner's wife squatting on the floor washing hotel sheets in her big bright plastic bowls, but on one occasion I was intrigued to find her husband there instead, busy boiling up syringes and needles in a saucepan. He explained that after every couple's one-night stand, in place of early morning tea they were offered a syringeful of antibiotic to ward off unwanted side effects.

In our sessions there we had to be strict with time. If we overshot our two hours, it meant that our landlord lost money on the next let. One day when we emerged from our room a few minutes late I was startled to find one of the municipal health officials whom I knew slightly sitting outside on the first of a row of chairs, a pretty young girl beside him. Without the least trace of embarrassment he rose politely to his feet and gave me an effusive greeting before disappearing into the same bedroom, partner in tow. We did not wait to see whether their allotted time-span was the same as our own.

It was not a comfortable way to spend a Saturday morning. The hot weather was approaching once again, and constant power cuts deprived us of the fan hanging uselessly above our heads. We had to pay extra for the generator, and in any case all it could handle was a single forty watt bulb. A large single bed took up most of the room, the narrow space beside it crammed to capacity with three members of staff and at least one patient, often several. The room's only redeeming feature was the view from the small window, straight out across the lake with its huge clumps of pink lotuses. But this, too, proved to be just a pretty face, as all too soon I came to realise. Happily most of what hides in the mud and filth beneath remains an enigma, but there is one inescapable fact; down there, in the marsh below that window, lie the naked needles from our first blood-letting session. I had thoughtlessly omitted to ask our staff how they were planning to dispose of syringes and needles; at least they had not pocketed them to use again.

Although there were no outright complaints, it gradually became obvious that morale amongst the staff was sinking. The novelty was wearing off and difficulties magnified proportionally. And then, one night, matters were taken out of our hands; a grenade exploded on the dyke. The Khmer Rouge had chosen three Vietnamese settlements in the city and had attacked under cover of darkness. Although we had some Cambodian prostitutes, many of our clients were from Vietnam, sent across the border by their families to earn their living in the age-old way. So the dyke was an excellent target for the guerrillas, hell bent still on expunging every trace of their hated enemies from Cambodian soil.

This was too much for the clinic staff, not surprisingly unprepared to risk life and limb. I was not too keen on it either, although the attack proved to be an isolated event. In any case, the following day we found our 'hotel' bolted and barred, for its medical-assistant owner was himself Vietnamese and had run for cover. And suddenly the street too was empty. There were no girls anywhere. Khmer and Vietnamese alike, they had disappeared. We heard that many of the latter had crossed the border and gone home.

So that was that, or so it seemed. It was very disappointing, not just because of the wasted effort but also of course that our main objective had died with the clinic. Although we were by no means the only group to be involved in the problem of AIDS, for there were others, notably the Cambodian National AIDS Authority headed by a very able Khmer doctor, we had been in an excellent position from which to take action. Now suddenly the focus of our efforts had been snatched away.

Chapter Twenty-Six

For some time I had been trying to interest the AIDS epidemiologist from the World Health Organisation in our prostitute clinic on the dyke, the expert who, right at the beginning of our two years, had invited me to join him in the cool detached World Health offices. I am not really surprised that he did not take us very seriously, for our contribution was small. But all of a sudden, just as it seemed that our efforts had come to naught, events took a mighty turn in our favour. A high official in WHO's Asia office in Manila in the Philippines decreed that war was to be declared on sexually transmitted diseases (STD) in his territory. Cambodia was to be the initial battleground, and the first skirmish fought in Phnom Penh. Where better to begin than in the biggest aggregate of prostitutes there, 'our' two thousand girls on the dyke?

And so it happened that VSO was approached by WHO and asked for co-operation in this effort. We were already there, working in that precise field and that exact geographical area, and although our attempts had been broken off this was for two reasons only. The first of these had been dangerous political activity, but already after only a few weeks life was beginning to return to the dyke. The second was financial. Our working conditions were almost untenable, and our budget for drugs, contraceptives and equipment nearly nonexistent. This could be overcome, and to counterbalance these things we did have some assets. Here was a partially trained Khmer team already in existence which had begun to make some headway, however slight, in a difficult and highly sensitive area. At least it was somewhere to start.

So what did WHO require of us? In essence, we were to do the work and they would pay the bill. They asked us to set up and run a full-time clinic for prostitutes, including both treatment of their diseases and education on how to prevent them. This education was to be extended to the brothel owners, in formal classes and in 'outreach', which simply meant casual visits and chats over the garden fence. But first we had to work out a budget, and only on acceptance of that could the project go ahead.

All of this seemed an enormously tall order. Although 'experts' would be flown in, each for just a few weeks, to help and advise on all aspects and to work out details, it was on the team already set up that the whole enterprise would hang or fall. WHO had caught us all at a low ebb. Even to work out a budget for premises, drugs, and all the rest, was a daunting prospect. By now, the hot weather was fully upon us, and with only a few months left before our final departure my energy was dwindling proportionately. There was the original clinic to think about, now humming with family planning activity, and I could not bear to say goodbye altogether to the hospital which was really where I was happiest. Also there was an unexpected difference of opinion amongst my superiors as to whether we should accept this offer, which I found hard to understand as surely it would mean a considerable boost to our organisation's image. After all, this could be just the first of a series of such clinics throughout Cambodia or even further afield, and to be instrumental in such an important pilot scheme would be very exciting.

Ultimately there could be only one answer, and that was yes. If we refused, WHO would have to start again from the beginning, which would waste too much time at this crucial juncture in the struggle against HIV.

So suddenly there was a startling change of scene as all sorts of important people came flying in and out at bewildering speed. It brought its embarrassing moments. A meeting was called at the health department offices, presided over by the Director of Municipal Health, Dr Abdul Koyaume, and with a number of WHO officials both from inside and outside the country in attendance. My Field Director and I sat near the bottom of the table, careful in this illustrious company to sit well below the salt. WHO had already visited the dispensary in which we had set up clinic number one, with its ample space and two shining new rooms restored for our use. This, they had decided, was the perfect place for the new enterprise. After all, it was less than half a mile from the brothel area, and had everything in its favour. They had got so excited about it that they had even drawn up a long document stating the precise changes that would be needed, right down to the number of chairs and where each one would stand. Although they knew of our difficulties in winkling the prostitutes out of their brothels and of the success of our

Saturday morning clinic, in their heart of hearts they felt that they could do better. Perhaps they could have done, in the end. But it would have taken a great deal of time, and there was no time to spare.

The meeting was opened by a handsome VIP from Manila who expounded with huge enthusiasm on this very subject, the suitability of the dispensary premises. I imagined this would be followed by a general discussion, into which I could gently dip my persuasive oar. But this was not to be. As soon as the beautiful Robert had finished, Dr Abdul Koyaume turned straight to me, handed me the document detailing the number of chairs and videos that were to attract custom like bees to a honey pot, and asked for my opinion. I somehow was once again taken completely by surprise. I supposed that I was simply there to be told what they wanted me to do. It was then or never, so I took a deep breath and told them exactly what I thought. In summary, the clinic would come to nothing if it were not sited right in the middle of the brothels. Of course I gave my reasons and told them of our various experiences which had led to these conclusions. They heard me out in silence, and to my astonishment gave in without a murmur. I think it was a great disappointment to them, for the dispensary could have been made into a real showplace once fully restored to its former glory. But that was not the point.

Most UN machinery moves slowly and ponderously, but for some reason never made clear this project was to be different. This time the World Health Organisation, although part of the United Nations, was in a hurry, and wanted us to act accordingly. This suited me in some ways as there was not much time left before our final departure. But there was a huge number of practical details to see to, and the pressure was relentless. A German specialist in sexual diseases, sent to set us on our way, was a formidable task master. Wolf was a lean, moustachioed young man of alarming energy who wielded carrot and whip to equal effect. He had considerable charm, sound knowledge and a great deal of experience, and certainly without his help I doubt whether we would ever have got the project off the ground. But there were drawbacks. He was only in the country for two months, was earning a large salary, and could afford to pull out all the stops. Admittedly unwell himself, he had absolutely no sympathy with weaknesses of the flesh, and I was within an ace of giving up on him when one day, as I struggled to give my report despite a high fever, he merely castigated me for what I had left undone.

Courtesy and gentleness were not his strongest points.

Another field in which WHO tried to help us was in the choice of premises. After that initial meeting, it had been unanimously decided to try to find a suitable building on the dyke. This was easier said than done, for it seemed that every one of the little wooden houses was either functioning as a brothel or in a supporting capacity. There were shops and stalls, hotels and even a laundry, but all these were fully occupied in their efforts to keep the area's main trade going. We had one hilarious day when several of the World Health bigwigs turned out in their limousines and wandered with us up and down the dyke, their drivers balancing the big cars on the precipitate edge of the road whilst doubtless enjoying this unfamiliar use of a working day. We trooped in solemn procession into various hopelessly unsuitable houses whose owners promised us the earth for a hyper inflated fee, banging our heads as we struggled up impossible staircases and getting our feet wet in the marshy ground as rotten planks leading to decrepit back doors gave way beneath us. Although that day we did not succeed in what we set out to do, at least it gave our paymasters some idea of the problems that were there to tackle.

But within a day or two, my own Khmer team had once again come

Going to work in a brothel for one

up trumps. Luckily for us, it was still only a few weeks since the grenade episode, when so many of the girls had run away. This meant that some of the bigger brothels were half empty, and we found one owner who was willing to accommodate her remaining employees elsewhere in return for a substantial rent. The building was solid; wooden, of course, but very spacious and in good repair. It would need internal alterations, the erection of a partition here and the putting in of a door there, but nothing too major. We needed rooms for consultation and treatment, for waiting and teaching. If in addition to all this we could even find space for some sort of social centre where the girls could get together for a little light relief, videos (strictly non educational) perhaps, or even table tennis, so much the better. This building held promise of all these things.

The ultimate view from the main room at the back was of course the lotus-filled lake, but several eye-catching structures came first. Obliquely to the left, built up on legs and leading by a plank bridge to the brothel next door was their lavatory. This was a platform about three foot square and open to the skies, with high screens sheltering it at the back and sides and a hole in the middle of the floor giving on to the marsh some ten feet below. But the front which faced our way was merely a hinged door only just high enough to screen the bottom of the squatting figure. It left almost nothing to the imagination. The girls knew they were overlooked, but they did not seem to care, and on occasion we even got a cheery wave. Then jutting out at right angles behind us was a very long narrow pier which led to a small hut. A constant stream of people walked backwards and forwards along it, and to start with I was baffled both by the obsessional cleanliness of the old lady who lived in the little house at the end and the number of visitors she had. She seemed to spend all her waking moments bent double over a bowl on the ground outside her front door, washing clothes. I must have been very slow on the uptake, for it was ages before I at last realised that she took in laundry, and that we clearly shared the same clients. Obliquely right and almost below us, built on a small peninsula of solid ground, was a tiny hovel in its own fenced piece of land. This was a minuscule brothel-for-one, (or two, in working hours,) an extension of the space that lay below us and that was contained within our four wooden legs. I was never invited to visit, but clearly the 'basement' had become the new quarters of the girls displaced by our takeover, the wide cracks between our floorboards making it impossible to ignore their presence and the trade they plied. Some of this we glimpsed on our first visit, but the only thing that mattered then was the obvious suitability of the premises, and the need to act quickly before our future landlady could change her mind.

We secured our brothel with money generously lent by our own WHO AIDS expert, who must have known that he might well never see it again. Then came the almost impossible task of listing and costing our needs. Building and plumbing estimates were one thing, (there was no water, so we had to install a complex system which pumped water up into an old oil drum on the roof and then allowed it to run down again into a beautiful modern basin through a beautiful modern tap) but to think up a sum for the purchase of drugs was quite another. We had no idea of numbers. Were we to cater for two thousand potential clients, or were we to expect just a handful? Which drugs should we use? The World Health team had given some guidance, but resistance to antibiotics was becoming a problem due to their ready availability to all and sundry, and hence their misuse. The injections of antibiotics by the hotel owner of our Saturday morning clinic was very far from being an isolated case, and many of the well-meaning Madams 'protected' their girls with the occasional capsule of this or that from time to time. Equipment was easier, for we had already begun to define our essential needs by trial and error.

Money came into every decision. There were for instance all sorts of extremely vexed questions concerning the faithful band of staff. I really could see no reason why these dedicated hardworking people should not be rewarded for their extra efforts, although they were still officially working for the municipal health department and receiving their princely salaries of anything up to $10 dollars a month. It seemed to me totally unjust. For some reason it was not official policy for the World Health Organisation in this particular context to pay even minimal wages, but I put up a huge battle if only to ensure that we did not lose our loyal helpers. The problem was eventually solved, and although the sums involved were small by Western standards it seemed that the staff were pleased. Then we had to think about transport for them. The dyke is well out of town, and they had to get there somehow. The provision of a small motorbike for each of them would be outside the budget, but could we perhaps buy them crash helmets in which to ride pillion on one of the numerous motorbike taxis or 'motos' as they were known? This would solve another difficulty at the same time; it would provide a disguise. Our lady workers were very worried that their friends might see them in this forbidden territory. It was not a place where 'nice' girls came, and they were truly concerned that if their presence was noted they would never receive an offer of marriage. But as crash helmets were virtually unknown it seemed in the end that they preferred discredit to ridicule, and anyway as they got used to the idea the problem seemed to evaporate. 'Travel allowance' was a useful way to add to their remuneration in any case.

And so it went on. After weeks of analysis and calculation, of arguments and consultations, of evenings spent poring over books, lists, and prices, we stuck a pin somewhere in the middle and came up with a budget of $26,000. This was well above the original ceiling set by WHO and more than three times the sum that had eventually been forthcoming for clinic number one, and seemed to me, at that time and in those circumstances, impossibly exorbitant. We could but wait and see if we had overreached ourselves.

In a surprisingly short time for an organisation so entangled in red tape, Manila signalled its acceptance, and we were to go ahead. Now. Immediately. The money, of course, would not be forthcoming for some time, but please would we get started. Our masters would brook no delay, and any such trifling details as running two clinics simultaneously half a mile apart with only one set of equipment were left to us to sort out. But overall we were delighted. Things were moving so fast that it was unlikely we would have long to wait for the promised funding, and after all we were well used by this time to carting our meagre supplies around the countryside. There were just a few more arrangements to be made and then we could begin.

There was something deeply significant about the ceremony of the sign. Exactly what were we going to put on it? What was the clinic to be called? Who precisely was it for? Any reference to sex, hidden or overt, would be totally out of the question in a culture where the subject was unmentionable in public, though only too acceptable in private amongst men young and old. The most important point to stress was that this was a Cambodian effort, most definitely under the auspices of the department of health of the municipality of Phnom Penh, but the logos of WHO and VSO must not be left out. Simple solutions are usually the best. In our minds, since its conception it had been the dyke clinic. Despite

Clinic staff beneath the all-important sign

the word's other connotation, probably not in the Khmer vocabulary anyway under that name, everyone knew what this meant, so we decided unanimously to let it rest. We nearly came unstuck, though, by putting in the word 'Community'. This was to be the Dyke Community Clinic, for we did not want to exclude the everyday illnesses of the children who lived there, nor of my washerwoman and her like. This was to have unexpected and unfortunate results and might well have spelled disaster in such a new enterprise but for the watchfulness of Monsieur Som An, our redoubtable medical assistant.

But back to the sign. At last we were agreed upon every inch and every letter of it, not to mention its exact site and the hooks it was to hang upon. And at last, as our design was skillfully converted into pale blue and white reality by a sign-writer in his primitive roadside cabin, just so was our project changed from concept into substance. The clinic came into being.

Chapter Twenty-Seven

Now the preparations were over and we could open our doors on to the busy, noisy road. Quietly and cautiously in ones and twos the local girls started to creep in, and then and only then did we begin to realise the full pathos of their situation. We had designed a simple verbal survey, and as each one arrived so Vathiny asked her a series of questions. The answers were extraordinary, and gradually we began to get some idea of the tragedies that lay behind them. Slowly we built up a composite picture, and as time went on and the girls felt easier in our company we were able to fill in the details of these young lives that had gone so badly wrong.

It seemed there were several categories. A very few were there because they wanted to be; they earned good money and were satisfied with their way of life. But to the question 'would you like to stop if you could?' the vast majority answered 'yes'. A number of the youngest ones, perhaps fourteen years old, had been sold into the trade by their mothers, for virgins were greatly prized and worth a great deal of money. Often these were Vietnamese, but many Cambodians too had been sold by mothers, husbands, even fiances; the tragic tales were unending. They were virtual prisoners until they had served enough clients to pay off their debt, usually over a period of about two years. But as the end of their slavery came near and hope began to dawn, the brothel owners got up to all sorts of tricks to keep these naive young people in their clutches. One girl might, for instance, be involved in some trumped-up infringement of the law. Her owner would pretend she had to pay off the police to keep the poor child out of trouble, and so would enslave her for even longer to work off the 'debt'. The police were only too happy to oblige in return for services rendered. Another would be sent to the doctor for a minor complaint, the Madam kindly promising to pay the bill if her protege would stay on just a little longer. But this apparent generosity was simply a cover for monstrous greed. The girl would be forced to continue working long after the debt had been cleared.

Those who were married with children fell into a slightly different category. The degrading service they were forced to give was of course exactly the same; it was merely the reasons behind it that were different. Almost always, this was the only way open to them to keep their family from starvation. I remember in particular one older woman, a farmer out in the country who came up to the dyke at weekends. Her husband had died and left her with four young children; the small patch of land she owned would not support the five of them, and what else was she to do? This really does seem to me the ultimate self-sacrifice.

Pregnancy was of course a constant worry. When I arrived, and I fear with little change by the time I left, the use of condoms was rare. Contraception was at that time almost unheard of, and in any case other medical problems made the choice of method difficult. Abortions were common. A young lady who lived and worked in our 'basement' became a frequent visitor and I got to know her well. One day she poured her heart out to Vathiny and me, and this is the story she told.

Although most of the UN visitors took themselves off to grander establishments than the dyke could offer, for they had more money to spend than they knew what to do with, a few of the brothels' clients did come from among their ranks. One of these, a handsome German soldier, had become very friendly with this particular young lady, and she showed me photographs of the two of them out and about together, arms around each other's waists like any young couple. She had really fallen in love with him, and when his regiment was finally moved away she found that she was to be the mother of his child. She never heard from him again. She was desperate to keep the baby as a part of him, but unable to afford the time off that the pregnancy and birth would entail was forced into getting rid of it. Plagued by headaches, she still lay awake at night thinking about him and carried his photograph with her everywhere. I remember we had a reporter with us that day, a young woman from the States getting copy for her paper. This particular story and others that she heard while she was there shocked her deeply; they evidently made a lasting impression, for she took the trouble to send us prints of her excellent photographs when she got back to New York.

So gradually we built up a routine in our new surroundings. Vathiny took each girl through the questionnaire, asked a little about her history, and told her of the dangers of unprotected sex. We were alarmed though not so very surprised to find that initially scarcely a single one of our patients had even heard of AIDS. Of course this involved a discussion on the use of condoms, and although it seemed that a few of the brothel owners did have reasonably enlightened views, most of them certainly did not. We made what seemed the obvious suggestion that if her client failed to oblige, the girl should withdraw her services. This was met with floods of tears, the reason quickly becoming only too clear. If her partner was sent away unsatisfied, she said, her owner would beat her. So the alternative evils with which she was faced were an immediate thrashing or the possibility of death in ten years time from a vague and unknown illness. If I was fourteen years old and far from home, I know which I would choose.

After the theory came the practical. Often there was no electricity, and for intimate examinations I would be forced to don the head-torch I had brought from England. It was impossible to buy the right batteries and the necessary rewiring, sprouting like entwined blue and yellow antennae from the shining proboscis, no doubt added greatly to the effect. I must have frightened the poor girls to death. Next came any tests that our microscope could interpret on the spot, followed by decisions on treatment and dispatch to our pharmacist sitting behind her rows of bottles. Finally the patient was presented with the totally arbitrary number of four condoms, all we could initially afford, and sent upon her way.

No money changed hands in our dealings with either the prostitutes or the general population on the dyke, and this is where we nearly came unstuck. Slowly we became aware that there seemed to be a change in the nature of the traffic passing our open front door. Although the narrow road was always clogged with motorbikes roaring up and down, aspiring customers choosing their prey from either the driving seat or the pillion of moto-taxis, at the beginning cars were rare. But though the red jeep remained unique, the numbers of other four-wheeled vehicles were definitely on the increase. None of us working there was on social terms with any of the local residents, and it took us some time to realise that the proud proclamation on our sign of a Community Clinic had been taken in its widest possible sense. We discovered that strangers were registering with us. Word had evidently got round that here was a group of idiots providing free medical treatment, no questions asked. People were coming for miles, well-heeled folk in fashionable white Toyotas, and taking us too for a ride. I never did find out how he handled it, but as soon as it was discovered, Som An, our medical assistant, had the problem completely under control. He was a forceful character and though I know that he had a gun at home for he had threatened to use it more than once I do not think he resorted on this occasion to anything more alarming than rigorous entry requirements.

The hierarchy on the dyke was an interesting one. As we had found, most of the girls wanted nothing more than to get through this period of their life as quickly as possible and move on to better things. But there were a few whose one ambition was to rise through the ranks and become that most respectable of dyke-dwellers, a brothel owner. There seemed to be two ways of reaching these lofty heights. The first was to save up enough money to put up your own plate, but the second and far more possible route was to marry your boss, given of course that he was of the male gender. This certainly happened once while I was there, and my attention was drawn to the happy event by rather unusual means. While carrying out an internal examination on the bride I came upon something not normally associated with the female anatomy, a common or garden elastic band. Baffled, I held it up for inspection and explanation. It seems that her new husband, more well-informed than most and knowing full well the dangers of his wife's previous career, was determined to protect his own health. What better than an elastic band for keeping on a condom that was not a perfect fit? Certainly an unusual variant on the theme of wearing belt and braces, and I never did hear whether it was both of the restraints or only the secondary one that let the bridegroom down.

A condition imposed by WHO in the setting up of the clinic was that we undertake the education of the brothel owners in matters of health. Wednesday afternoons from two to four p.m. had been set aside for this purpose; but how could we persuade them to come? As always, it was a member of our Cambodian team who found the answer. Som An's cousin was the district chief and was persuaded to cycle round his parishioners and instruct them to attend. Thus it was that on Wednesday, 5th July 1993 we held our first educational session for the brothel owners of Tuol Kork. Even in our later years, any of us can be faced with a situation so ludicrously new that it is impossible to think about it in advance. This was most definitely one of them; nothing I had ever done before seemed even remotely relevant to these particular circumstances. The plan was that I would speak, and that the faithful Vathiny would then translate my words of wisdom into Khmer. As I left the house that morning, remembering that I had no paper on which to draw diagrams I had seized off its hook on the wall a calendar that my brother had sent us for Christmas. Carefully chosen to assuage homesickness, its twelve pictures of English wild flowers were about to be put to a use as far from the unfortunate artist's intentions as could be. Certainly it came in extremely useful. Contrary to all our expectations, about thirty men and women, not to mention several children, turned up. They did not look like ogres, and it did not seem too difficult to embark on my prepared speech, such as it was. But one phrase nearly stuck in my gullet; it seemed to me important to feign interest in the business in hand, making out that we wanted to keep 'their' girls healthy in order that they could bring in more money. It was, I knew, absolutely no good appealing to our audience's better natures and asking them to set their captives free. This was a business meeting with hard-headed business executives, and our immediate purpose was to gain their co-operation, not to antagonise them. The whole thing was an enormous strain, and my hand shook as, with a big black marker pen, I drew on the back of paintings of primroses and violets wobbly pictures which left nothing whatever to the imagination. When we finally departed, I left the calendar hanging on the brothel clinic wall, pretty side out. I wonder whether it is still there, wobbles and all?

That first session finished with the inevitable and vital discussion about condoms. A wrinkled old man in the back row became very vociferous, entering into a long discussion with Vathiny which I was as usual unable to follow. It turned out that he had a street stall just along the way which amongst other things stocked these useful items. He explained to us that he found it necessary to keep a number of different kinds in stock, as his customers' tastes differed. The one that he was proudest to display was very expensive, he said, and could only be afforded by the rich. The wearing of it was supposed to improve the owner's performance. When he passed me the packet and I opened it, I was horrified to find that in the tip of it were incorporated three hard little knobs looking just like seed pearls. I shudder to think of the agony it must cause. But I had to smile and thank him, though it took me a minute to realise that he was not going to leave until I had paid for it. After all, it was no good to anyone else now I had opened it, was it? The session finished with the formal

Vathiny and a recalcitrant brothel owner

distribution of several free condoms, sealed in their packets, to each of our students. There were smiles all round, and our little party left feeling that, given the circumstances, perhaps we had not done too badly.

We continued with our weekly meetings, attempting to attract a different group of listeners each time. It soon became apparent that Vathiny was much better at the lessons than I was, and once more I became a figurehead, sitting in the front corner and admiring her good natured verbal battles with recalcitrant customers. There were never any really awkward moments, and I think that gradually we began to have a little effect. It was no good trying to be too ambitious. Even if we could persuade just one owner to see the light, it would be worth the effort. One man did say that he had found the talks so useful that he had attended all of them and that now eighty per cent of his girls' clients were using condoms. Perhaps he just wanted to be teacher's pet, for teacher was very attractive, but he promised Vathiny the last time we saw him that from now on any customers who refused to use protection would be turned away.

Prostitution is a very emotive subject, and our efforts on the dyke quickly began to attract more and more attention. Representatives of other non-government organisations came to see what we were doing, and journalists from both East and West started to take an interest. A long article appeared in the Bangkok Times, and, more importantly, local Khmer newspapers started to comment on our activities. Our press reports were neither always accurate nor always totally favourable, but at least we were drawing attention to the problem of HIV.

Few people are prepared to back a non-starter, but once a project is up and running the cash begins to flow. This one was no exception. Save the Children were particularly generous, and we had a happy little ceremony at which we were presented with money to buy a television and video for the entertainment and instruction of our patients, with enough left over for minor running expenses outside our original budget. The World Health grant materialised just two weeks before I left for home. This presented no problem, for my successor from England had already arrived, and I knew that she would spend the money wisely. What a marvellous girl she proved to be. Under her guidance, the clinic thrived mightily over the next couple of years despite all sorts of difficulties which would have felled a lesser mortal. She did not have half the fun that I had in setting it all up, and not only did an excellent job but won all hearts as well. Largely through her efforts I have been able to feel that my own were not wasted, but far more importantly many CSWs have been given the help that they so badly need. And who, the reader may well ask, are CSWs? The letters stand for Commercial Sex Workers, a title given to the prostitutes by that section of the international community involved in women's rights. Although, along with such catch-phrases as Gender Awareness, there was considerable sardonic raising of the eyebrows at the time it was introduced, I suppose that it is a less contemptuous label. At any rate, the word 'prostitute' is no longer part of the local vocabulary.

Chapter Twenty-Eight

Now it is very nearly time to go. But before we draw a line across the page, two groups of people deserve more space than they have so far been given. The first is the German contingent of the UN that ran the Field Hospital on the road to Pochentong airport, the hospital to which Tim nearly went when he lost his memory. Although there primarily to look after their own troops, they immediately put themselves at the disposal of anyone and everyone in need, of whatever nationality. The doctors were not from the regular army, but were skilled specialists in all areas who had offered their services for a limited period, usually six months. One of these was a chest surgeon, who earned the undying gratitude of a simple Cambodian lady whom I came to know all too well.

One day, Panita was brought into the 'Reanimation' ward at the hospital by a worried husband carrying in his arms their two-year-old daughter. She was one of the prettiest children I have ever seen, her head a mass of dark curls and her little face permanently wreathed in smiles. I never once heard her cry in all the three months that she was with us. But despite her long stay, it was not she that was ill, but her poor mother, clearly in serious trouble with a high temperature and rapid laboured breathing. Our X-rays despite their inadequacies showed that one of her lungs had collapsed, its shrunken outline surrounded by fluid. When Dr Chuoy attempted to draw this off with a syringe and needle, he found not the watery straw-coloured liquid that can often be drained away to allow the lung to expand again, but thick pus. This is a life threatening complaint called an empyema, dangerous and difficult to treat at the best of times but in conditions like these next to impossible. Though we struggled within our limited resources for a day or two, it was clear that she was getting worse and I went to the UN hospital to see if they could give us any advice. What followed was I suppose made all the more surprising and wonderful by its contrast to the constant background of pessimistic resignation that we had become so accustomed to.

The German chest surgeon had only arrived two days before. Despite the gravity of Panita's condition and his private conviction that she would not survive, he set to work with a will, employing all the sophisticated X-rays and machinery that the unit had imported into their dilapidated premises. It proved impossible to admit her for he had no spare beds, and so the poor dying girl was subjected to constant ferrying to and fro for treatment. It was not surprising that she made little progress, and finally the surgeon put a call through to Germany on his field telephone, seeking the advice of no lesser person than the president of the German Chest Surgeons Association. I do not know what this eminent gentleman said, but from then on, slowly and against all odds she began to recover. After a while, her husband became a familiar sight in our ward as, syringe in hand, he sat at her bedside washing out the infected chest cavity several times a day, first injecting a disinfectant fluid and then withdrawing it again. I do not think the little girl ever took a turn, though I would not have put it past them. Panita made a full recovery, gained more weight than was good for her, and was discharged cured before I went home.

It was not just Panita and her family whose lives were transformed by the Germans. As we got to know them better, we were bold enough to ask for more and more. We knew that our own treatment in the poor little municipal hospital could be vastly more effective if only we had the right drugs. The UN had converted a huge shed into a pharmacy, putting up shelves and loading them with enough drugs and dressings to turn us green with envy. I asked one day if they could spare us a few crumbs. 'Make a list', they said, 'of what you want and we will see what we can do'. Chuoy was our man in charge, and when I passed on this suggestion he set to work with a will, covering a piece of cheap A4 paper with an almost endless catalogue of requirements. Together we drove the jeep back along the airport road, turning right through the guarded gates of the UN compound where we were carefully scrutinised by a blue-bereted soldier, rifle at the ready. My white face allowed us access without question, and I felt sad that my medical colleague would need a pass signed by a senior camp doctor to allow him through the barrier should he ever come here without me. We handed our embarrassingly long request to the army pharmacist, who asked for time to gather up what he could spare. 'Come back tomorrow', he said; and when we did, there were so many boxes waiting for us that there was scarcely room for them in the jeep. That was just the first of many occasions on which Dr

Chuoy and I drove along the familiar road, each time bringing in much needed supplies. He used to store the most precious drugs under the 'on call' bed in his office for want of a better place in which to guard our booty against theft.

The other people who benefited greatly from the UN's generosity were the sex-workers on the dyke. It was becoming increasingly clear that gonorrhoea was rife amongst them. This in itself is an infection which can cause a great deal of distress, but there is another problem associated with it which perhaps is not generally known. Intact and healthy membranes to some extent put up a barrier to the passage of HIV, but if these become inflamed and sore, this barrier becomes correspondingly less efficient and the possibility of HIV infection greater. So for several reasons it was vital to treat the girls' gonorrhoea, but it seemed that the more we tried the more we failed. It soon became apparent that what we had feared had already taken place, and resistance to all but the most sophisticated antibiotics was already widespread.

With the help of the World Health experts and a local Khmer doctor who had been working in this field for some time, it was decided that the only effective treatment would be a drug called spectinomycin, very expensive and far beyond the means of a struggling third world clinic. We had bought a small quantity of ampoules, but with injections priced at ten dollars each even our grant would not go far towards the necessary supplies. There in the UN pharmacy was carton upon carton of spectinomycin. It was almost time for the UN to go home. They had been in the country for the specified year, and were leaving at about the same time as we were. We had only to ask, and the young pharmacist's assistant, clad in full battledress, was once again hard at work loading the jeep to the gunwales, this time with the antibiotic that would, to its future recipients, be more than worth its weight in gold. But until the day comes when reinfection can be prevented by the routine use of condoms, the effect of even this wonder drug will be temporary. Funding for a continuous supply of expensive antibiotics will remain a constant drain on limited resources.

It was really through the UN hospital that I forged another important link, this time with Mother Teresa's Sisters of Charity. Admittedly I had made their acquaintance when I deposited my kidnapped prostitute on them, but that had been a very brief encounter. Each morning, the army hospital held an outpatient clinic, open to all. I used sometimes to take a patient there, and so did one or other of the nuns. We would line up together, waiting for the receiving soldier to take our name and business. Sometimes it was a very long wait, for while the doctors, when we eventually got to them, were courtesy itself, the same did not always apply to the ordinary soldiers who worked with them. One day, a young bespectacled Sister came up to me in the queue to ask a favour, she said. Would I be prepared to take a clinic at their house occasionally? When would it be, I asked. My heart sank when she said 'on Saturday afternoons'. It was only to be once a month, but with every Saturday morning already firmly booked for the sex-workers at the Hotel Clinic on the dyke I could see our precious weekends shrivelling to nothing before my very eyes. She explained that their usual doctor had left the country and that it was important for her replacement to be a woman because otherwise the Khmer ladies would keep their intimate problems to themselves. She looked at me soulfully with her great big brown eyes. Before I knew what I was doing, I said yes. And so it was that every fourth Saturday came to be divided equally between the two groups, the nuns and the prostitutes. Diversity is all.

As happens so often, things that promise badly turn out to be the best, and though it was very hard work it was an experience I would not have missed. Every single day of the week, this same young nun, a nurse from the Philippines, held a 'surgery' for about ninety of the most poverty-stricken Cambodians, families who were too poor to consult doctors from amongst their own people. They would queue halfway down the street and file in one by one to see her. It was only on Saturdays that she was given medical help by one or other of the expatriate doctors and by young Khmer students who had been trained in the Thai border camps in the recognition and management of tuberculosis. I was officially there to see only the gynaecological cases, but it was not long before I was faced with every sort of medical problem, and finally found myself to be the only doctor there at all. Usually I would see about fifty patients for approximately two minutes each, any conversation limited as much by my appallingly bad Khmer as by the time constraint. Not surprisingly, language difficulties led to a number of misunderstandings, as I was soon to discover. The Cambodian people derive great enjoyment from their language, and find inversion of words and sentences a highly entertaining pastime. One of the first phrases we were taught was 'sok se bye?', a familiar greeting roughly equivalent to 'how are you?' and I had long since learnt that by turning it round to 'sye se bok' I was always rewarded with a laugh. One afternoon when we were not too busy I decided to try it on an old man who hobbled in for a consultation. He laughed so much that I think we both forgot what he had come for. His response seemed out of all proportion to what was after all only a literary joke, and it dawned on me that perhaps it actually meant something. Later I found that I had conveyed to this octogenarian my pious hope that he would become the father of many children. Once again, I had tried to be just too clever by half.

In the specified two minute consultation time, I listened to the complaint, made an examination, reached a diagnosis, and wrote the treatment on a tiny slip of paper. On his way out, the patient would hand his prescription to the jolly little plump nun sitting in the doorway with her bottles of tablets and tubes of ointment. It was against the rules to prescribe more than three days' treatment to anyone for fear that any surplus would be sold. Sometimes the patient was too ill to stand and would be carried in by one of the family. Once I was asked to go into the room next door to look at a lady who was lying on the floor because she felt faint every time she stood up. Nobody could understand why until I pulled back her clothes and found her soaked in blood. It was obvious that she had lost a great deal, and we had to whisk her into Tim's hospital nearby where fortunately she survived. Some of the patients came in by a bus which drove round neighbouring villages to pick them up. This only happened on Saturdays, so there was no possible way they could be seen again until the following week, and most of even the most severely ill refused to stay behind for hospital treatment. It follows that even the malarias and heart failures had to be sent home unsupervised, and often we remained ignorant of the final outcome. Some came back next week; others did not.

Although I was supposed to stick to two-minute appointments, of course I went over the allotted time and it was often dark before the last few stragglers came in. I do not remember that we ever had electricity there, and out would come the candles. There were only two of them, and it was a most peculiar brand of medicine that one way and another was practiced at that clinic. But the atmosphere was wonderful. My Philippines companion was never out of temper, and had a glorious sense of humour. Her Khmer, though better than mine, left a lot to be desired, and we got ourselves into some fine old language pickles. It was

My nursing companion (in spectacles) with a colleague and patients outside
Mother Teresa's House

always hot, even clad as I was in a thin cotton blouse and skirt, and I
asked my colleague what it was like to be incarcerated from top to toe in
heavy swathes of thick material with only her face exposed. She cheerfully
explained that within minutes of dressing she would be soaked with
sweat, and she needed to change her habit at least once during the day.
I enquired then about the laundry; surely they had a local girl splashing
away in the background? Oh no, came her airy reply. I do all my washing
myself. The clinic can have done little good medically. But to the poor
of Phnom Penh, the obvious love and devotion that radiated from my
saintly and hilarious companion must have meant a great deal.

All of a sudden there was only one Saturday left, and it was time to start
saying our goodbyes. There was no chance of slipping away unnoticed.
Last clinic at the dispensary, last sessions with the sex-workers on the
dyke and with the Sisters of Charity, last round on each of 'my' wards at
the hospital, last chamber music evening, all had to be got through. Our
feelings were very mixed. There is no doubt that Tim and I were both
tired and more than ready to go home. But we knew too that we might
well never see some of our Cambodian friends and colleagues again, and
the memory of the preparations for imminent departure as we struggled
through nightmares of packing and farewells is mercifully blurred by the

sheer congestion of events and emotions compressed into those last few days.

Three occasions nevertheless do stand out, and the first of these was the farewell party held in my honour at the municipality hospital where I had worked throughout the whole of the two years, though for fewer and fewer hours each week as the clinic work increased. Long white-clothed tables were erected in the Directors office, that same room where I had first met the assembled doctors two years previously. On that occasion, faced with a sea of brown unsmiling faces and fearful of their unfamiliarity, I had been a complete outsider. Now, as the hospital staff filled the big room, it was difficult to remember that I had not known them all my life. We drank the inevitable cans of beer, Coca Cola and 7-Up and ate milk-apples and bananas, and then the speeches began. Dr Veng Thai, the hospital director, delivered a long harangue in Khmer. It was fortunate for me that, because of his language skills, it was Dr Chuoy who had been chosen to act as interpreter, for this made it seem as if it was he who was bidding me a personal goodbye. Mutual respect and liking, together with the sharing of so many clinical dramas, had bridged the gulf of age and race between Chuoy and myself and we had become good friends. That speech encapsulated for me the meaning of my two year transplantation to another world in a way that nothing else had done. Suddenly I saw clearly just what a privilege it had been. Both professionally and personally, not only had I been made overwhelmingly welcome, warts and all, but I had been allowed to share in the problems of this troubled country's people in a way that is quite out of the tourist's reach. That was the beginning of realisation that this had been an experience of an unanticipated depth, something that would stay with me for ever.

My attempt to answer in their own language failed miserably, so once again Chuoy had to officiate. And after that came the presents. It was just like my birthday but ten times better. I was led to the front, and one after another up came my lovely colleagues, each bearing a gift and each with a little prepared speech of thanks. Chuoy, unable to contain his excitement, had already shown me in the ward office a few days previously what he had bought. He had taken out of its woven straw case a beautiful little Cambodian silver box before carefully locking it up again in his cupboard; it lives now on my dressing table at home. Vathiny's gift was a two-headed silver bird. She pointed to each head in turn; you and me, she said, with her infectious giggle. And so it went on. When the dancing started, surely at last it was time to go home. But no; I was not allowed to get off so easily, and had to cavort round the room in the arms of not just the staff but of their friends and relations as well. It was an evening to remember.

The farewell party that we gave at home was equally memorable in a different way. We had invited eighty people, hopeful that the rainy season which had officially only just ended would abide by the rules, for our little wooden house would have been hard pressed to accommodate so many. The first Cambodian women's NGO by the name of Khemara had recently been set up to promote women's industries, and we had asked some of its members to do our catering for us. Just half an hour before the party was due to begin, in swept an army of ladies who took over the kitchen, erected in the garden tables covered with blue and white checked cloths, and in the twinkling of an eye had piled them high

Traditional Khmer musicians bidding us farewell

with mouthwatering delicacies. Dozens of cans of beer and soft drinks had been packed in ice-filled dustbins, our landlord had lent us strings of coloured lights which he had draped along the front of the house, and for once in our lives we found we were ready too early, left with nothing to do but await our guests. The first to arrive exactly on time was Ben. 'Where would you like the band to sit?' he asked. We laughed at the pleasantry, for we certainly had not organised any such thing. But he persisted in the question, and when we too persisted in our answer he told us to look down the drive towards our gate. Sure enough, there, just coming in, was a stream of Cambodian musicians each carrying a different traditional instrument. Then he explained. Our expatriate friends led by Mary the flautist who taught at the College had passed round the hat, and provided us with one of the few remaining traditional Khmer bands in the country to entertain our guests throughout the evening. And so they did, by the light of a full moon in a cloudless star-filled sky. They were, without any doubt whatsoever, the making of that farewell gathering of brown and white faces in our little garden, amongst the bougainvillea and banana trees.

The third event that remains riveted in my mind was not such a happy one. After some difficulty, we had agreed on the sale of the now notorious jeep to a poverty stricken NGO who could afford nothing better. The handover was to be on the very morning of our departure, but when the time came to leave for the airport nobody had arrived to pick it up and pay for it. Part of the proceeds was vital for a holiday we had planned in a Thai jungle resort on the way home, a necessary halfway house before facing the Western world again, and major panic set in. It took a crazy drive right across Phnom Penh to the car's new home to sort out what was simply a misunderstanding as to where the exchange should take place and finally all was well. The problem was solved in the nick of time, and we were ready to face the final sad hurdle of a farewell committee assembled at the airport to see us off.

There were nine people to wave us away, five Cambodians and an Irishwoman, a Scotsman, a Welshman and an Englishman. Someone had brought a bottle of Russian champagne and plastic cups to drink it from, and we whiled away the period of waiting sipping at the warm bubbles. At first it seemed that Vathiny was going to be conspicuous by her absence and this worried me, for we had had our first ever serious falling-out just a few days previously, blemishing an otherwise unsullied partnership. However, suddenly there she was, clutching a stiff and formal presentation bunch of flowers, and our little group was complete. How strange that at the sad parting from our real family two years before we did not even know of the existence of the people round us now, and here we were faced with a separation that came perilously near to giving the same pain. Then suddenly the time was up, and we were being pushed through the little departure gate. It was all over.

Epilogue

One

People

Cambodia compels you, clutches at you, caresses you, drives you mad. It makes you love it, hate it, long to be there, long to leave. It makes you sweat and scratch, soar with the sunrise, sink in the slime. It is beautiful beyond belief and ugly beyond hope, and yet not so, for it will not let you go.

In September 1993, our two-year enterprise came to an end and we made our slow way home. Aware that inevitably demands would be made on us as soon as we got back, we took a short time out at Tamen Negara, a safari camp in Malaysia. To us, it was luxury; all things are relative. We imagined then that, for better or worse, this chapter of our life was over. How wrong we were.

For a while, events took their expected path. Four years went by, recovering, satisfying the curiosity of others with endless talks each more nerve-racking than the last, and self-debriefing in the writing of this book. And then, in the autumn of 1997, a sudden phone call from Cambodia brought an unexpected invitation. Please would Tim come back, next week, for three months to help his colleagues write a manual for the treatment of obstetric emergencies, a practical guide to be used in hospitals throughout the country. And 'do not at all forget to bring Liz'.

In the West very little happens spontaneously; on the whole we make plans in advance. So seven days was, we felt, somewhat unreasonably short notice. But appointments were cancelled and diaries changed and within a month to our own surprise we were on our way. We went in trepidation, because we did not know what we would find. News had been sparse; Cambodians are not letter writers for language is a much greater barrier when it has to be written down. But once again we need have had no fears. Nothing could have prepared us for the warmth of our welcome, from Cambodians and expatriates alike. A surprising number of old friends and acquaintances were still there, and continued to materialise throughout the whole of our stay.

My meeting with my colleague, Dr Vathiny, was dramatic to say the least. In the years after our departure contact had not been close and I had failed to warn her of our return. Conspiring colleagues had decided to give her a surprise and under some pretext had asked her to come to the office where I was working. And so it happened that one morning when I was sitting at my desk two brown arms were suddenly thrown round me from behind and an astonished 'my God!' trumpeted in my right ear. I was grateful for the hug; the exclamation alone could have been open to misinterpretation.

Though faithful to our clinic on the dyke for some time after I had come home, Vathiny had eventually been tempted away to work with a big UN family planning organisation. This in turn led on to greater things and my tireless colleague became head of a large organisation specialising in sexual health. She started working particularly amongst teenagers, treating more than 400,000 people a year and reaching out far and wide into the community. Hundreds of thousands of youngsters benefited, learning the hitherto taboo facts of life and how to deal with them.

Gone were the days when together we scratched for pennies. By 2001, with a string of efficient purpose-built clinics across the country, she had annual funding of over a million US dollars from USAID, and a staff of a hundred and twenty doctors, midwives, pharmacists and lab technicians. She had great plans for the future and I was and still am inordinately proud of her. This of course is an impertinence on my part. She is extraordinarily able and was destined to succeed.

But I am moving too far ahead. On this our first return visit in 1997, Vathiny and I went together to see the clinic on the dyke where it had all begun. Amazingly, it was still there; that was the first surprise. Even more remarkable was the fact that it was still in the hands of almost exactly the same team as we had appointed at the beginning. The staff had no idea we were coming, and again the effect was electric. We found the clinic statistics neatly chalked up on the blackboard; two hundred and sixteen new sex-worker patients had been treated the previous month. Once again, I felt very proud of them.

On that occasion the building looked much the same as when I had last seen it, and there was little to mark the passage of time. But nothing lasts for ever. Seven years later on our second return visit, Vathiny and I drove once more down the road along the top of the dyke. This time almost everything was different except, I'm glad to say, for my friend and colleague. Perhaps she was a little plumper and a little older but the infectious sparkle was still there and we took huge pleasure in each other's company. But nothing else was even recognisable. Vathiny's new status was reflected in her car, a limousine on a par with those that, right at the start, had carried their cargo of World Health Organisation dignitaries, come to inspect the initial possibilities of setting up a clinic here in the middle of the Red Light district.

Instead of the bumps and pot-holes that the red jeep and I had got to know so well, the road we drove along was smooth and surfaced, so that I did not even know where we were and had to ask my companion. And although we went up and down it several times, we could not find our clinic. It had evidently been pulled down. Along with most of the brothels and their occupants it had totally vanished.

Not that this means the end of prostitution in Cambodia. There is another group of sex-workers who continue their sisters' work but under cover. Amongst them are the orange sellers, young ladies innocently squatting by their plastic bags of fruit in the parks and open spaces, peddling their wares to the young men strolling by. Sadly it is not just the flesh of the orange that is for sale. These penniless youngsters have more than their fair share of sexually transmitted diseases, increasing the risk of passing on HIV for the two go hand in hand. A more elite class of workers are the beer promotion girls, in very small skirts and very large sashes inscribed with the name of a well-known brew. They move between the tables in the more glitzy restaurants advertising their wares, the hems of their skirts, such as they are, dangling at the eye-level of their seated customers. The invitation is obvious, and the higher prices demanded for a cleaner encounter can well be afforded by the affluent customers only too ready to avail themselves of the offer.

But the vital achievement does seem to be that, whether brothel- or beer-based, the message has got through to most of these girls that condom use is essential if they are to remain healthy, and indeed alive. And better still, recognition of the epidemic has cut down men's use of prostitutes; the government's efforts at education have born fruit, though there is a great deal more to do.

I suppose I should be devastated by the closure of the dyke clinic, the wooden shack that had served the prostitutes in two such contrasting ways, first as workplace and then as treatment centre. But somehow it doesn't seem to matter. Events have moved on apace since we left, and it is only right that individual efforts like ours in Tuol Kork should be absorbed into the whole.

Strangely, although the building is still standing, the story of our first clinic, where the sex-workers could or would not come and which thus led on to the little wooden building on Prostitute Row, is less happy; progress seems to have passed it by. This large concrete house, once the property of a Cambodian physician murdered by the Khmer Rouge and the site of our initial challenge, was the next port of call on our journey into the past.

As soon as we drove through those same shabby double gates with their arching faded blue dispensary sign, we should have guessed what was in store. But still I wasn't fully prepared for what we found. It truly was as if someone had waved a magic wand and banished the intervening years in a puff of the black smoke from the ice factory next door. The vast cavernous entrance hall was exactly as it had always been; incredibly, even the ornamental fish-pond in the corner remained, still floored with the same blue tiles broken in the same places, the same grime encrusted in the same cracks. We wandered up the familiar wooden staircase and along the maze of corridors, the lick of clinical white paint we had paid for before we left peeling off the walls to reveal the original grubby blue. We peered through the keyholes in the myriad of bolted doors; sadly even our old waiting and consulting rooms were locked against us.

So far we had encountered no one, but back in the entrance hall we found a teenaged girl who declared herself in charge in the temporary absence of more qualified staff. The teddy bear clutched to her budding bosom did nothing to allay our fears that the whole clinic had reverted to its original indolent squalor, that we might never have been there at all. She was able to point to a whiteboard listing the dispensary statistics, and to tell us that the team from the dyke were ensconced here once more. The ghosts of the brightly clad girls that had once thronged the hall awaiting their turn in our busy family spacing clinic wafted their presence about us; I can only hope that the originals have been absorbed into other contraceptive programmes, for I saw nothing about birth pills and coils on the posted list.

Probably expatriates like ourselves can and often do make some contribution to the countries in which they operate. But most of us work no miracles, and we are totally dependent on the local counterparts whom we leave behind to carry on where we left off. This is where Tim and I are both so very fortunate. Dr Vathiny is a perfect example of how this should be; she has done and is still doing so much in the field of sexual health and I am so grateful to have had her as a colleague. But Tim, too, had a devoted disciple during those two years, who also has gone on to achieve remarkable things.

Like Vathiny, Dr Chhun Long had been amongst the very first batch of medical students to be trained in 1979, after the end of the Pol Pot era. Highly intelligent, an exceptionally hard worker and with ambition to succeed, it seemed that he was the only one to realise just how much could be learnt from an experienced Western consultant. He became both Tim's interpreter and his right hand man, and at the end of our two years Tim was able to persuade the British Embassy to bring Long to England and finance his four-month stay in our local district general hospital, where he could observe for himself all that he had been taught. In itself such a prestigious visit would have given a big boost to his career. But even more importantly and largely as a result of that experience, twelve months later Long spent a year in London on a scholarship from the British Council at the School of Tropical Medicine, studying for and gaining a Master's degree.

It was he who had telephoned Tim in 1997 to ask him to go back to help with the writing of a manual for the treatment of obstetric emergencies, and on that first return visit we were able to see for ourselves what rapid progress he had made. By this time, the Japanese government had built a magnificent new women's referral hospital in which Long and his colleagues were happily ensconced. The contrast with its predecessor was breathtaking; apart from anything else, it was so startlingly clean. Although funded entirely by its donors, administration and staffing are Cambodian, and the morale of its doctors and midwives have soared as a result.

The only barrier to Long's even greater advancement at that time was his relative youth, for in Cambodia it is hard to supersede your elders, even if they do not happen to be your betters. But now the years have released him from that stranglehold and he is in a senior and greatly trusted position. A few years after we left he was asked by the World Health Organisation to spend some time in Papua New Guinea where he was to help them to set up their health service, a remarkable turnabout when only so recently the cries for help had been coming from his own country. There can surely be no better illustration of Cambodia's growing maturity in the eyes of its neighbours. Now he is working in the field of maternal and child health in Bangladesh, applying in that country the lessons learnt the hard way in his own. Like so many responsible Cambodians, he has for a long time taken on his thin shoulders the burdens of his extended family. Now those, too, are lessening as his financial status improves, and it is a real pleasure to see the smile on his face and a little more flesh on his slender bones.

But nothing is perfect; there are some sadnesses too. The municipal hospital where I had seen so many interesting cases with Dr Long Key and Dr Chuoy, and where in the end I had enjoyed the work so much, is I fear nearing the end of its life. A new charity hospital has been put up by expatriates on the grass actually inside its grounds, and patients have been tempted away. The doctors that I had seen busily and happily at work were playing draughts when I visited at ten o'clock in the morning. The building was visibly more decrepit than before; what a contrast to its glittering Japanese cousin just down the road.

Dr Chuoy is no longer there. Determined to do the best for his three children by giving them a fresh start in a fresh country, he won a scholarship to Australia. This was no easy task, demanding an almost impossibly high standard of English. He certainly deserved his scholarship. He had worked incredibly hard, getting up at four in the morning and spending literally hours each day struggling with overcrowded English classes; and all this on top of a full programme at the hospital, where our ward rounds often ended with grammatical gymnastics or the analysis of obscure Shakespearean quotations.

Somehow, against all the odds, he made the grade but it breaks my heart when I think of the consequences. Though his beloved children are receiving the sort of education he could only have dreamt about at home, he tells me that he has been forced to leave medicine altogether for more financially rewarding work to cover his family's increased needs. What a waste of one of the best doctors I know, on either side of the world.

Very little has been said about Tim's original achievements, not just in teaching the doctors and midwives at his hospital, but also in his study of the reasons behind the disastrously high maternal mortality rate throughout the country. He is not one to boast about his work, but there were big changes for the better as a result of what he did. I am still waiting for him to write his side of the story; people do say that miracles still happen. The most obvious memorial to his time there is very much a living one, perhaps more so than is usually meant by that term. The manual for use in obstetric emergencies that was begun on our first return visit was at last finished through a lengthy exchange of e-mails between Tim on our side of the world and Dr Long and his colleagues on theirs, each shaping and suggesting until both sides were satisfied. Translated into Khmer, it is now in full use in district hospitals throughout the country. I suspect it has saved many lives, of babies and of their mothers.

What of the others who flew out with us in September 1991? Most of them stayed in Cambodia longer than the statutory two years, and I admire them for their stamina. Few have been able to settle back in this country, and this is understandable for there is so much that needs to be done elsewhere. Of the eight of us who started out together in September 1991, seven survived the course. The exception was of course poor Iain, whose cautionary tale the reader has already heard. Caitlin and Bill remained inseparable throughout all the exigencies of the three years they spent there, and are inseparable still. They numbered among the very few working outside Phnom Penh, and in their posting to Battambang, a pretty town in the north-west where we were able to visit them once, there was often the sound of shelling as the Khmer Rouge and government forces continued to bombard each other. Several times they were unwillingly evacuated to the capital, where they would stay in our spare room and cheer us up with their stories of country life. Caitlin's unending Irish flow of tales from a vet's case-book was better than any television, particularly seasoned as it was with flashes of brilliant humour from Bill; when he could get a word in edgeways. Soon after they got home they were married in a beautiful Dublin church. Now they have four children and are job-sharing in a veterinary practice in north Wales. With a large family, a house-move and almost no help Caitlin continues to rush off to operate on accident-prone cows; when she isn't preparing a course of sixty lectures or studying for a higher veterinary degree.

Peter, who helped us buy mattresses and who restored the dispensary, moved after a few months to another agency in Phnom Penh. He too achieved remarkable results, teaching and supervising his able Khmer colleagues in a number of important building projects. Now he has fulfilled his life's dream; after taking a teaching degree, he lives and works in Ireland, running greyhound kennels in his spare time. He too is married with a family.

Our electrician friend, a tough little fellow in his fifties and the kindest man you could hope to meet, exchanged his English Lake District village for permanent residence in Cambodia. Within weeks of our arrival, he had made his own personal arrangements with the assistant manageress of the Asie hotel, our first home, for private tutoring in the Khmer language. She was an elegant and cultured Cambodian widow with a small daughter, speaking fluent and beautiful French but at that time without a word of English. Harry was no linguist, but somehow between them they found the right language with which to become betrothed, and within a few months they were wed in true Cambodian style. Sadly, it was to be a short partnership. Though Cumbria and Cambodia are as far removed from one another as they could be, old habits die hard and fell-running had been thirsty work. It was the drink that over several years undermined Harry's health, and when he developed pneumonia all the fight had gone out of him. Somaly, his widow, still works today as secretary in our agency Field Office.

Christopher, the corpse with the feather in its ear, taught English to a group of would-be interpreters, joining the mine disposal group Halo Trust in the school holidays for light relief. At the end of his original commitment, he turned his hand to demining full time, training and working alongside his Cambodian team. With almost no sophisticated equipment at their disposal, together they poked at the soil with sticks and exposed any suspected mines with garden trowels before detonating them. He left Cambodia with all four limbs intact, and is now living and working in Scandinavia where he has a small daughter.

So much for our immediate group. Of others who came before and after us I will mention just four. Tom, my honeymoon partner on our weekend trip to Vietnam, also left our agency early, headhunted by the World Health Organisation for higher things. After taking a second degree, he went with his wife and two children to Kenya to work with the government health service there. Since then, gaining another son along the way, he has moved successively to India, South Africa, where he was advisor on health and HIV/AIDS to the whole of southern Africa for

Britain's Department for International Development (DFID) and now to Geneva.

Angus, seconded to WHO, worked on malaria throughout his two year term. Miraculously he managed to avoid infection himself, despite numerous unprotected visits to hospitals in the high-risk forested areas. Another degree, a spell in Africa still working on malaria and a variety of other adventures preceded a desk-job in DFID's London office. The world seemed at his feet. Ahead lay a two-month spell of accumulated holiday and then a DFID posting back to Africa on a new and exciting project in Uganda as regional health advisor for the east and central sections of the country. But that winter brought near disaster. It wasn't the malaria that got him, or the dengue, or the typhoid; it wasn't even an earthquake or a tidal wave. It was a thirty-foot Alpine precipice that caught him and his ski-board unawares. The impact of his fall crushed one of his vertebrae to smithereens; the wonder is that he avoided paralysis for a sharp chip of bone had lodged itself within a millimetre of his spinal cord. Two months and two operations later he was back on his wobbly feet, facing a year away from all he loved doing most and, as he said, giving him time to think; nothing that had happened was to change his way of life in shape, though perhaps in degree. Perhaps. At any rate he got to Uganda as planned, and is now the proud father of a beautiful baby daughter.

My replacement, Jenny, has not been wasting her time either. By taking over from me she missed all the fun and excitement at the start of the project, but in spite of that by all accounts she did a magnificent job in the dyke clinic and elsewhere after our departure, with many additions of her own. She, like Vathiny, has remained in the field of sexual health, both in the Isle of Man where she lives, and overseas. After leaving Cambodia and a spell at home, she went with Medecins Sans Frontieres to Azerbaijan where she worked with the government in reproductive health, and where, as in Cambodia, the sustainable supply of condoms was of primary concern and one of her many successes. Less dramatic but equally important is her work in her home island, where the young are every bit as much in need of guidance as they are in every other country in the world. But they should make the most of her there now for I somehow don't think she will stay for long; I'm willing to bet that before long she will be off, for there is too much to do elsewhere in the world.

The fourth person whose achievements demand attention is Catherine, the young violin teacher at the College of Fine Arts. Her interest had always lain with traditional Khmer music, and increasingly as time went by she encouraged her students to go back to their musical roots. In those early days she came to visit us, and as we sat together in our garden under the mango tree she told us of her plans. She had a dream, a vision of setting up a Traditional Music School for disabled young people in the south-west near the sea. She had no money and little support, but a lion's share of determination..

On our return to the country four years later, we found her dream. In the seaside town of Kampot, tucked away in a pleasant building set in a lovely garden, there was her music school. She herself had moved on, but the halt and the lame greeted us, and the young man in charge proudly unlocked the door of their big music room. In a circle on the floor stood a wonderful array of all the traditional instruments, just like those that had made our own leaving party such a special occasion. We left her a note to say we had visited. I know little more about her movements, except that she was in Bosnia when that too was a notorious trouble spot. Rumour has it that she lives now in Italy and for health reasons has not been back to Cambodia for some time.

In the summer of 1995, two years after that unforgettable period of our life had come to an end, twenty-five young people met in our English garden for a weekend of memories, reminiscing far into the night. We shall never again gather together so many who have shared so much, for the friends that we made in Cambodia have scattered all over the world. There is no doubt that the experience and the will to take part in the destinies of other poorer countries will remain with all of us and no one, whether we like it or not, will ever be quite the same again. Perhaps because it was the first overseas assignment for most, or perhaps because of its heart-rending history, Cambodia seems to hold us all in its sway; we can only hope that, sooner or later, those that guide its destiny will help it to become the place of peace and beauty that it ought to be.

Looking forward to the future must be more important than backward at the past, and it seems appropriate that the end of the story proper should rest with Cambodia's young people upon whom that future depends.

Back in December 1992, in commemoration of International Human Rights Day, a competition sponsored by UNTAC was held in which children all over the country were invited to submit paintings entitled 'What Human Rights Means to Me.' There were more than ten thousand entries, and through their pathos, their fear and yet their intense optimism, one thing became overwhelmingly clear, summed up in the preface to a booklet reproducing the prize-winning pictures. 'Cambodian children, like all children, instinctively know what human rights means. It is a dream, a hope for a better tomorrow... The children of Cambodia are indeed the nation's soul. They are also its witnesses. Will they witness a return to peace? Will they live in a nation guided by the ideals expressed in their drawings? Creating such a future is the charge of these drawings.'

That was seventeen years ago. Those children are the young adults of today. Have they witnessed a return to peace? Is their nation guided by their childish ideals? Perhaps a 'yes' to the first, but a 'no' to the second, for the moment. But that they have fresh ideas on the future of their country is not, I think, in doubt. The hope for a better tomorrow is alive and well.

The preface to the collection of pictures ends with these words. 'Creating such a future ... is also the challenge to those who experience them.' Most of us have not seen their drawings, but that does not exonerate us from responsibility. The challenge is to all of us.

Two

Problems

Cambodia is a country of contrasts: wealth and poverty, kindness and cruelty, blazing sun and bucketing rain, despair and, sometimes, hope.

Sometimes. On our last visit it seemed that perhaps, just perhaps, hope had actually arrived. It had always been there in the background, in our time at least. But fifteen years ago hope had been a bloodless wraith, riding on the shoulders of the ever-increasing numbers of Westerners that were flooding in, eager and willing but often lacking in circumspection and sadly disunited. Now there is at least some local enterprise. Gifted individuals are racing ahead. The vacuum left by the killings of twenty-five years ago is beginning to fill, the new generation of 'intelligentsia' beginning to take the place of the layer of leaders creamed off in the seventies by Pol Pot's murderous regime. Other governments, the Japanese in particular, are pouring money and commodities into the country, presumably with the hopeful assumption that help given now will pay dividends later.

But there is no doubt that Cambodia's full recovery is a still a long way off. After Pol Pot's flight in 1979, the physical destruction that had taken place was all too apparent, and Herculean efforts were made both by Cambodians and, later, by the international community to put things right. But it is impossible to plumb the depths of the moral damage that was done during those four awful years. The destruction of all things sacred and beautiful and of those that upheld them, the loss of the wise and the learned, and perhaps above all the tearing apart of families, of mother from child, has left a bleak and empty chasm whose barrenness is out of all proportion to the relatively short time span of the Pol Pot era. Corruption, child prostitution, the recently uncovered trade in unwanted babies, these are just three of the things that tell us how far the country is from a reasonable equilibrium. Such wrongs are vastly more difficult to right than dirty drinking water and eccentric electricity and the fight must go on to remedy them. Thankfully there are a great many people both from inside and outside the country who have taken up the cudgels and one can only hope and pray that gradually, over the years, their efforts will be rewarded. It will certainly take a very long time.

Not all Cambodia's present problems can be blamed on Pol Pot, tempting though it is to try, and of these AIDS must top the list. Over a quarter of a million Cambodians have been infected with the HIV/AIDS virus, and although Pol Pot was responsible for the demise of far greater numbers, the two disasters are still comparable in their numbers. Most of the victims are young adults, a huge drain on the workforce that is so badly needed to build up the country so soon after the previous tragedy.

If anyone is to blame for the Cambodian epidemic, now amongst the worst in Asia, it could be said to be us outsiders: largely the UN 'invasion' of 1992, but also experienced world AIDS-watchers who perhaps should have seen it coming and acted accordingly. But it wouldn't have worked. The alcoholic must be desperate to stop drinking before any one can help him; the desire for change must come from within. Despite the efforts in those early days by Cambodians as well as non-government organisations, these were too feeble and too few. It was several years before the truth sank in and the scattered skirmishes were combined into a force formidable enough to tackle the problem head on. But it was already too late for many; a major epidemic was well under way.

Most infections took place in the brothels. By 1997, half of all prostitutes and one in ten of their clients were infected with HIV. A remark made four years before, in those early days when the worst could only be guessed at, has stuck firmly in my mind. 'Our only hope is to change the behaviour of Cambodian men' said Dr Tia Phalla, a far-sighted and idealistic young Cambodian who headed the newly formed National AIDS Committee. I remember being both touched and sceptical. How was that possible? The habit of visiting brothels was so common amongst young Cambodians that it had almost become a rite of passage. There certainly came a moment in the life of our young guard, So Peap, when his brisk early morning arrival was exchanged for a bleary-eyed appearance halfway through the day and we realised that he had been inaugurated into the mysteries of manhood. In any case, AIDS itself was an unknown and invisible illness which would not make itself felt for at least eight years. So why should the ordinary man in the street suddenly change his ways?

But that is exactly what has happened. As the truth sank in, the authorities really got their act together and by the end of the 1990s the number of men visiting sex-workers had been cut in two. At the same time, a huge effort on all sides to teach the importance of protected sex was meeting with amazing success, an almost unimaginably far cry from our early days on the dyke. The meagre ration of four condoms that we dished out to each girl at the end of every weekly clinic had of course been laughable, but the best we could do at the time; the fact that there is now almost 100 per cent condom use seems little short of miraculous, and I can only hope that the old condom-seller down the road lived long enough to benefit. Perhaps the technique learnt by the girls of putting them on with their lips and tongue had become an added inducement. The proportion of men using condoms in those early days rose to greater heights in Phnom Penh than elsewhere in Cambodia, starting its increase back as early as 1993. I like to think that some of this could have been due to our efforts.

The reader may remember that when we left the country in 1993, the clinic that we had opened for sex-workers on the dyke was just beginning to come into its own. After our impecunious battles, the to us unheard of riches from the World Health Organisation were about to flow into its coffers and the VSO succession was guaranteed. My own struggles were at an end, and time alone would show what would happen. That was a long time ago, and much has happened since then.

In our day there were no AIDS drugs available anywhere in the world. For some time now, medication has been used with success in the West though not in the East; it is simply too expensive. But in Cambodia at least, thankfully times have changed. It seems now that 80 per cent of the HIV positive population do receive antiretroviral drugs.[5] Admittedly these are largely paid for by international aid groups, but such success is due to an unusually strong partnership between the government, the UN, NGOs, donors and other groups from both inside and outside the country, a conglomerate known as UNAIDS. The fall in infection rate, from 3.2 per cent of the population at its height to 0.8 per cent in 2008[6] has resulted from a very comprehensive national programme aimed at the epicentre of the epidemic, the sex-workers and their clients.

But this successful combined approach was a long time in coming, and in the early days it was left to NGOs to do what they could to help. Srey Vy was one of the lucky ones. An AIDS widow herself, she looked after a niece and nephew tragically orphaned in the epidemic as well as her own four children She too had AIDS and it looked as if very soon all six children would be without anyone to care for them. Frances, an English friend of mine then working in Cambodia, went to see her. Previous visits had been increasingly depressing as she watched the poor lady visibly fading away.

But this time a huge surprise was in store. Srey Vy was busy at the cooking-stove, boiling rice for herself and her family, and actually ran to greet her visitor.

'Look at me!' she said, proudly lifting her blouse to show Frances her invisible spare tyre. 'Twat nah!' ('Very fat!')

'What on earth has happened? You look wonderful!'

'Two foreigners came to visit me – French, I think they were. They asked lots of questions, and then they made me lie down on my bed mat and pushed and poked me all over. Ever so gently, though. Then they said they could give me pills that would make me better if I liked. I couldn't afford them, so I shook my head. They were ever so surprised, and asked why, so I told them we didn't have enough money for food let alone medicine. One of them laughed, and patted me on the shoulder – so kind, he was. 'You don't have to pay,' he said, and gave me some tablets, just like that. Now watch me!'

She skipped across the wooden floor of her one-roomed house and picked up a bowl.

'These days the only trouble is I get so hungry that this isn't big enough. Can you imagine - I have to pile it this high five times a day!'

She was quite right; her saviours were indeed French. Medecins Sans Frontieres, as well as other NGOs, had set up a number of clinics across the country to provide free treatment. But there was not enough money to go round; only one in ten could benefit, and in those sad days the other nine were left to die. But now, thanks to UNAIDS, out of those ten only two will be left to their own devices.

Srey Vy's own children were lucky but thousands were not so fortunate. Much of the care of AIDS orphans is left to the NGOs and once again it was Frances who told me about Sokhon.

Sokhon ('Auntie' to her charges) is a redoubtable Cambodian lady who runs a small Dutch concern. Her two hundred orphans still live in the comfort of family homes with friends or relatives, but are supported in various ways by the organisation. Frances and Sokhon are old friends and they went together one day on Sokhon's rounds, ending up at the project office in time for a late lunch.

'That was absolutely delicious!' Frances delicately pincered one last grain of rice and regretfully laid down her chopsticks. She smiled up at the young woman who had served them. 'Sokhon is extremely lucky to have such a good cook. Is this what you do all the time?'

Laughing, the girl shook her head and pointed pouted lips through the window, in true Cambodian style.

'No, I work next door. Would you like to come and see?'

Together they went towards the little wooden house just down the road, the unmistakable clackety-clack of sewing-machines growing louder with each step they took. The child opened the door and ushered her in, and for a second Frances, dazzled from the bright light outside, could see nothing. Then as her eyes recovered it seemed to her that she was catapulted from deep darkness into a fantastical world of illusion. The single shaft of sunshine that poured in from the unglazed window coned out into a million dancing points of light before it splintered and came to rest on each of a dozen shining heads bent low over their work. For a fraction of time, Frances suffered one of those strange and fleeting dreamlike moments when nothing is what it seems. Was this hallucination or a vision of the Buddhist acceptance of fate, a tableau of bowed heads silently, unanimously, acquiescing in all that had been and was yet to come? But the feeling passed almost before it had been, and as the smiling faces one by one turned towards her, she pulled herself together and listened to her guide's explanation.

'This is where Auntie teaches us to sew. Tira here is trying to make a school uniform for one of the younger orphans' and she held up a half finished navy skirt for inspection. Frances took it, and looking at the puckered seams and Tira's perspiring anxious face, felt a surge of pity for the youngsters.

'It's so hot in here. Do you have to work so hard? Does anyone pay you for what you produce?'

'No, but we do get our food. Anyway, if we learn to sew, when we leave we can get work in the market making clothes for customers, so most of us turn up most days. Auntie doesn't have time to make all the little ones' clothes, so she likes us to help.'

It doesn't take much to set the ball rolling; an idea, a helping hand and a modest sum of money.

And Cambodia does play strange tricks with your mind.

AIDS is an accidental addition to human tragedy. Devastating though it be, it is rarely a positive act of evil. Cambodia's intrinsic woes, though, stem not just from its appalling history but also from its present lack of good stewardship. The difficulties could be overcome if only the will in high places were there. But is it?

Take law and order. Police there are in plenty, their smart khaki uniforms standing out from the crowd: if only their actions matched their looks. Like virtually all those in authority, they are only too open to bribery. Corruption, violence and crime are in free-fall. You can get away with anything, provided you know the right people. And it happens, all the time, in every walk of life. There is a cycle of violence and trauma in the country dating like so much else from its recent past and until everyone from the top to the bottom stops turning a blind eye, this will not cease.

I am thankful to say I have never witnessed a vigilante killing; I wouldn't know what to do and strongly suspect I would just cut and run. But photographs I have seen. In strip cartoon format, the photos show a group of young people standing round a man lying on the road; they kick him, stone him, and beat him with sticks; he clutches his head. Next, a small group of police appear and simply stand watching; they wander off. And then the final scene. The photograph is taken from further away and in the centre of the picture the camera focuses on a small crumpled heap. The street is empty of any life.

This was a killing by a group of university students, possibly unprovoked, certainly paid for not by prosecution but with hard cash slipped to the right quarter.

There are so many more examples of careless unpremeditated violence, witnessed but totally ignored for fear of retribution. A brothel owner beats a prostitute to death. A boy of sixteen is tortured and shot for stealing chickens. Ten fishermen are suspected of the theft of a cow; nine are shot. A holiday celebration is deemed too noisy; five party-goers are gunned down, one by one. All these incidents were observed; no one was prosecuted. This will go on, until the legal system is completely overhauled and judges are given a proper wage. But here things really do seem to be beginning to improve. Efforts are being made to increase the numbers of trained lawyers, run down to almost nothing in the Pol Pot era. At a recent ceremony of the Bar Association of the Kingdom of Cambodia, fifty new lawyers graduated and joined the two hundred and forty or so who had already trained within the last few years.

Corruption is everywhere; it has simply become an acceptable way of life. According to the government's legal adviser, money pouring in from foreign donors merely 'plugs the gaps caused by the leakage (from corruption)'.[7] There has been a draft anti bribery law in the pipeline for some time but there always seems to be a reason for yet further delays; whisper it not that many prefer it to stay there.

When a group of students was interviewed recently and asked which party they would like to win the next election, one twenty-two year old gave the following reply:

'I hope CPP (the present ruling party) wins. They have been corrupt for a very long time and have a lot of money already, so they are able to change their character. But if a new party wins, they don't have money yet so they will have to become more corrupt'.[8]

It is not beyond teachers in certain schools to give advice on the art.

Sihanouk summed it up very poetically in one of his monthly bulletins:

'In today's Cambodia, the God of Impunity reigns side by side with the King of Corruption'.[9] He has a nice turn of phrase.

But corruption is a wider moral issue, not just concerned with bribery, and where could this be more in evidence than in the trafficking of women and children? This is another huge and particularly obnoxious problem. During the last decade almost three million women and children have been sold for sex across South-East Asia, of the same order as the African slave trade. Cambodia is a vital link in the area's trafficking network, the regional thoroughfare between Vietnam and the lucrative people markets of Thailand and Malaysia. Well-organized crime syndicates lure their unsuspecting prey with promises of good jobs or marriage, instead of which these poor girls find themselves in brothels or karaoke parlours, or, if they're lucky, working for a pittance on plantations or as chambermaids.

Dina Chan was not originally sold into slavery. The intentions of her parents had been entirely honourable; she was to earn her keep while at school in Phnom Penh by washing up in a local hotel in the evenings. All went well for a while; it seemed she was one of the lucky ones. But it was not to last. One evening as she was going back to her lodgings she was raped; the downhill slide into prostitution had begun. She was trapped, as surely as if her body had been exchanged for money at the start.

She talks of her experiences. 'This man' (not the original rapist) 'took me to the pig slaughterhouse where he worked and locked me in a dirty smelly cell. Then he came back with six other men. They all, one by one, raped me; one man raped me twice. After a whole night of gang rape I was faint with pain... In the morning I heard the pigs being pushed into the pens, they were screaming. I knew what that feeling was like... the men could have killed me. Something inside me did die, and I will never be the same...My life has become this way now; for me there is no turning back.' She has written a poem, which I quote in part.

I am not a person
You see me as a virus
I am invisible
Your eyes do not see me
You hate me
You blame me
I do not want your pity

I do not want your charity
I want my rights
Not your lies and abuses[10]

Dina is a member of the Sex Workers Union of Tuol Kork, where our Dyke Clinic used to be. I suppose a Union has to be a step in the right direction, until these appalling abuses cease. And there is another shred of good news. As far as trafficking is concerned the legal system is slowly grinding towards reform.

An endless list of Cambodia's dilemmas must make for very depressing reading; writing it is even worse. But although of course there is no way in which I can hope to make the picture totally complete, there are a few more problems that do demand attention

Deforestation is certainly part of that bad news. The Cardamoms, a hidden and forested mountain range deep in south-western Cambodia, are almost untouched by human life. The reason, once again, is the Khmer Rouge. This was one of their strongholds; once heavily mined, it is a treasure trove of rare plants and strange creatures that have been preserved by war in a virtually pristine time capsule. Efforts are being made to promote ecotourism, and with a few days to spare on our last visit we attempted to sample a jungle trek. Unable to discover much in the way of information locally, we tried the internet. This only served to whet our appetite. The article that Google found for us told us of the exploits of a British group of scientific researchers who, in the company of Cambodian wildlife experts and guided through the landmines by the guerrillas who had laid them, spent two months in the early spring of 2000 exploring the region.

Tim's reaction to their report was one of extreme excitement, turning rapidly to frustration as it became ever clearer that there were no guides, trained or untrained, to lead us.

'Just look at this', he said, stabbing the report with his finger. 'Herds of elephants, white ones as well, leopards, golden cats, jungle cats, fishing cats, tigers. Even this what's-its-name, khiting vor, whatever that might be.' We read on and discovered that this strange animal is half sheep, half antelope, the only large mammal on the face of the earth that is positively known to exist but has never been officially documented.

Perhaps there are organised expeditions into this animal utopia; if so we failed to find them. Perhaps in any case we might have been disappointed. We might have found our way barred by one of the powerful logging companies, defying half-hearted attempts to keep them in check by devastating great tracks of jungle with their noisy machinery and new roads. We might have glimpsed an unmapped lake through the undergrowth, the work of dam builders for illegal hydroelectric companies. If our jungle craft could have matched theirs, we might even have witnessed the wiles of poachers; sundry assorted tiger parts remain vital ingredients of Chinese medicines and the corpses of elephants and a multitude of other wild animals provide rich bounty for trophy-seekers and restaurateurs seeking unusual dishes. Ecotourism versus financial greed has a hard fight on its hands.

In any case, we didn't have much time. We did manage a couple of mini treks in a much smaller reserve in the south-west, near the seaside resort of Sihanoukville. They were interesting and fun, but the only man-eaters we encountered were the mosquitoes, presented with an unexpected feast when our newly 'trained' guides lost their way as dusk fell.

These little trips were safe enough. Exploring without knowledgeable guides in wilder parts of the country could have cost us an eye, a leg, or even our life, for landmines are a much greater hazard than wild animals and still present a huge and ongoing challenge. Experts believe it will take them at least another decade to finish the job of getting rid of them. So experienced are the Cambodian deminers that in 1998 they were invited to Kosovo to help clear land to which refugees were returning.

Demining is a dangerous job; it is expensive, but vital for the future of a country where so much land must still be out of bounds. But the army is another matter altogether. The payroll is almost endless, and includes a huge list of 'ghost' soldiers, long since dead or otherwise gone. The spare salaries have no difficulty in finding homes. The army gets a great deal more than it gives: more than double, in fact, than schools and hospitals together.

Ceremony, too, ever an important part of Khmer culture, costs dear. The Royal Palace is allotted four times the amount spent on justice; looking back to its extravagant face-lift when we were first there and the God-King Sihanouk was expected back from exile, and now at the recent coronation of the new King Sihamoni, I am not surprised.

Where does the cash come from?

Despite loans and donations pouring into the country, Cambodia seems to be slipping deeper and deeper into poverty. Most foreign companies are frightened to set up shop in Cambodia; dodgy deals, graft, military-run smuggling schemes, labyrinthine custom and port charges are not the most inviting of prospects. Oil has been discovered; the only snag is that much of it lies under Angkor Wat. Agriculture seems the obvious source of income, but until government reforms turn from fiction to fact too much of the profit finds its way into someone's back pocket.

It is the home-grown clothing industry that wins all the honours and makes more money for the country than anything else. Its factory conditions passed muster with the UN and favourable trade agreements followed. But at the end of 2005 these came to an end and now Cambodia is in free competition with the rest of the world including of course the colossus of them all, China.

Tourism is definitely up and coming. The ancient temples of Angkor draw thousands of visitors each year to worship at the shrine of culture. But Cambodia, with its glorious past history of man's creativity, has become one of the world's major centres of man's ignominy; sex tourism. Our merry-go-round of misery seems doomed to run and run as it takes us round again to the little girls snatched from their homes, to Dina and her like, to virgins sold for a song. What tune, I wonder, does it play?

Despite tourism, despite garment factories full of overworked and grossly underpaid women, despite huge sums of money donated to the country by the outside world, Cambodia gets steadily poorer. It is poverty that kills young children; and more of them rather than less are dying as the years go by. This will not cease until corruption ceases.

In 2003 SARS, the Sudden Acute Respiratory Syndrome, struck South-East Asia. But Cambodia was lucky, thanks to a baby with miraculous powers born in Siem Reap Province. Or so the story goes.

Imagine the scene. A few hours after the birth, the exhausted mother rests in the torrid heat, the traditional charcoal burner glowing beneath her bed to keep her warm. Her brand new baby is at the breast. She dozes. They are very close. Suddenly, her tiny son speaks to her.

'Mother, I have something important to tell you. There is a very bad new illness coming here, but I can save you. You must send father to the market to buy Mung beans, and you must cook them and eat them before midnight. Otherwise you will die.'

The story spread like wildfire. Cellphones worked overtime and within hours the entire population of Phnom Penh, well over a hundred miles to the south, was wolfing down the magic vegetable. Clutching a bowlful, neighbour banged on the door of neighbour:

'Wake up! Wake up! You must eat this now, or you will die.'

By midnight, the price of beans had gone up tenfold. No one in Cambodia died of SARS. But the story does nevertheless have a tragic ending. Worn out by its efforts, the poor baby died, a martyr for the greater good.[11]

I can vouch for the truth of this tale, or rather the part of it that deals with beans, for our daughter was in Phnom Penh at the time and e-mailed us that Mung beans were out of stock.

But it is not all doom and gloom; every now and again, the sun comes through with a brilliance that is all the greater for the black clouds. There are many areas where things are getting better. Some, though not all, of the health services, for instance, are improving. Immunisation, the treatment of TB, psychiatry, have all made advances. Even heart surgery is on the agenda. The Cambodia Trust, an NGO born from a quiet after-dinner chat amongst dons at Oxford University about fifteen years ago, has made enormous inroads into the problems of the limbless.

Cultural activities, too, are struggling back to their rightful place.

In 1998, a troupe of Cambodian dancers toured Europe for two months, meeting with great acclaim everywhere. The phoenix had truly risen from the ashes; self-destruction of their own culture by the Khmer Rouge could well have spelled the end of the centuries old Apsara tradition of dance, passed on in all its intricacies from one generation to the next. But by a superhuman effort from those dancers that remained, those few 'unwanted leftovers from a decadent past' in Khmer Rouge terms, a new generation came into being and stunned audiences everywhere with their grace and elegance.

A year later, for the first time one of the South-East Asia Write Awards was won by a Cambodian, pen-name Tum Kravel. The word Kravel means 'to make a hole in my ear to remember something in my life', he explained with a chuckle. He said his name change marked Cambodia's bitter history, particularly the Khmer Rouge genocide. 'I took this name as a memory of past events in our country'.[12]

Even landmine injuries can be a factor for good. In 2002, the Cambodian volleyball team won the gold medal in the FESPIC disabled games in South Korea; not altogether surprising, perhaps, with Cambodia's vast number of amputees to choose from. And four of their able-bodied compatriots entered for the 2004 Olympics in Athens.

Another success story comes from the world of music, so dear to the Cambodian heart. A quarter of a century ago, nine-year-old Khoun Sethistak was rescued from the Khmer Rouge labour camps by the arrival of the Vietnamese. By singing his way on to local radio, he gained the ear of those that mattered and was eventually sent to study piano at the Moscow Conservatory. Despite the ending of his grant with the fall of communism and an ensuing diet entirely of potatoes supplied by local farming friends, he managed to achieve his piano diploma. The story goes that so overjoyed was he that he burst into a Khmer song of such brilliance that once again he attracted the attention of his professors and found himself embarking on a second diploma course, this time in singing. A stomach full of spuds cannot be the soundest basis for voice production, but in spite of all he won a major award before his return to the poverty-stricken home he had left four years before.

The American opera lover exploring the back streets of Phnom Penh in his cyclo could hardly believe his ears when he heard, flooding out of the glassless windows of a small undistinguished wooden house, the glorious rendering of a famous tenor aria. This lucky encounter took Khoun to San Francisco and further training until, once again, the funds came to an end as a result of the events of September 11th and he had to return home.

Now he sits, and sings, without money or work, waiting and longing to complete the coaching that would launch him as an international tenor. He knows he has the voice. There are two great ambitions in his life; to bring opera to his own stricken country, and to create a marriage between the music of East and West. He has not forgotten the sounds of Cambodia.

Three

Politics

With apologies to those readers well versed in Cambodian politics and to help others who are not, I venture to start this chapter with an alphabetical list of the names that dominate it.

Chakrapong. Prince. Son of King Sihanouk, half-brother of Prince Ranariddh.
CPP. Cambodian People's Party. At present the ruling political party.
Duch. Khmer Rouge leader. Previously in charge of Tuol Sleng prison, or S21.
Funcinpec. Royalist political party, until recently headed by Prince Ranariddh.
Hun Sen. Prime Minister. Leader of CPP.
Khieu Samphan. Senior member of Khmer Rouge.
Lon Nol. Previous leader of Cambodia, before Pol Pot. Ousted Sihanouk.
Nuon Chea. Senior member of Khmer Rouge.
Ranariddh. Prince. Son of King Sihanouk, half-brother of Prince Chakrapong.
Sam Rainsy. Heads his own political party, now in opposition.
Sihamoni. Cambodia's new king. Son of Sihanouk.
Sihanouk. King, then prince, then king again. Now abdicated in favour of Sihamoni.
Ta Mok. The One-Legged Butcher. General in the Khmer Rouge.
UNTAC. United Nations Transitional Authority in Cambodia.

No government can please everybody; that is why democracy was invented. For us in the West, the system of voting gives us the luxury of choice, however much we may change our minds later. But others are not so lucky. To have a permanent leader foist upon you, to be hamstrung in an endless regime that you fear and hate, is to us almost inconceivable. And then for the miracle to happen; to see the prospect of change ahead and to be a part of that change, that too must be beyond belief. No wonder excitement gripped the whole Cambodian nation with such fervour when in 1993 the first elections for over twenty years took place.

Here at last was to be the great turning point in the country's story, a historic moment when Cambodian people could at last determine their own future. The timing for us was perfect; the four months that were left before our departure would surely give us time to witness the start of this brave new world.

This was the first of the five-yearly elections, as laid down by the new constitution. Since then there have been two more. But right from the start nothing ran smoothly and by the time we left the country there was little sign of even the beginning of the end of conflict. Prince Ranariddh's royalist party, Funcinpec, had won the election, but only just. It was thus forced into an uneasy coalition with the Cambodian People's Party, or CPP, its bitter opponent and close runner-up. Everyone was aware that the influence of Prince Sihanouk would be crucial during this time as the only Cambodian able to command the respect and allegiance of both sides. But when immediately after the election Sihanouk, dismayed by the closeness of the vote, took it upon himself to assume full powers in a government of one, there was a general outcry. This, said the affronted Funcinpec as well as several foreign governments, was going too far, and the attempt to go solo collapsed in twenty-four hours. But only a few days later, the new temporary government voted unanimously to reappoint him to the position he had held twenty-three years ago, that of Head of State. It passed a resolution declaring 'null and void' the illegal coup of 18th March 1970, when Lon Nol had ousted him and condemned him to death. So great was Sihanouk's sway that they invested in him full and special powers 'in order that he may save our nation'. Sihanouk, who had been waiting all this time to avenge his overthrow, was deeply moved. Ordinary mortals, such as members of UNTAC and other international diplomats, were puzzled at this turn of events but delighted at anything that would pour oil on troubled waters. Perhaps, after all, like the Tonle Sap, things would turn about. And only three months later when the new government came into being events took another unexpected turn; a vote was taken which firmly endorsed the restoration of the monarchy and of Prince Sihanouk as King once more. Nearly forty years previously he had abdicated in favour of his father so that he could expand his own political role. Now that role had been passed on to his son Ranariddh as prime minister while he himself would retain as king only the nominal powers of a ruling monarch in a democratic state. But they could not do without him.

A major factor in such a heartfelt plea to Sihanouk for help must have been the antics of one of his other sons, Prince Chakrapong. Chakrapong was Ranariddh's half brother, and a long sharp thorn in that gentleman's ample flesh. He seems to have been in the habit of changing sides, previously abandoning his brother's party, Funcinpec, for his rivals, the CPP, with a failed attempt to join the ranks of the Khmer Rouge in between. The Khmer Rouge would not have him. So now Chakrapong, doubtless to get his own back on his victorious brother Ranariddh and declaring the election totally unfree and unfair, led a Cambodian People's Party splinter movement, taking with him CPP troops that had become disenchanted with their present masters. Less than two weeks after the result of the voting was announced he attempted a takeover of seven eastern provinces, proclaiming the secession of the whole of this zone from the rest of the country. In the absence of a capital city from which to function, Chakrapong took to his helicopter, no doubt to gain a unique overall view of events. Hundreds of Funcinpec supporters in the area fled into the jungle or escaped to Phnom Penh, and a number were killed. With a considerable show of bravado and strength the rebel movement demanded that all UNTAC troops leave the area, an order which the UN as peacekeepers had little choice but to obey. 'Let the King Father resolve Cambodian problems without any interference from foreigners,' said Chakrapong.[13] But the attempt at secession was short lived, and the prince took himself off to Vietnam. They did not want him either so where could he go but home to the Palace? There, we are told that Sihanouk, after his initial outraged burst of anger against his errant son, finally freely forgave him, embraced him and welcomed him back into the fold. We do not know whether the fatted calf was killed. But we do know Sihanouk's words. 'This is a very Third World situation,' he said. ' I'm so sorry'.[14]

We left the country just at the point of the brand new government's first sitting, and any attempt to give a comprehensive account of the goings-on since would clearly be grossly misguided. A great deal has happened and in politically capable hands would bulge the covers of several more books. So the best I can do is to take you on a short guided tour through the ups and downs of the intervening years.

The post of First Prime Minister went to Prince Ranariddh who had won the election by a short head. This, though, was not at all to the taste of the Second Prime Minister, Hun Sen of the Cambodian People's

Party or CPP, who proceeded to make life as difficult as possible for his Number One. The coalition was an uncomfortable one, and as the years passed became increasingly so. Finally Ranariddh, feeling the need for material support in the way of arms and ammunition, concocted a plan. He made an alliance with the rump of the Khmer Rouge, still holding their own in the north of the country. In return for the Prince's backing, the Khmer Rouge would publicly recognise Cambodia's constitution and would dismantle their own provisional government. Or so they said. In fact, from secret papers found later, it was a trick. They intended to gain strength by this union with the Prince, but later to betray him and plunge Cambodia back into their own regime. 'Ranariddh wants to use us as a water buffalo to get across the mud, but we have to ride on the water buffalo'.[15]

The alliance, whatever lay behind it, put terror in the heart of Hun Sen. With the Khmer Rouge and Funcinpec joining political and military forces, he might well not achieve his heart's desire of an outright win in the following year's election, the second in the series, and thus achieving sole control of the country. So on Saturday July 5th 1997 the citizens of Phnom Penh awoke to the rumble of tanks along its bumpy roads and the sound of gunfire as CPP troops attacked Funcinpec's party headquarters and royalist soldiers throughout the town. For forty-eight bitter hours, there was shelling and shooting across the streets of Phnom Penh as once again Cambodian shed the blood of Cambodian. About a hundred people died, most of them local civilians. Several of our own friends had a narrow escape, staying firmly under the bed until it was certain that all was over.

But although Hun Sen had well and truly won the battle, he refused to call his action a coup d'etat. He had no wish to be christened a dictator and so lose the goodwill of the international community. He planned to allow the royalists to appoint a substitute for the errant Prince Ranariddh, and thus to preserve the frills of democracy. But Ranariddh himself, who, duly warned by his generals of impending events and fleeing abroad the day before the shooting taking with him one suit, one pair of shoes and one daughter, was banished from the country. His son refused to go with them. He preferred to stay at home with his girlfriend.

Time passed and in March the following year the exiled Ranariddh was tried in absentia for importing illegal weapons and for colluding with the Khmer Rouge. A lifetime prison sentence was imposed, together with a hefty fine. However in true Cambodian style all had been planned carefully in advance; Ranariddh was needed at home for the next elections, so what could be easier than to engineer a full pardon, granted by his kingly father? The prince lost no time in returning to the fold.

So now the elections had come round again. The first attempt at creating a democracy five years previously had met with dismal failure; Hun Sen's coup had seen to that. Prince Ranariddh's popularity was waning. Surely this time Hun Sen could sway the voters, and his Cambodian People's Party become the outright winners, achieving the necessary two-thirds majority and taking their legal place as the elected government of the country? The voting had already been held up by all the shenanigans over the coup, and now there was serious risk of not just one but two further delays. The late delivery of the three tons of indelible ink for marking voters' fingers to prevent their owners coming round again arrived only in the nick of time, and just three days before polling Hun Sen developed acute appendicitis and the offending organ had to be removed. However he managed to hobble to his ballot box, and at last the show was on the road.

And what a show, employing all the artfulness dear to the world of fiction. But this was no fiction. This was life, and death, that were all too real. From the violence and bribery that led up to the voting through to the final count, interested election watchers everywhere were kept in anxious suspense. The final result was the last thing either party wanted; a win for Hun Sen but once again with insufficient votes to function without embracing his main rival in a coalition. The aggressive cries of 'unfree, unfair' from the defeated parties, and the snowballing violence that followed, took months to untangle until at last a new coalition government was formed.

This, of course, was just the start. Faced with the overwhelming problems of AIDS, lawlessness, impunity, corruption, deforestation, poverty and malnutrition and everything else, how well would it cope? How well could any government cope? Cambodia, compared with most countries in the West, was a country in chaos. There was no blueprint to follow; problems beset the new government on every side. Hun Sen to his intense dismay still had the millstone of Prince Ranariddh's Funcinpec party around his neck. His ambition to achieve total control, not by force this time but legally and democratically, had failed. It seemed to the country and to the rest of the world that for Hun Sen there could only be one way forward; to do all he could to improve the lot of the people, so that next time round the vote would be his and his alone.

And so he embarked on the next five years of his tenure. To what extent he and his government did or did not succeed in making the radical reforms so essential to the country's welfare is a matter of opinion; hopefully the content of the previous chapter will have gone some way towards giving the answer.

Meantime, a new political party, small at its conception but growing rapidly in importance, had been born. Sam Rainsy is in his late fifties. Slim and bespectacled, he looks what he is, an intelligent and astute man. His father was Sihanouk's Deputy Prime Minister fifty years ago; his mother was the first Cambodian woman to pass the baccalaureate examination. A lawyer, he also has four university degrees to his name, in business, politics, economics and accountancy. After spending over half his life in France he returned to Cambodia in 1992. He set up his own party six years later having previously been a founder member of Funcinpec. Watch this space.

So now there were three political parties battling it out, planning their strategies for the third election, due in 2003. As time went on, many people become disillusioned with the CPP and were looking to the opposition parties as their hope for the future. The propaganda put out by both of these had been encouraging, particularly from Sam Rainsy who spoke most clearly to the young and the urban, promising an end to the corruption and impunity from legal redress that was still ruining any hope of progress in the country. Perhaps at last the voters would put matters right.

As the elections approached, all seemed at first to go reasonably well. Over ninety per cent of those eligible registered to vote. There was less overt pre-election violence; in fact a false impression, for more sophisticated forms had sneaked in instead. It was in the rural areas, the CPP strongholds where the poorly educated country folk could more easily be hoodwinked, that most of the deceptions took place. In the countryside, primitive superstitions are still rife; there remains, for instance, a strong belief in witches, punished in vigilante fashion by death and the eating of the victims' demon-tainted livers. Black magic and democracy are not comfortable bedfellows. So it is not surprising that simple farmers and their families are easily swayed by those with a mind to do so. In many areas of rural Cambodia, where fear and superstition go hand in hand, local rituals were performed to secure votes. One village chief 'invited' everyone in his parish to a ceremony. Attendance was compulsory, no matter what the guest's political leanings. Each villager was handed a glass of 'sacred' water from the pagoda and told to drain it to the last drop, and all were made to swear allegiance to the CPP. There can have been few that were brave enough to refuse, for from the bottom of every glass there shone a gleaming bullet.

Again, in the countryside particularly, vote buying and bribery were rife. A few kilos of rice go a long way towards helping you make up your mind. After all, material things had improved. The road to town was better; the bridge over the river had been rebuilt. No matter that all the promises for improved education had vanished with the wind; at least the school roof didn't leak any more. So why not take the line of least resistance and vote for what you know? What's it all about, anyway?

In the towns, particularly in Phnom Penh, things were different. There is a huge generation gap between the youth and their parents as Western influence waxes and the personal memories of the Pol Pot era wane. But even here, it remains unwise to discuss openly. '…it would be too dangerous for (the prime minister) to debate with other leaders. It would open a Pandora's Box of his political platform, judicial system, even his personal affairs'.[16]

Something is rotten in the state of Cambodia.

The build up was over; the people voted. The result was only too familiar. Hun Sen and his CPP won the 2003 election by a straight vote, but once more with just insufficient numbers to achieve the necessary two-thirds majority. Yet again, a coalition was no longer the dreaded spectre but a certainty. Although Rannnaridh did defeat Sam Rainsy by a short head, this was a huge advance for Rainsy who, last time, had trailed far behind. In Phnom Penh, he actually cornered half the vote, appealing as he did to the young and the educated. And poor Ranariddh was in all sorts of trouble, with leadership arguments and major defections. A cheeky comment in the press summarised the state of play of the three parties; if a road race were held between them, Hun Sen would drive a four-by-four (for gains in the countryside), Sam Rainsy a sleek sports car (for gains with the young and upwardly mobile) and Prince Ranariddh a motorbike with a flat tyre.

Le Mal Cambodgien takes many forms. Not long after the 2003 elections a spate of shootings took place on the streets of Phnom Penh.

Famous as a video star and popular karaoke singer, Touch Srey Nich lay for months in a Bangkok hospital, paralysed and on a ventilator. While walking along the street one day shopping with her mother she was shot and seriously wounded; her mother was killed outright. The soloist in songs used in Prince Ranariddh's election campaign and the star in a film directed by the prince himself, she could well be looked upon as a political target. Now a refugee in Los Angeles, USA, she is said to be wheelchair bound and grossly overweight but starting to sing again. And Srey Nich was not the only one. Her attempted murder was only the first of several, all of which could well be regarded as political killings. It did seem that no real attempt had been made to find those ultimately responsible for these crimes. There are many who connected them with the July election that had so recently gone before.

It took eleven months and a great deal of arguing between the three parties before, in June 2004, a new coalition between CPP and Funcinpec was formed. In the meantime, as there was no functional government, nothing could advance, and much, including the parlous state of the economy, regressed. The hope that, faced with the prospect of a much more demanding electorate at the next election in 2008, the new government would behave itself and get on with a good job took several backward steps. Funcinpec's influence was rapidly fading, along with Rannariddh's interest in his own party. He spent more and more time out of the country, and his personal problems increasingly overwhelmed him. He had fallen for the young and beautiful dancer Ouk Phalla, and on 13th September 2006 divorced his wife, Princess Marie. A month later, possibly prompted by a nudge from Hun Sen's CPP, the rank and file of Funcinpec snatched their presidency from the hitherto evergreen Ranariddh and gave it instead to his sober brother-in-law, Ambassador Keo Puth Rasmey. Poor Ranariddh. Flat tyres are one thing; a total mechanical meltdown quite another. It looks as if the motorbike may well be off the road for good.

For some months, King Sihanouk had been issuing warnings that, on the grounds of ill health, old age, and the general misbehaviour of the political parties he might well abdicate. This news was not popular, and unfortunately for Sam Rainsy, head now of the opposition, it seems that quite unintentionally it fell to his lot to precipitate matters. Rainsy maintains that through a tip-off from an 'unidentified source', he had learnt that should the ailing king return from Beijing where he had been staying he would face dangerous demonstrations. A letter from Rainsy to Sihanouk is said to have been posted on the king's website, warning him not to come back for fear of destabilizing the country yet again. Sihanouk promptly abdicated. The 'unidentified source', says Rainsy, was actually the government who planned to use his actions as an excuse to arrest him and thus get rid of him.

Facing criminal defamation charges and stripped of his parliamentary immunity, it is not surprising that he suddenly felt an urgent need to visit his old haunts in France, where he remained for a year. As time went on, he worried that his position as leader of his own party at home was in danger in his absence and that he must return. His apology to Hun Sen was accepted, but only on far-reaching terms, terms that may well be the turning point in recent Cambodian history. Certainly all charges against Rainsy were dropped, but in return Rainsy was to move an amendment in Parliament that could change the whole face of Cambodian politics. In order to form a new government, it would no longer be necessary to gain more than two-thirds of the votes; a simple majority would do. On 2nd March 2006 the National Assembly overwhelmingly voted in favour of Rainsy's resolution. Verghese Matthews, former ambassador in Cambodia from Singapore, wrote 'Historians will look back at 2006 as a defining year for Cambodian politics, the year that changed the political landscape'.[17]

At last Hun Sen had got what he wanted. Now more than ever he was the single most powerful person in Cambodia. Ranariddh had gone. Rainsy, though catching up, was still far behind. For Hun Sen, the tarmac on the road stretching ahead to the 2008 election must have appeared singularly free of potholes.

But before looking forward, and before making the all-important introduction to the new king appointed by his father to take his place, we should complete the past story by taking a backward look at the Khmer Rouge. Are they really finished? Nobody knows for sure. One thing, though, is certain. The era of the black clad soldiers and their mastermind, Pol Pot, those four awful years the horrors of which are etched for ever on the pages of world history, are well and truly over. The beginning of the end had been on the 2nd January 1979, when the Vietnamese drove Pol Pot and his Khmer Rouge out of Cambodia. However, pockets remained and in June 1997, almost twenty years after their major defeat, an isolated jungle town in the north close to the Thai border erupted. A major power struggle in Anlong Ven hit the headlines, a fight to the death between the Khmer Rouge leaders, from which the one-legged General, Ta Mok the Butcher, emerged victorious. Pol Pot escaped into the jungle.

But not for long. Old and ill, a mere shadow of his former self and carried in a hammock by his supporters, he was recaptured a few days later and brought back to face his captor. A 'people's tribunal' had been hurriedly set up to 'try' their tormentor; and the crowds did not mince their words. His walking stick clutched in his hand, their helpless target, old, tired, and silent, faced a torrent of anger and abuse. His wrists were manacled, his eyes full of tears. 'I am wrong…all the mistakes were made by me, alone' he said. And in the end, he was not convicted after all. 'Let's not have our hands covered in blood' said the prosecutor, one of Ta Mok's generals, 'A little longer, and he is old already, he will die anyways'.[18] There was not to be so very long to wait.

In Anlong Veng Ta Mok now reigned supreme; for a little while. With the help of Ritha, the Mata Hari of Cambodia, a Khmer Rouge breakaway group were about to make an attempt to unseat him. In her everyday life, this lady ran a vegetable stall in Siem Reap market. She was always immaculately dressed, gold bracelets drawing attention to her nail polish, diamond earrings nestling against perfectly tended hair. An unlikely spy, her qualifications were tailor-made for the task. Her cousin, a top Khmer Rouge commander, was one of the plot's masterminds. Her husband and brother were involved in the CPP and its army on which the rebel group were relying for support. She was the perfect messenger, suspected by no one, riding her motorbike to and fro along the rough roads of the wild Khmer Rouge territory. She was not afraid, she said; with friends on both sides she ignored the threat of certain death had she been caught by the wrong party. For a month and a half she risked her life, carrying messages on tape and film asking for support and for weapons to fight against the one-legged Butcher.

Ta Mok, getting wind of the breakaway, fled to a hilltop; uncrowned king of the castle of cards, he crowed his cleverness to the world. But Ritha had done her job well, for the rebels followed him there and the fierce fighting that broke out virtually spelled the end of the Khmer Rouge.

For the time being, Ritha stayed on at her cousin's command base, where, still dressed in her finery, she cooked over a campfire for the secessionists in their fatigues and Mao caps. Ritha has been promised a medal. And now if you visit the marketplace in Siem Reap, perhaps you will find, behind her shining pyramids of tomatoes and rows of succulent beans, an unusually elegant vegetable seller, gold bangles jangling as she serves you with your half-kilo of carrots.

On April 15th 1998, Pol Pot died at home. Whether or not it was a natural death will probably never be known as there was no autopsy. Worn-out tyres were heaped into a funeral pyre together with the offcuts from a coffin knocked up by soldiers from old planks. His only mourners were his second wife Mea Son and their fourteen-year-old daughter Mea Sith.

'No ceremony, just burn. Just burn,' said the soldier standing by.[19]

Towards the end of that year the Khmer Rouge's forty-seven year war was declared officially over. There had been massive defections from the lower ranks and Ta Mok and other top leaders, Khieu Samphan and Nuon Chea, were detained in Thailand. But then came another of those extraordinarily gymnastic turnabouts unique to Cambodia. On Christmas Day, Khieu Samphan and Nuon Chea themselves decided to defect, to change sides leaving the sinking ship of the Khmer Rouge and in its place joining Hun Sen. In response, Hun Sen not only granted them their freedom but invited them on a tour of the country, visiting him in his own home and staying in luxury hotels at the cost of the government. Not a bad Christmas present from yesterday's bitter foe. Says Hun Sen 'the real success is not killing all the enemies but peacefully stopping the fight.' All that Khieu Samphan managed in return was 'Yes, sorry. I'm very sorry' for so much death. Comfortably installed in Phnom Penh's Royal Hotel he adds 'Let bygones be bygones'.[20]

For the first time in nearly fifty years, Khmer was not fighting Khmer.

And so began the endless discussions about the trial of the Khmer Rouge. Should it be held by Cambodians only, or should there be an international tribunal? Should it be held at all? Despite all the procrastination, it seemed that the trial was essential if the people were ever to recover from their wounds, often unrecognised because they lie so deep. The argument seemed endless. It became clear that limiting the judges to Cambodians alone would not do, and the problem lay in reaching a formula that would please everybody; the United Nations, the Cambodian people, the international community and both Hun Sen and Ranariddh. That this was actually an impossibility goes without saying.

For more than twenty-five years, the Cambodian people have waited for justice; it seemed that the day of reckoning might never come. The arguments have swung backwards and forwards, from this side to that. There are many that question Hun Sen's motives. After all, he himself had been a member of the Khmer Rouge before the going got too hot and he sided with the Vietnamese. There are those who have argued that simply trying the Khmer Rouge leadership will be impossible, for in the process the deeds of others lower down the ladder will inevitably be uncovered. This Hun Sen clearly does not want. Stalling would also help to keep China sweet, China which was heavily involved in financing the Khmer Rouge and has not been anxious to have its name pulled through the mud of an international trial. Hun Sen does not want to cross swords with China.

To attempt to bring all those connected with the Khmer Rouge to trial would be an impossibility, for there are huge numbers of them living now as normal Cambodian citizens. But after years of fruitless discussions and arguments, decisions were finally been taken and a tribunal actually set up. The Extraordinary Chambers in the Courts of Cambodia (ECCC) where Cambodians and the United Nations work together to achieve justice finally came into being.[21] The Cambodian government decreed that it is only the senior leaders of the Khmer Rouge who will be tried. The choice will be made by the court; it is not thought that there will be many, and in any case they are all old men now. As with Ta Mok, the 'butcher', none will be judged posthumously. Ta Mok was arrested at the wedding of Hun Sen's daughter in 1999. Admittedly he languished for seven years in prison, but he avoided the final ignominy of judgement in the full glare of international view by conveniently dying 'from natural causes' in July 2006. He was well into his eighties.

So, at long last, after much song and dance, discussions, disappointments, signing ceremonies, blessings of buildings and court-rooms, inauguration of a spirit house to shield Lokta Dambang Dek, the 'Lord of the Iron Staff', and the appointment of a mixed bag of international and Cambodian judicial officers by a Decree made Royal by no lesser person than HM King Noradom Sihamoni, the first notorious criminals were brought before the court.

On 13 July 2007, history was made by the ECCC; the first of the pre-trials was held. Kaing Guek Eav, otherwise known as Duch, was charged with crimes against humanity and placed in provisional detention.

Duch, already in prison for some years, had been the gaoler of Tuol Sleng or S21, the notorious centre where fifteen thousand people had been tortured and finally murdered. Just seven of them had survived. During his time in captivity he had apparently become an ardent convert to Christianity and seemed resigned to whatever fate comes his way.

'It is God's will I am here' he said. 'For the trial of myself, I don't worry. It is up to Hun Sen and Jesus'.[22] The Cambodian pastor who baptised him, in total ignorance of his real identity, forgave him despite the death under his 'care' of members of his own family. However in his opinion it was right that Ta Pin, as Duch is now known, should stand trial, if only to teach others the difference between right and wrong.

Six weeks later, on 19 September 2007, it was the turn of Nuon Chea, Brother Number Two. Described as Pol Pot's shadow and possibly the most cruel of them all, he it was who was ultimately responsible for Duch's fifteen thousand prisoners, personally putting his signature to the death warrant of each and every one. Seemingly amused at the very suggestion that he should knowingly have taken part in the mass killings, he was brought before the court and charged with crimes against humanity and war crimes, and was likewise placed in provisional detention. He told the court that he was 'not of a cruel nature' having been a Buddhist monk, and that, although in his simple wooden house on stilts he lived close to the Thai border and so could easily have escaped, he did not intend to tarnish the honour of his country by fleeing. The charges stand and the full trial will presumably eventually take place. Although he is eighty two years old, short of breath and with high blood pressure, in the opinion of his three doctors he is mentally and physically capable of standing up to everything that will be thrown at him. Perhaps.

Two months later, on 12th November, the husband and wife team of Ieng Sary and Ieng Thirit were arrested at their home in Phnom Penh, both charged with crimes against humanity and, in the case of Sary, with war crimes. Two days after this, Khieu Sampan suffered a stroke at his home next door to his erstwhile neighbour Nuon Chea. After a helicopter ride and a week in the Calmette Hospital in Phnom Penh under heavy police guard he was discharged and immediately taken into custody, again charged with war crimes and crimes against humanity.

So now there are five of them, all detained by the Extraordinary Chambers in the Courts of Cambodia. And there they stay, until such time as the Court sees fit to try them. It does now seem possible that the trials will begin in earnest in March 2009 with Duch of Tuol Sleng. We shall see.

But whether or no the trials turn from fiction into fact, the Khmer Rouge will not go away. 'It's always dangerous to say that this is the end of the Khmer Rouge. As long as the leadership is existing....you can never say it is finished'.[23] So said a local Khmer Rouge expert at the time of Ta Mok's overthrow. It is a fact that the party is inextricably linked with the CPP senior leadership of today. The present prime minister Hun Sen and both the party chairman and the honorary chairman all held positions in Pol Pot's ruling clique before fleeing from the purges of 1977 and 1978. Immediately after the election in 2003, King Sihanouk wrote:

'The Khmer Rouge is now more powerful than ever....the future will show even more clearly that Pol Pot's Cambodia is alive and well. It is immortal...'.[24]

Let us fervently hope that he is wrong.

Pon Sovachana, a previous government minister, gives us food for thought.

'Cambodia now is a country weary of hopeless existence. It is a country where the impossible becomes possible, the immoral becomes acceptable and the insane becomes normal...Can the people change and adapt to the Buddhist way of living in peace, compassion and harmony? Yes. Effective, competent and strong government is the surest way to prosperity. Humility, not arrogance. Hard and honest work, not complacency; the goal of shared prosperity, not winner-take-all. Make it happen before it is too late'.[25]

Buddhist and Christian alike, that is the heartfelt prayer of all of us.

*STOP PRESS. Hun Sen did indeed win the 2008 election.

Trial of Kaing Guek Eav, alias Duch: After a nine month trial the prosecution has finally demanded a sentence of 40 years. This is supposedly lenient; responsible for the execution and torture of 16,000 people, he is said to deserve twice as long. As he is 67, the choice seems somewhat academic.

November 2009

A Royal Introduction

The call of the conch, the hollow echo of its thrice repeated note cut short by a single drumbeat; the golden palanquin with its royal burden borne aloft by guards in silken uniform, sunlight glistening on ceremonial spears; the fifty-two tiny silver trees, each one carried by a monk in his bright habit; the sprig of orange blossom, for longevity, tucked behind the royal ear. The pomp and circumstance of the coronation of His Majesty Preah Bat Samdech Baromneath Norodom Sihamoni, King of Cambodia, on the twenty-ninth day of October, was as different from our own as the East is from the West. Even the year is not the same; 2004 in the Christian calendar, 544 years on for the Buddhists.

The new king is a ballet dancer. This comes as a surprise, even a shock, to us Western philistines. But from time immemorial the Khmers have believed that art, especially dance, has spiritual associations; it is the soul of their country. Not that they are alone in this, for imaginative Christians, too, have allotted to Christ a lead in the dance of life. Legend has it that the Hindu god Shiva danced his heavenly influence over the kingdom's rulers of long ago; The pure form of the Khmer court dancers in ancient times linked them directly to God, their dancing giving special honour to their god-king. 'Music, dance and art can help Cambodian thinking, minds and feelings to become peaceful. Art can help – if our king's an artist, that's a good symbol.' So says Sophy, a professor at the University of Fine Arts. 'The Khmer Rouge tried to break Khmer culture. People without culture are like machines – they have no humanity.'

King Sihamoni was fifty-one years old at the time of his coronation. He is not married. Says his father 'he loves women as his sisters. He dares not make a deep relationship – he is a simple man'.

From an early age he showed artistic promise, and when he was nine years old was sent by his father to school in Prague. It soon became evident that he had unusual musical talent, and at the age of eighteen won first prize in classical dance at the Prague Conservatory. Then came five years in North Korea where he joined his father in the study of cinematography.

At home in the early 1970s the Khmer Rouge were gaining ground on Lon Nol and the entire royal family were finally put under house arrest in the Royal Palace. In April 1976, Prince Sihamoni was tricked into a return to Phnom Penh, about to be occupied by the Khmer Rouge. A fake telegram, ostensibly from his father but in reality from a high official in the Pol Pot regime, had him rushing home where he too was arrested and joined his family in their confinement. As a fit young man, it was his regular job to clean the Throne Hall; from force of habit did he, I wonder,. look for cobwebs as he processed up the aisle on his coronation day?

There, in the palace but living in penury, the family remained for the four years of the Pol Pot era. In the last days of 1978, it was clear that in the face of the Vietnamese invasion the Khmer Rouge would be routed; what would happen to Sihanouk should he fall into the hands of the country's age-old enemy? China decided it was high time to intervene and sending in a special plane whisked the whole family away to China just before the Vietnamese army entered Phnom Penh.

Two years later, Prince Sihamoni left for France where during the next decade he became professor of classical dance at no less than three conservatoires in Paris. Since then, he has added to his public service by becoming Cambodia's Permanent Representative to the United Nations and to UNESCO.

'King Sihamoni has all the attributes to be a great king. What he needs for now is time.' So says Vergese Matthews, former ambassador to Cambodia from Singapore. Not flamboyant and more predictable than his father, it seems that on all sides he is recognised and welcomed for his quiet charm.

> Dance, then, wherever you may be;
> I am the Lord of the Dance, said he,
> And I'll lead you all, wherever you may be,
> And I'll lead you all in the dance, said he.

A Short Bibliography

Elizabeth Becker, *When the War was Over: Cambodia's Revolution and the Voice of its People*. New York: Simon and Schuster, 1987.

William Shawcross, *Sideshow: Kissinger, Nixon and the Destruction of Cambodia*. London: Chatto and Windus, 1986.

Dawn Rooney, *Odyssey Illustrated Guide to Angkor; an Introduction to the Temples*. Hong Kong: Odyssey Publications.

Michael Hayes, *The Phnom Penh Post*. Thailand: Phnom Penh Post Publishing, Ltd.

Notes

1. P. Jeannerat de Beerski, *Angkor, Ruins in Cambodia*. Houghton Mifflin, Boston and New York, 1924, p. 20.
2. 'Moving Tribute to Dominic, Kellie and Tina', *Phnom Penh Post*, Volume 3, Issue 23.
3. 'Journey Through Gunfire for Peace'.
4. 'Voters Mob Polling Station', *Phnom Penh Post*, Volume 2, Issue 12.
5. Roy Byrne, Voice of America, 4.09.2007.
6. Tony Lisle, UNAIDS co-ordinator in Cambodia, *Phnom Penh Post*, Volume 13, Issue 8.
7. *Phnom Penh Post*, Volume 12, Issue 13.
8. *Phnom Penh Post*, Volume 2, Issue 12.
9. *Phnom Penh Post*, Volume 8, Issue 12.
10. *Phnom Penh Post*, Volume 8, Issue 19.
11. *Phnom Penh Post*, Volume 12, Issue 10.
12. *Phnom Penh Post*, Volume 8, Issue 20.
13. *Phnom Penh Post*, Volume 13, Issue 2.
14. *Phnom Penh Post*, Volume 13, Issue 2.
15. *Phnom Penh Post*, Volume 7, Issue 10.
16. *Phnom Penh Post*, Volume 12, Issue 15.

17. Verghese Matthews, On Line Opinion, 9.01.2007.
18. *Phnom Penh Post*, Volume 6, Issue 16.
19. *Phnom Penh Post*, Volume 7, Issue 8.
20. *Phnom Penh Post*, Volume 8, Issue 9.
21. Website of the Extraordinary Chambers in the Courts of Cambodia.
22. *Phnom Penh Post*, Volume 8, Issue 9.
23. *Phnom Penh Post*, Volume 7, Issue 7.
24. *Phnom Penh Post*, Volume 12, Issue 16.
25. *Phnom Penh Post*, Volume 8, Issue 14.